TrendWatching

Don't Be Fooled by the Next Investment Fad, Mania, or Bubble

Ron Insana

HarperBusiness

An Imprint of HarperCollins*Publishers*

HarperCollins books may be purchased for educational, business, or sales promotional use. For information please write: Special Markets Department, HarperCollins Publishers Inc., 10 East 53rd Street, New York, NY 10022.

FIRST EDITION

Designed by Nancy Singer Olaguera

Library of Congress Cataloging-in-Publication Data
Insana, Ron.
    Trendwatching : don't be fooled by the next investment fad, mania, or bubble / Ron Insana.—1st ed.
        p.   cm.
    Includes index.
    ISBN 0-06-008462-6
    1. Wall Street.   2. Investments—United States.   3. Speculation— United States.   I. Title.
HG4910 .I476   2002
332.6'0973—dc21   2002027567

02   03   04   05   06   RRD   10   9   8   7   6   5   4   3   2

Photographs in the insert are courtesy of the Collection of the Museum of American Financial History, New York City.

For Emily and Thomas

CONTENTS

ACKNOWLEDGMENTS

No book is ever written by a single individual. Many people influence, both directly and indirectly, the shape and scope of the final product. From other authors who influence both style and substance, to the great economic thinkers who frame the arguments made in this book, to the colleagues and friends who offer their unique insights that aid the effort, to my family who provide support and inspiration. With that in mind, I'd like to thank and acknowledge the contributions made by many to the completion of this work.

My old friend Mary Ann Koory was an invaluable asset in the writing of this book. Her painstaking research, meticulous and highly scrupulous sourcing, and editorial insights turned a cursory examination of bubbles into a far more thorough and satisfying project. Ever since our days at Chaminade College Preparatory, Mary Ann has set the intellectual standard for our class. While I can never hope to attain her level of intellectual achievement, I can certainly try to imitate it.

To my closest friend and mentor, Doug Crichton, whose high editorial standards and commitment to excellence force me to work harder, and sometimes longer, than I would otherwise like. But his tireless efforts to educate me in both the subject of this work and in life in general remain, as ever, a generous gift for which I will always be grateful.

To my brother, Art, my mother, Adelia, and my sister, Lisa, for their constant encouragement and support, without which I would have been a weaker spirit.

To my good friend Art Cashin, who has for 15 years now lent me his insights and inspiration to keep writing about matters that we both find interesting, exciting, and instructive.

To my good friend and great analyst John Bollinger, whose charting work helped me illustrate with pictures what it takes too many words to describe.

To several of my colleagues from academia and the business world who provided information, insight, and intelligence that enriched the project most noticeably: Richard Sylla and Michael Moses of NYU, Bob Shiller of Yale, and David Cowen.

To my friend and editor, Glenn Coleman, of *Money* magazine, who generously provided the material on the bicycle mania of the late 1800s.

To John Kenneth Galbraith, Charles Kindleberger, Edward Chancellor, and Peter Bernstein and Jim Grant, whose writings on the topic helped inspire me to find my voice in this ongoing conversation about markets, money, and manias.

From Wall Street, Barton Biggs, Ed Yardeni, Robert Farrell, John Roque, Jim Bianco, Marc Faber, and Jeremy Grantham and Karlheinz Muhr, all of whom shared data or offered insights that helped to complete the contents of this book.

To Timothy M. Meehan, who helped identify sources on obscure bubbles that enriched the manuscript.

To David Conti, the editor with whom I have worked now for several years. David's constant pushing and prodding, cajoling and caring keeps me focused and on track throughout the writing process. As I have told David many times before, wherever he goes I go, assuming that I have more writing to do in the future and there is a willing and paying customer.

To all the others whose names I have, through errors of omission, left from this page, thank you for your patient and constant support of my efforts. I am forever grateful.

My most important acknowledgment, as always, is saved for my lovely wife, Melinda, and my children, Emily and Thomas. Under almost unthinkable circumstances, through pregnancy and delivery of our second child, Melinda graciously and generously allowed me to complete this project, despite the obvious and powerful pull of more important obligations. My daughter, Emily, who greets the world with an enthusiasm and freshness I find compelling, never complains when her father is forced to sit at a computer rather than with her. And Thomas is a strong young man, who I hope will not recollect the first few weeks of his life, when his dad spent more hours composing than cuddling. The scars, I hope, will be few.

INTRODUCTION

Wall Street's vaunted reputation as the bastion of capitalism lies in tatters. The nation's most highly respected business leaders, once lionized, are now scandalized by their self-dealing and duplicity. Shares of some of the biggest companies have fallen by 50 to 90 percent thanks to a savage bear market that mauled one of the biggest bull markets of all time. The most promising new technologies are failing to fulfill their promises of a smaller, better, more efficient, and more interconnected world. Legislators and regulators are investigating all manner of fraud and deception in corporate America, leading to great investor disaffection and a generalized malaise among those individuals who had put their faith and hard-earned savings into the stock market. The investigations, congressional hearings, and subsequent lawsuits have led to resignations, high-profile firings, and, sadly, a few suicides.

Sound familiar? It's not 2001 being described here: it's 1931. The headlines in the aftermath of the great stock-market Crash of 1929 read remarkably like the headlines of our own time. Some 70 years ago, the nation dealt with a Wall Street catastrophe much the same way as we are dealing with one today. And I suspect some 70 years from today, another set of investors, Wall Street professionals, regulators, and legislators will act out a similar script as a result of their own generational investing mistakes. Moreover, given the almost uniquely American interest in speculative excesses, I am sure the scenario will play out more than once between now and then.

The mood of the country in 1931 was decidedly worse than it is today. The great crash ushered in the "Great Depression," a condition we can, happily, say has yet to materialize today. But investor disaffection may, in fact, be greater now than it was then, since so many more Americans, both in absolute and relative numbers, have involved themselves in this latest and greatest episode of "irrational exuberance."

Still, the lessons of the 1930s and the script written then are instructive. The bear market that followed the "Roaring Twenties" was savage. By the summer of 1932, the Dow Jones Industrial Average had been stripped of 90 percent of its value, falling from a high of 381 in September of 1929 to 41 in July of 1932. The bear market, as it progressed, exposed all manner of financial shenanigans, from corporate self-dealing to accounting irregularities to extreme conflicts of interest among brokers, bankers, and investment bankers. Some banking CEOs were investigated for selling short their own shares in the weeks leading up to the crash. Others were investigated for manipulating stocks, trading inside information—in short, any type of abuse that allowed the professional investor to profit at the expense of the individual investor.

Believe it or not, regulators and legislators demanded that Wall Street become more transparent about its dealings in the years immediately following the 1929 crash. It was the Wall Street elite who, as author and historian Ron Chernow suggested in a 1999 *Wall Street Journal* editorial, had a "historic monopoly on information." The Securities Act of 1933 changed all that. The Glass-Stegall Act separated commercial and investment banking, creating more than just a "Chinese wall" between what had become two very cozy but conflicted businesses. Deposit insurance was created in the 1930s to protect the savings of banking depositors from being plundered by speculative bankers who made reckless forays into the markets using depositor funds to finance their antics. When the banks failed at a record clip in the 1930s, the hard-earned savings of a nation were wiped out in one fell swoop. The loss of wealth in the 1930s exacerbated the economic downturn and created a level of distrust toward Wall Street that took a generation to disappear.

That climate has many parallels in our own time. Regulators and legislators are contemplating remedial action designed to make companies in the post-Enron, post–Global Crossing, post–Arthur Andersen, post-Tyco world more transparent, more accountable, and more concerned with the long-run interests of their business than with the short-term fluctuations of their share price. New York State attorney general Eliot Spitzer has been hell-bent on ridding the big brokerage houses of Wall Street of the wild conflicts between their research and investment banking divisions. In the 1990s, analysts were prized less for their objective research than for the hypocrisy they displayed in promoting stocks and bringing in lucrative investment banking business. That two-faced hucksterism enriched many an investment banker, CEO, and analyst, but cost the individual investor billions of dollars, thanks to the extraordinarily and unforgivably bad advice doled out to the masses. Corporate CEOs, once held in high esteem for their entrepreneurial enthusiasm and wealth-creating prowess, are now viewed, as Woody Allen once described politicians, as "just a notch above child molester." Unlike the big bankers and CEOs of the twenties, today's CEOs didn't short their own company shares (at least we think they didn't), but they sold billions of dollars of their own stock options at the peak of the cycle, at times when their own employees were forbidden to do so. Indeed, as they sold their own shares, those same executives were exhorting their employees to buy even more! Wall Street analysts, cheerleaders without the pompoms, did the same "favor" for the investing public, inviting them to get in as CEOs quietly slipped out.

The public got snookered, just as it did in the 1920s. Of course, the public gets snookered in all of these bubbles. They are the last in and the last out of the game. It has ever been thus. The professionals practice a different kind of market accounting. They are first in and first out. That's the way the game is played, whether it was the 1920s in America or the 1720s in Britain or France. Financial market bubbles, manias, and subsequent crashes repeat themselves with great regularity in this world. They emerged simultaneously with economic man from the primordial soup of early civilization. Since humans have engaged in collective activity, there have been moments of mass economic delusion, crowd behavior, and then disillusion. It happened in ancient times, during the Renaissance, in the colonial period of Western nations, and again as the industrial and information ages began to unfold. There is no period in history when new economic developments haven't attracted the attention of the investing public. Most certainly the objects of speculation change from period to period. Sometimes the mania is for hard assets like gold, oil, or real estate. Still other times great works of art, beautiful flowers, or even small novelty items capture the popular fancy. Most frequently financial instruments create a mania among the masses. These recurring episodes of mass delusion have both profited and perplexed the world's great civilizations.

Remarkably, despite the great body of knowledge about these historic events, few individuals pay heed to the lessons of days gone by. Countless books have been written about bubbles, panics, manias, and crashes. Each generation produces a classic text that captures the most recent flight of fancy and puts it into some historical context, usually offering some admonitions about how to deal with future moments of financial temptation.

But it is not enough to study, observe, and comment on financial folly. One must not only recognize that these events *have* taken place with great frequency in our past, but also understand that they *will* take place, and with increasing frequency, in our future. The question is what to do about them. How should the individual investor view those potential rewards and risks? And how should they be dealt with? That is where this book hopes to be different from its predecessors. *TrendWatching* is not merely a collection of anecdotes about the grim events of the past and their similarities to the grim realities of the present. Instead, *TrendWatching* hopes to offer an intelligent framework in which to understand moments of madness in the markets, offering some objective criteria that can guide an investor's behavior into the future.

Recognizing these bubbles or manias, as they form, is a difficult task, to say the least. Participating in a bubble and profiting from it is even more challenging. Some professionals have been able to do just that. Unlike the individual investor, who has been badly burned by his most recent foray into the financial markets, savvy professionals do not lose all reason when confronted with bewilderingly new opportunities. The best investment professionals I know use historical guidelines and valuation parameters to control the greedy voices that whisper within them. They study historical parallels to make sure their own desire to reap rewards does not cloud their judgment about the attendant risks of a given enterprise. They actively recall those peak moments in other markets when the frantic behavior among investors became symptomatic of an irrational environment. At that point these "trend watchers" depart the scene, content to let others try to catch the last leg up. As they move to the sidelines, others less grounded in the lessons of history lose themselves in the emotions of the moment. They come to believe that this market event is different from all others and that, somehow, all involved will receive the riches they so justly deserve. Bubbles, however, do not behave that way. Bubbles inflate wildly until all investors are floating in the light and airy environment. Then they burst, and the weightless bodies inside come crashing to earth.

Those who stay outside the bubble stand at the ready, picking up the pieces they knew would eventually litter the investing landscape. Such trend watchers were able to exit safely because they understood that all bubbles inflate beyond their ability to maintain their integrity and form. All bubbles burst. Only those who understand the true nature of these financial phenomena will survive to invest another day. As in war, only those who study the history of markets will escape the errors of the past.

1

"IT'S NEVER DIFFERENT THIS TIME"

Federal Reserve chairman Alan Greenspan has a favorite stock-market joke that he tells which describes how to know if a stock-market bubble is about to burst.

> A friend of mine decided to get into the stock market and called his broker. "Buy me 100 shares of XYZ." And sure enough he bought 100 shares and the price went up. He says, "This is great. I'm making money." He picks up the phone three days later. "Buy me another 100 shares." The price goes up again. And this goes on for weeks and the price is mounting and he's building a huge block of stock in his portfolio. My friend says, "You know, I've gotten to the point where I don't want to be too greedy. I want to sell." He picks up the phone, once again to call his broker. He says, "Jim, I've had enough. I want you take all my stock and sell it." The broker responds, "To whom?"

The joke, as Mr. Greenspan recalls, was told by an old vaude-villian, George Jessel, the man known as "the Toastmaster General" to his contemporaries. Jessel, famous in his day for emceeing the Friar's Club roasts, was a Roaring Twenties raconteur and a show-man whose name many still remember. He, along with other noted entertainers of the time, like Eddie Cantor and Groucho Marx, was badly burned by the stock-market crash in 1929.

In fact, in the Broadway version of the Marx Brothers comedy *Animal Crackers,* Groucho paused onstage to lament the plunge in stock prices the very day it happened. In an unscripted moment on the night of the crash, he moved upstage for a brief soliloquy, a tactic he frequently used, much to the surprise of the audience and his fellow actors. While commenting on the possibility of marrying his usual foil, actress Margaret Dumont, Groucho threw in a gag about plunging stock prices, a line not easily lost on a New York crowd in October of 1929: "Living with your folks, the beginning of the end . . . drab dead yesterdays shutting out beautiful tomorrows. Hideous, stumbling footsteps creaking along the misty corridors of time. And in those corridors I see figures, strange figures, weird figures, Steel 186, Anaconda 74, American Can 138 . . ."[1] In *The Marx Brothers Scrapbook,* Groucho recalls that everyone he knew "was affected by the crash. They were either wiped out or became very poor."[2] As is the case today, the stock market in the 1920s was not just a Wall Street phenomenon, it was a part of pop culture. It is not surprising that the crash left an indelible imprint on those who witnessed it first-hand.

The Jessel joke, however, has a serious point . . . when everyone who wanted to buy stock has bought it, there's no one left to sell to. That, by the way, is also the point at which financial market bubbles burst, when the buying power in a particular market has been exhausted. It was as true in the 1920s as it was in the 1990s. It is that moment in time when the great opportunities and riches created by a financial market bubble turn into great risks for Wall Street and Main Street alike. The downside of the bubble threatens to undermine the very prosperity on which it was purportedly based and hurt the greatest number of investors. Throughout global economic history, the bursting of a speculative bubble leads to great hardship. Whether it was the damage inflicted on the Dutch economy in 1636, when the famous "tulip-o-mania" was deflowered in Holland, or the ossification of the Japanese economy in the 12 years since the Nikkei-225 hit its historic highs, bubbles and their aftermaths are watershed economic events that require—and reward—both intense study and, more important, intelligent action. As a good friend of mine often says, "Forewarned is forearmed." That should be the mantra of all investors who hope to make, and keep, money in the market.

Salutary Effects

Of course, the innovations, economic growth, and general euphoria that seem to help inflate the bubble can be positive developments. Massive technological change often lays the foundation for a burst of creative economic renewal and creates previously unthinkable opportunities for the rich and not-so-rich alike. Venture capitalists, financial professionals, individual investors, and even governments often reap great rewards from the flowering of new industries, thriving markets, and turbocharged economies that emerge during a period of speculative euphoria. By the same token, it is the very excitement that creates so-called new paradigm thinking which, in turn, leads to "irrational exuberance" and the great expectations that can never be completely satisfied by the most marvelous inventions or strongest economic expansions.

Bubbles, fads, and financial market manias are, by their very nature, double-edged swords. They can help to finance entirely new industries, such as automobile, radio, biotechnology, and the Internet. But overinvestment and instability pose great risks to national and global economies if left to spin out of control. We have, in recent years, again witnessed the fallout from a financial market meltdown. Thanks to the work of monetary policy-makers in this country, the collapse of the technology bubble has not and most likely will not cause the same sort of economic dislocation that cripples the Japanese economy today or led to a global Great Depression in the 1930s. But that's not to say that there won't be long-term consequences for stock-market investors, who should not expect the market to provide the unprecedented returns of the peak bubble years.

Borrowed Robes

One of the great problems in both identifying and dealing with bubbles, fads, and manias is that they all appear to be "different this time." Old rules of investing and old laws of economics seem archaic and inapplicable to the current trend. Policy-makers may fail to appreciate how an emerging market crisis, dressed in borrowed robes of prosperity, may ultimately undermine an economy's long-term ability to grow in a healthy manner. Investors, blinded by the promise of easy money, fail to recognize obvious similarities to previous moments of financial folly and are, often willingly, led to the slaughter by less-than-scrupulous professionals who, as economist John Kenneth Galbraith would say, "blithely separate them from their pocketbooks." It is the latter issue with which I am most concerned. It seems to me, after covering financial markets for nearly 20 years, that the individual investor or retail client, as he or she is known on Wall Street, has failed to study the lessons of financial market history. As a consequence, they are condemned to repeat the mistakes of the past. For those unfamiliar with economic history, the consequences can be just as devastating as it is for those who fail to pay heed to the lessons of political or military history. Indeed, such was the case in the stock-market bubble just recently concluded. Few, if any, individual investors, and maybe even fewer professionals believed the great Internet bubble to be, in any way, analogous to previous market experiences. It was, as you will soon see, nearly identical to past market bubbles that burst disastrously in both recent and distant times.

Of course, critics will contend that I say these things with the benefit of 20/20 hindsight. Anyone familiar with my reporting on CNBC knows that not to be true. Both I and many of my colleagues in the financial media often demonstrated how typical this mania was. Of course, some of the details were different. The size, scope, and life span were thought to be different from any other. But again, they were not. The object of affection (or object of speculation, as Galbraith describes it) is almost always different in some seemingly meaningful way. That's what throws most investors off the course of prudent action. The Internet, for instance, doesn't appear to be remotely similar to the turnpikes, canals, railroads, or radio industries that established this nation's physical and communications infrastructure over the last 150 years. But as many insightful economists have shown, it is truly quite similar. Like the infrastructure plays of the past, the Internet provides a new highway over which goods, services, and ideas can travel. It is faster and more efficient than the railroad, but the railroad was faster and more efficient than the turnpike. Each in its day represented a transformational moment in the development of this nation's economy. Instead of recognizing another in a series of speculative infrastructure episodes, investors chose to believe that this time it was different. In reality, this time is never different.

Within a matter of years, we will witness another bout of market mania. It won't occur in Internet or technology stocks, to be sure. But it will occur again. It is the aim of this book to train investors to spot the similarities, even as they attempt to capitalize on a "brand-new" investment opportunity. When you hear that "it's different this time," or that there's a "new paradigm," run for the hills, it's time to get out of that market, whatever market that may be!

> **Insana Insight:** By the way, it is the very appearance of dissimilarity from bubble to bubble or market to market or era to era that allows investors to suspend their disbelief in the mania's ultimate fate and overstay their welcome on Wall Street. That same dissimilarity also invites the fiscal- and monetary-policy mistakes that lead to wholesale economic dislocation. We have seen this time and time again throughout economic history. It was true in the United States in 1929, true in Japan in 1989, and true for a host of other manic events that dot the economic landscape. A recent example, possibly one less well known to the general public, points to how constructive and destructive market manias can be.

Toothless Tigers

Witness the intense political and social strife that has plagued Indonesia after the collapse of the emerging market bubble in late 1997. For those who don't recall, the economies of the so-called Asian tigers—Thailand, Indonesia, Singapore, Malaysia, and South Korea—experienced rapid economic growth in the mid-1990s. The boom was fueled by foreign investors who, despite recent catastrophic investment experiences in Japan, believed they had found a market frontier that was entirely new and not subject to the normal rules of investing. Billions of dollars were poured into these emerging markets amid the promise of rapid economic growth and extraordinary investment returns. And, of course, for several years investors were more than amply rewarded for their risk-taking. Asian stock markets boomed, inviting more and more investors, both professional and individual, into emerging market funds. But as is the case in all market manias, the underlying economic fundamentals could not sustain and support the gains. Many of the rapidly growing Asian countries were not as healthy as billed. As their economies boomed, the "tigers" borrowed heavily from overseas investors to keep the growth going. They saddled themselves with tens of billions of dollars in debt and ran huge budget deficits and even bigger trade deficits. Yet despite the mounting imbalances—which were plain for many to see, by the way—investors continued to buy emerging market stocks and bonds.

Adding to the strains that ultimately cracked the tiger markets and economies were the fixed exchange-rate policies of the Asian governments. The Asian tigers tied their own currencies' values to that of the U.S. dollar. Whenever the United States raised interest rates, they had to, just as they had to lower interest rates every time the United States did. Fixed exchange rates help maintain stable prices in emerging countries, keeping a lid on inflation and smoothing out fluctuations in international trade. The problem with such a policy, however, is that when economic imbalances occur, it is very difficult for the country in question to keep its currency exchange rate fixed. Foreign and domestic investors will begin to withdraw money as the country becomes troubled, putting downward pressure on the value of its currency. To keep its currency from going lower, or being radically devalued, the country will offer very high interest rates to encourage investors back in. If the currency doesn't get devalued, rates go so high as to cripple the economy. We have seen this recently in Argentina. If a currency is devalued, then the money owed to foreign investors increases dramatically, since it takes more bahts, won, or pesos to pay the debt.

In the summer of 1997, every Asian tiger was suffering from the same problem even as their stock markets careened higher. By July, the pressures from a slowdown in economic growth and an explosion in debt triggered a crisis. Currencies all over Asia collapsed. Stock and bond markets plunged and economic growth ground to a halt. To this day, few of the countries have resumed the rapid pace of growth they experienced during the boom and bubble years.

In Indonesia, for instance, inflation immediately skyrocketed as its currency collapsed, plunging the economy into a crippling recession. The Indonesian currency, known as the rupiah, was worth so little that it could buy only a fraction of the goods or services it bought before the crisis. That's just another way of saying inflation spiraled out of control. For a time, nearly half the country's 200 million people could not even afford basic food supplies, like rice or cooking oil. Violence erupted in the streets, and the government of Prime Minister Suharto was toppled. Indonesia has yet to regain the type of economic stability, much less the dynamism, for which it was becoming quite well known. In that country, as here, both participants and observers failed to appreciate the historical lessons that might have helped them avoid the ruinous aftereffects of an uncontrolled episode of financial market speculation. Indeed, recognizing a bubble as it is forming can distinguish a successful investor from his more numerous, less fortunate counterparts. In the case of Asian markets in the mid-1990s, investors were again told that this experience would be different from all others. But it turned out to be exactly the same as all others. While an emerging bubble most definitely creates early and exciting opportunities for investment gains, it also presents unique risks as it draws to its usually violent close.

By definition, a bubble cannot form, expand, and burst without the uncritical participation of the entire mass of available investors. It is that very crowd psychology, the willing suspension of disbelief and the "Jessel-style" accumulation of positions, that both inflates and deflates the bubble. In the sense that its goal is to save at least one soul from financial damnation, this book can almost be called a religious exercise. All too many investors lost their hard-earned dollars in the last great market debacle, even though many could have been saved. And despite the complex nature of markets and the perceived difficulty in recognizing speculative episodes, even a brief study of bubbles by novice investors can prove helpful in protecting their profits.

Parallel Problems

One of the most interesting lessons of financial market history shows that new bubbles may very well be created by bubbles taking place simultaneously in another market. For example, the bubble in Impressionist artworks in the late 1980s may well have been an outgrowth of the bubble in Japanese stocks that occurred at the same time. Japanese investors, flush with cash from their huge winnings in the stock market, used that excess profit to buy expensive, museum-quality art in the late 1980s. Japanese collectors spared no expense for Monet, Cézanne, Gauguin, and van Gogh. The mania for Impressionist masterworks was the biggest bubble the art world had ever seen, even to this day. Tens of millions of dollars were spent on trophy pieces, only to have the art market crash with the Nikkei at the end of 1989.

Unintended Effects

In other instances, new bubbles may form from the policy responses to a bubble just recently passed. The most recent mania for tech stocks is a case in point. The full inflation of the bubble in technology stocks may well have been exacerbated by the Federal Reserve's response to the collapse of Long-Term Capital Management, a Connecticut-based hedge fund. Long-Term Capital was an investment fund for rich and well-heeled professional investors. It made large, and often risky, bets on the direction of global interest rates, hoping to make big profits when the markets did what they expected them to do. In the summer of 1998, Long-Term Capital or LTCM, as it was known, bet a trillion dollars that interest rates around the world would converge, or come together, over a relatively short period of time. Sophisticated funds like LTCM often make money by betting on anomalies in many different markets around the world. During periods of global economic stress, global interest rates diverge; during times of calm, they converge. However, an unanticipated event, the collapse of the Russian economy and financial markets in 1998, caused an unexpected amount of turmoil. Instead of converging, as

LTCM had expected, global interest rates diverged more wildly than they had in decades. The hedge fund's big bet on global interest rates went sour with alarming speed. Had the fund only bet its investors money on its highly speculative trade, the world at large would probably have never known about Long-Term's failure. But Long-Term wanted to magnify its big bet even further, so it borrowed heavily from some of the nation's biggest banks to, as they say in Vegas, "double down."

By the time the "geniuses" at LTCM were done, they had borrowed and lost so much money that not only their investors were at risk, but the biggest banks in the country were threatened with insolvency. As a consequence, the New York Federal Reserve, with Fed chairman Greenspan's approval, arranged a rescue plan that would save the banks from their own folly. The Fed supervised the liquidation of the hedge fund, and also slashed interest rates to improve the financial condition of the troubled banks. Rate cuts allow banks to borrow more cheaply and lend that cheap money out at higher rates. Thus banks can earn fatter profits on their bread and-butter business of making loans, thanks to the generosity of the Fed. In addition, lower interest rates make bond prices go up. As rates fall, the value of older bonds, sporting higher yields, goes up, pushing up bond prices in the process. Since banks own a lot of bonds generally, that rally in bonds makes the banks' investment portfolios worth even more. That, too, helps restore the profitability of the banks.

While indemnifying the financial system from an economy-threatening event, the Fed inadvertently provided the liquidity, or fuel, for a huge run-up in stock prices. Low interest rates not only help the banks, but lower interest rates make it cheaper for investors to buy stocks and make it cheaper and more profitable for all businesses to make profits. In essence, low interest rates spur the economy, which the stock market anticipates with a big, old-fashioned rally. So, the response to falling rates on Wall Street is, 99 out of 100 times, a bull market. When rates are cut quickly and dramatically, as they were in response to the Long-Term Capital crisis, the stock market takes off like a shot.

The response to the bursting of the Russian market bubble and the associated collapse of Long-Term Capital helped to create the final, and most manic, phase of the bubble in U.S. equities.

Many economists, though not all, believe that the cheap cost of money, coupled with the ready availability of credit, provide the environment in which bubbles can thrive. Some go so far as to say that the great and final leg of the technology bubble occurred when the Fed provided additional money to the economy in preparation for the year 2000. The so-called Y2K crisis, which never occurred ultimately, prompted the Federal Reserve to increase the nation's money supply dramatically in the months leading up to January 2000. In the event of a computer-driven disruption to the nation's financial system, the Fed wanted to provide enough cash to cover the potentially irrational activities of consumers who might have hoarded hard currency. The Fed increased the broad money supply by upward of 20 percent as the millennium approached while printing $50 billion in additional currency, just in case consumers rapidly withdrew money from the nation's banks. A Y2K run on the banks could have had disastrous consequences for the economy, so the Fed anticipated the potential irrationality in a way that would have helped to soften the blow. But the crisis never came. Still, the extra cash coursing through the economy made its way into the stock market. The explosion of money that occurred in the months leading up to Y2K created tens of billions of dollars of what economists call "excess liquidity." That excess liquidity had no useful economic purpose, since the economy was already growing as fast as it could. Rather than use the money to build more plants or to buy equipment, businesspeople used the cash for speculative investments in the stock market. They poured as much money as they could into stocks, hoping to capitalize further on the run-up that had already taken place. The extra cash helped to drive the NASDAQ Composite 25 percent higher in the first two and a half months of the year 2000!

Elements and Style

Emerging markets expert Marc Faber, a Hong Kong–based money manager and analyst, believes that overextension of credit and low interest rates provide the fuel for an asset bubble and, in many ways, an artificially induced economic boom. (Some would describe the 1990s just that way.) In his December 15, 2001, letter to clients, Mr. Faber quotes famous economists Frederich Hayek and Irving Fisher to support his arguments. Hayek discusses credit expansion as one of the ills leading to an unstable boom in both markets and the economy. While Fisher, a highly praised economist of the 1920s, identified low rates and excess borrowing as two of the main reasons that stock prices rose so high and then crashed so violently in the Roaring Twenties.[3]

Throughout *TrendWatching* we will examine the historical analogues that prove not only that are bubbles frequently occurring phenomena but that they share common characteristics, ingredients, and life cycles. We will also show that if one recognizes that bubbles occur in different asset classes and in different regions of the world with increasing regularity, then one can become a far better investor . . . one who is not taken in by the current fad or blindsided by an unexamined episode of speculation in some seemingly far-flung corner of the globe.

We will also further explore how some crises, real or perceived, help to lay the groundwork for future moments of speculative excesses. And that may be true again today. The policy responses to both the burst technology bubble and, later, the economic impact of 9/11 may be setting the stage for another bout of speculative excess, although the object of speculation has yet to be identified. To be sure, there will be another bubble in the relatively near future. It may not look like the previous one. It may not even involve the same investment vehicles. The trick for the investing public will be to recognize the similarities among the bubbles and not act irrationally as the new asset grows in value and stature. Investors will hear the same arguments promoting the "new, new thing," to borrow a phrase from financial writer Michael Lewis. Its champions will speak of the asset's immense promise. They will describe its value in glowing terms, suggesting that somehow its growth potential and durability have never before been seen.

It may be a hard asset like gold or real estate. It may be a collectible object. It may even be another kind of stock-market investment like a biotechnology or nanotechnology play. It will likely hold out hope for large-scale change in the way we work, live, or invest. It will be to investing what the perpetual motion machine was to science . . . something that seems logical and possible while still being magical. And, after a period of initial skepticism, the mania will capture the fancy of both natural devotees and most hardened cynics, before it comes to a crashing close.

Bubbles, fads, and manias come in a variety of guises. They can come wrapped in big, impressive world-changing packages or they can also involve far more modest vehicles. Beanie Babies were a popular fad, and they also saw their market values rise to levels well above their intrinsic worth. As was the case with Internet and technology stocks, a large group of people believed that the eBay auction market for Beanie Babies would continuously bid up the prices of these little dolls until they became enduring investments. The little beanbag dolls were actively bought and sold, often fetching eye-popping prices that were expected to rise still further. But like Pet Rocks, Cabbage Patch Kids, or even Furbies, the market for such collectibles shrank considerably, and Beanie Babies became another short-lived novelty item for children with naturally limited attention spans. So, too, Internet stocks, Silicon Valley real estate, Japanese equities, or Dutch tulips.

Insana Insight: And therein lies the key to successful investing. It is not enough for an adult investor to believe that all investments are for the long haul. That may be true of your home. But stocks, bonds, commodities, and investment real estate should never be socked away for the long run. As economist John Maynard Keynes once noted, "in the long run, we are all dead." Even during protracted, secular periods of expansion and bull markets, your investments require constant monitoring. Legendary financier Warren Buffett is often mistakenly described as a "buy and hold" investor. But contrary to Wall Street's billing (which, by the way, serves brokers' own profit-making needs), Mr. Buffett does not merely buy and hold stocks. He buys and watches. He often sells when a particular investment no longer provides the growth or value opportunities that led him to make his initial investment. That was a technique lost on many investors during the great technology bubble of the late 1990s. Too many people assumed that despite prices that far surpassed the utility value or even terminal value of most firms, stocks would ascend forever. Many assumed that it was "different this time." They also assumed that new technologies require new valuation parameters, new metrics for assessing success, and new thinking to understand how the world is changing. In point of fact, the bubble proved exactly the opposite. Valuation parameters remain remarkably constant. Success metrics rarely change. Simple measures of revenue and profit still determine the market value of an enterprise. And new thinking often obscures the old, time-tested rules of supply and demand.

Market history is replete with examples of such rationalizing. Sir Isaac Newton, as the story has been often told, was taken in during the great investment folly of his day, the South Sea Bubble. The noted physicist, famous for being the first to comprehend the law of gravity, suspended his belief in the centrifugal forces that work in the financial markets. He lost a fortune investing in the joint stock company that was a forerunner of the modern corporation. Enticed by the promise of easy riches, the gravitational expert failed to comprehend the iron laws that govern economics. "What goes up must come down" governs the world of finance as well as the world of science.

While the literature on financial follies has more than adequately covered the South Sea Bubble, there are examples of more recent vintage that bear examination. It is remarkable how similar they all are. From this country's early fascination with canals and turnpikes to its love affair with the automobile to an age-old fascination with precious metals, there is no shortage of illustrations of people making the same investment mistakes over and over and over again. Some previous speculative episodes seem so remote that current market participants believe old rules no longer apply. That is simply not the case. While one can travel back in time to ancient Mesopotamia, Greece, and Rome to find examples of monetary excesses, one needn't take such a long journey.

History Lessons

The history of this country alone provides ample evidence that bubbles, manias, and fads recur consistently and in similar form. The bubble in personal computer stocks that ended in 1983 was similar in style, though not in size or scope, to the period of excess just witnessed. There were instant millionaires, the promise of sweeping changes in the way we work and live, and, of course, financial scandals that punctuated the bursting of the bubble. To be sure, the wholesale change that was brought about by the introduction of the PC was monumental. Twenty years later we are still reaping the benefits. But of the hundreds of companies that went public hoping to capitalize on the emerging trend, only one remains. And the most dominant name in the PC business, Dell, was not even established when the bubble burst. And in the decades immediately preceding the 1980s, electronics stocks enjoyed similar popularity and were themselves part of a broader mania in stocks that ended in the late 1960s. There are obscure passages in then-popular finance books that describe those stocks in much the same way that Internet stocks were described just a few short years ago and PC stocks not two full decades ago. I will share with you numerous anecdotes and statistics that reinforce the notion that the game never changes, only the players. (Sometimes not even the players change. Some of the biggest players in the 1960s "go-go markets" were the biggest players in the stock-market mania that gripped Wall Street from 1982 to 1987. There will be more about that bubble a bit later.)

You can begin to see the serial repetition with which these bubbles and manias occur. It is mystifying to professional observers why the public falls for the same trick time and time again, despite the many examples of previous manic episodes. Maybe the lesson has not been taught in accessible enough language. Maybe, as Alan Greenspan strongly suggests with respect to bubbles, the greed that accompanies speculative manias is part and parcel of human nature. And until human nature changes, these moments of financial hysteria will dot the economic landscape. (By the way, Mr. Greenspan doubts that human nature has changed much over the course of the centuries and is unlikely to change in coming years. It is his strongly held belief that very few variables beyond human nature have any impact on the formation and collapse of these strange market phenomena.) Despite that view, there are smart ways to play this game. But assuming that the game never ends is certainly not one of them.

It is in that spirit that this book is written. In *TrendWatching*, I hope to show you how to identify the onset of a major secular move in any investment class. I aim to show you the list of ingredients that often help to fuel a bubble, but also to help you recognize when the bubble or even a major market move is threatening to deflate.

Some say it is impossible for the masses to profitably time their entrances and exits from the markets during these momentous periods in market history, since it is only with their unwitting enthusiasm that such events take place. But I do not believe that all lambs need be led to the slaughter. Will it be enough to identify the major ingredients of a bubble, both at its beginning and its end? I don't know for certain, but I certainly think so. As tempted as I was to invest in fad stocks, start my own Internet company, or leverage the bubble to my own advantage in some way, I was always quite reluctant to do so. The studying I had done over the years had suggested to me that this was just another moment in time when investors were taking leave of their senses and leveraging their futures on a temporary phenomenon. That is not to suggest that the changes wrought by technology and the Internet are transient. I don't believe that. But I do believe that immediate and permanent financial satisfaction as a result of investing in that change is a far too risky gamble unless—and this is a big unless— one is willing to recognize that the market environment is unstable and requires constant supervision. One cannot simply let profits ride as the bubble begins to deflate. One has to protect one's investment: take profits, sell, or otherwise hedge. Very few people who participated heavily in the technology bubble hedged their bets. Instead, they lashed themselves to the masts with no intention of manning the lifeboats. Having no exit plan is the mistake most often made when the crowd believes in the permanence of a new era market.

Buffet Service

There are smart money players who often manage to enter and exit the markets with great skill. Some, like Warren Buffett, never even play that game at all. Both techniques are viable options in my mind. Those who sat on the sidelines during the greatest bull market of our time would have done as well, or better, than those who got in late and failed to exit before the crash. Between 1998 and 2001, the return on the Standard & Poor's 500 was nil, underperforming cash, bonds, and real estate. Some of the hottest stocks of the era performed far worse over that same period. So it is imperative for individual investors to understand the origin, nature, and life cycles of bubbles. It is possible to invest wisely during explosive periods of market and economic growth. But that is so only if individual investors take the necessary time and assume the necessary responsibility to monitor their investments themselves because, quite simply, no one else will. Those who profit from your participation want you to believe that, in market parlance, trees grow to the sky. Sir Isaac Newton found that not to be the case, both in science and finance. As coming chapters will show you, in examples too numerous to note, market bubbles that promise eternal reward offer only temporary success.

Irrationally Rational

I should take a moment to note, however, that bubbles are not completely destructive events. Noted venture capitalist Roger McNamee points out that many, if not all, great industries benefit from the vast amounts of capital made available to entrepreneurs during market bubbles. That capital finances the development and deployment of new technologies, many of which radically alter the future shape of the economy and raise the general level of prosperity. Of course, setbacks occur along the way. But in McNamee's view, the destructive market implications of burst bubbles take a backseat to the productive implications of the widespread distribution of new goods and services. There would have been no turnpikes, canals, railroads, autos, radio, computers, or Internet without these moments of madness. Great innovations, he argues, require vast amounts of capital. That capital is pried loose from investors during periods of speculative excess in the markets. Unusually high rates of return invite investors of all stripes to play capitalism's lottery. Bets are placed on many horses in the hope that the fastest horse in the innovation race will sprint to the pole, producing even greater returns for the jockeys and gamblers who placed their bets and took their chances. McNamee takes a fairly cavalier attitude about the losses that come with the big bust. "Who cares," he says, "if he and other investors overstay their welcome in the markets and lose money?" That's the game. But in the long run, new productivity-enhancing industries are built. The losses of investors, though painful, are secondary to the economic revolution that comes from the rapid deployment of new technologies and new ideas.

And with few exceptions, he is right. And while we will examine that aspect of the bubble phenomenon, this book will deal principally with the market cycles that are described by the terms *bubble* and *mania*. That is because true bubbles and manias have implications and consequences beyond the market in which they are occur. They can, as McNamee suggests, usher in entirely new economic environments where progress and productivity transform the landscape in a meaningful and positive manner.

The emergence of the 1990s financial market bubble occurred coincidentally with one of the strongest periods of economic growth in U.S. history. Along with that longest-ever bull market in stocks came the longest-ever peacetime expansion. Economic growth was positive from early 1991 until the second quarter of 2001. Over 22 million jobs were created in the period, many in high tech and high-tech services, which, of course, represented the hottest area of growth in the stock market as well. The unemployment rate plunged from a recession high of roughly 7 percent to a 40-year low of 3.9 percent at the end of the boom.

Statistics like these led many noted economists to talk of a new economic paradigm that allowed for quite rapid economic growth without the usual annoying companion . . . inflation. This "new para-digm" thinking was, for a time, embraced by Alan Greenspan and the Federal Reserve, which allowed the economy to grow in the last part of the 1990s at a faster than normal clip. The thinking associated with the new paradigm suggested that the fast-growth/no-inflation scenario was made possible by the rapid change wrought by technology and the Internet, and as such, the life cycle of this expansion was likely to be markedly different from those that preceded it. From 1995 to 2000, the economy grew at a better than 4 percent annual clip, one of the strongest periods in the post–World War II experience.

But while bubbles can be friendly companions to sustained periods of rapid, noninflationary growth, the bursting of those very same bubbles, which is inevitable, can also rip entire economies apart. The mania in Japanese stocks and real estate in the 1980s, the biggest bubble of all time before 1995, and the subsequent crash has kept Japan in an unrelieved state of recession since 1990. So, too, have other Asian and Latin American economies suffered when unstable and unsustainable market events produced problems. Many well-known economists have rather dire views of the consequences of burst bubbles. Government officials, likewise, worry about the policy implications of market distortions and how they affect the population at large. I recall a conversation I had with then–Treasury Secretary Robert Rubin, who worried about the implications of the tech bubble that was in full swing at the time. "These things never end well," he told me. And ultimately he was right. The biggest bubble of all, the tech bubble of the 1990s, ended badly, just like all the rest. Whether it leads to the same sort of calamity for the population at large, as other burst bubbles have in the past, remains to be seen. To be sure, plenty of wealth was destroyed in the bursting of this bubble. From its high to its low, the stock market lost approximately $4 trillion in value. The NASDAQ Composite plunged 70 percent. Many individual stocks in technology and the Internet collapsed by 90 percent or went out of business altogether. It was a painful experience for those who participated and believed that in the long run, they would always make money. That, as the George Jessel story illustrated, is what all people think during the peak moments of speculative episodes. And they are always, without fail, wrong.

The highly repetitive nature of market cycles is what we hope to deal with in this book. All cycles, great and small, repeat themselves in financial markets. But it is the big cycles, the bubbles and manias, with which we are most concerned. They are the most spectacular events, the supernovas of the financial world that burn bright and explode violently. And like their cosmological counterparts, they should receive an inordinate amount of attention, since they have the potential to have the greatest impact on society as a whole.

But before we begin to examine the origins, ingredients, nature, and consequences of bubbles, we should first seek to define them. While the strict definition of a bubble tends to be universally recognized, there are variations on the theme, as a further exploration will show.

2

WHAT IS A BUBBLE?

I am also as poor as a Howlet, and that, perhaps, the Witch knew. Well, I repulsed her once and twice, but she put by my Repulse, and smiled. Then I began to be angry, but she mattered that nothing at all. The she made Offers again, and said If I would be ruled by her, she would make me great and happy. For, said she, I am the Mistriss of the World, and men are made happy by me. Then I asked her Name, and she told me it was Madam Bubble.

John Bunyan, *The Pilgrim's Progress*

The textbook definition of a bubble not only describes what a bubble is in nature, an ephemeral, floating object, but also describes the strange financial market acts of levitation that occur on a regular, if not spectacular, basis. The explosions of asset values that are the hallmark of a bubble are followed by equally violent crashes. The presence of inflation and deflation, takeoff and crash landing not only define but also bracket the stages of a bubble.

Investors, economists, or speculators, however, tend to emphasize one aspect over another. Federal Reserve chairman Alan Greenspan, whose job it is to guide and protect the nation's economy, says a bubble is an asset that, without an external event, declines by 30 to 40 percent in a relatively short period of time. Other economists emphasize the upward movement of asset prices, an inflation of values that defies conventional valuation benchmarks and then, inevitably, declines in value. Still others, like venture capitalist, Roger McNamee, emphasize the result of that asset inflation, focusing on how bubbles are used in capitalist economies to deploy vast amounts of capital to create new and highly productive enterprises or technologies. NYU historian Richard Sylla has a more strict definition of a bubble. Very simply he focuses on the characteristics of market bubbles in which both the upside action and the downside result are unusual movements in an asset's price, wholly detached from the underlying economic fundamentals.

SOME EXTRAORDINARY DELUSIONS

The process of defining, identifying, and discussing bubbles began with a wonderful book called *Extraordinary Popular Delusions and the Madness of Crowds*. Written by Charles Mackay in 1841, *Extraordinary Popular Delusions* is widely recognized as the first modern attempt to chronicle the world's most famous speculative endeavors.

The must-read sections for students of market history include the wonderfully written pieces on the tulip-o-mania that gripped Holland in the 1630s, the South Sea Bubble that hit England in 1719 and 1720, and a coincident bubble in France known as the Mississippi Scheme. Future generations would use Mackay's examples as the benchmarks by which to judge future bubbles. As my colleague John Bollinger pointed out to me many years ago, Wall Street traders acknowledge the emergence of a new bubble in the market with one word: tulips. The smart money understands, without further explanation, that the crowd is losing its rationality, and values, whether for an individual stock or an entire market, are rising to an unsustainable extreme.

Be that as it may, the fallout from the crash in tulip values was widespread, given the vast participation in that speculative episode. For those of you unfamiliar with the tale, tulip-bulb prices soared in Holland between 1634 and 1637, thanks to a growing belief that those rare (at the time) and beautiful flowers would rise in value in perpetuity.

The excitement over the many varieties of tulips, originally brought to Holland several hundred years before by enterprising traders and crusaders who ventured to Arabia, was such that prices were bid up to astronomical levels by 1636. Initially, there was some justification for the tulip craze. The highly prized flowers remained the province for the rich after they were imported from the Middle East. As tulips were cultivated more successfully and broadly, the available supply increased greatly, making them available to the general public for the first time in Dutch history. In normal times, when the supply of a commodity expands, prices tend to fall. The more tulips there are, the less frantic consumers will be to buy them at any cost, knowing they can always buy more at a later date, as they become available. Prices fall, consequently, until buyers find the commodity not only attractive but a bargain as well. But since the demand for tulips among the average Dutch citizens remained pent up for quite some time, they willingly bid up the prices of the newly planted bulbs in an effort to be the "first on their block," if you will, to own one of these exquisite novelties.

In a major innovation of financial engineering that corresponded to all of this, the Dutch developed a futures market for tulips that essentially tracked the planting and flowering cycle of the bulbs. Tulips are planted in November and emerge in May. Dutch citizens purchased and traded tulip futures back and forth to capture the rights to the higher-quality flowers that bloom in May. The rarer the tulip, the more vibrant the trading in the market. But even common tulips commanded lofty prices as the craze intensified in 1636.

Individuals mortgaged their farms, livestock, and homes in order to buy but a single bulb in the hope that someone else would come along and pay even more. The rarest bulbs commanded premium prices that, in today's dollars, would equal a couple hundred thousand dollars or more. As tulip futures were traded ever more actively on the Dutch Stock Exchange, all forms of credit were extended to facilitate the buying and selling of actual bulbs and bulb derivatives. But that first bubble crashed like all other subsequent bubbles would do, and in the process it did at least some harm to the Dutch economy. The stories of tulip-o-mania became legend after MacKay published his book, and remained a vivid reminder of market excess for centuries to come. While economists and historians will differ over the economic implications of the mania, it remains among the most important examples of "irrational exuberance" in market history.

First, the tulip-o-mania remains the benchmark by which all subsequent bubbles have been measured. Second, the mania itself was an important financial innovation since it helped create and expand the market for liquid, or tradable, securities. That financial innovation would lay the groundwork for other European countries to develop their own liquid markets, which, in turn, became homes to even larger bubbles.

Going Dutch

The Dutch, by the way, were the true financial innovators of Renaissance Europe. Where the Lombards were innovators in banking, the Dutch were the originators of highly efficient capital markets. There was a very good reason for all this. The English and French traditionally financed their wars with short-term, high-yield debt instruments in which the debt was serviced by an array of taxes that depressed their respective economies. Most of the debt issued by England and other powers to finance their wars was irredeemable, meaning it could not be called. Hence investors could not trade their debts to other speculators or reap the implicit capital gains as they do in modern markets. Today, when governments issue debt—whether it's Argentina, Russia, or some banana republic—the debt, even bad debt, is often traded actively among investors who speculate that at a certain price, it is a worthwhile gamble. The debtor often restructures or replaces the debt with more generous terms, though repayment is stretched out over a longer period of time. The government can thereby improve its financial position while debt holders will be, in some way, satisfied. Such was not the case in Continental Europe at

the time of the Thirty Years' War. Indeed, since European governments could not either redeem or restructure their debt in the absence
of a fully functioning debt market, the consequences tended to be severe.

The Dutch, on the other hand, figured out the problem early on,
thanks to countless wars that plagued them from the 1570s on. The
Dutch, who alternately fought the Hapsburgs, English, and French, financed their wars with the sale of long-term annuities. They were her-
itable but illiquid. When the war was over, the Dutch government
used taxes to slowly pay off the long-term obligations, while the outstanding issues were converted into marketable equity, a truly important innovation of the period. That new process allowed the Dutch to
fight wars and prosper economically, something the Europeans failed
to do prior to the late 17th century.

That innovation, the creation of a public market for long-term
public debt, was the template on which all other European and British
markets were built—again, leading not only to healthy public participation in investing and saving, but to some of the more spectacular
bubbles of the 18th century as well.

Big, Big Bubbles

The other bubbles described by Mackay have been written about
many times since. The South Sea and Mississippi schemes are equally
well discussed, most eloquently and recently by Edward Chancellor
and Ron Chernow, and I will not belabor those examples here. Suffice
to say that the South Sea and Mississippi bubbles were the consequence of such new thinking in finance. Economic historian Larry
Neal describes the bubbles rather succinctly:

> The Mississippi Bubble and South Sea Bubble arose precisely
> from the competing efforts by France and England to con-
> vert fixed-interest irredeemable debt into variable-yield
> securities that could be more easily traded and retired...
> Both the English and the French governments seized on the

weakened position of the once mighty Spanish Empire after the War of Spanish Succession to convert their annuity debts into equity of large monopoly trading companies that would exploit the riches of the Spanish Empire. . . . Placing the shares of these huge new companies on the relatively small stock markets of the time led to the famous bubbles of 1719 and 1720.[1]

As you will see in the description of the first bubble and panic in the United States, which occurred in 1792, those who opposed the creation of a national bank did so because of the lingering memories of the South Sea and Mississippi bubbles. The bank would be opposed by Thomas Jefferson and others. Such concerns were justified at the time. The British Tories of the 18th century, who derived their power from land ownership, were essentially unseated by the Whigs, who derived their power from finance and commerce. A similar schism in political philosophy occurred among our founding fathers, who were deeply divided over similar issues. The Jeffersonian ideal of a country composed of "independent yeomen" was threatened by the Hamiltonian interests, which backed not only a strong central government but a strong national bank as well. On this I will have more later.

I will spend much of my time examining the pre- and postindustrial bubbles in America that serve as more direct templates for the modern experience. Still, historians like Chancellor have shown that speculative moments reach even farther back than 17th-century Holland. Roman citizens traded aggressively and lost wildly in financial orgies not so well reported as their fleshly counterparts.

In all the examples throughout history, the message is basically the same. At some point humans are driven by either fear or greed in their economic behavior. The pendulum swings with some regularity to both extremes. Greed is the fuel that helps to create a bubble, though only after other ingredients are mixed to convince people that "greed is good," to steal a line from a movie. It is at that point that greed becomes a general public characteristic and that bubbles are allowed to form. Alan Greenspan would phrase it differently. He would suggest that it is the point when individuals become convinced that the economic outlook is nearly perpetually benign that a financial market bubble, or moment of mass financial delusion, can occur. The other ingredients—technological innovation, easy money, tax law incentives—are secondary to the moment when an entire population decides that the business cycle has been repealed and prosperity will become an enduring phenomenon.

With respect to the formation and collapse of bubbles, issues like these become chicken-and-egg questions. Do the ingredients that make up a bubble help lead to a generalized belief in perpetual prosperity or is it the other way around? For our purposes, the matter will be left unanswered. What is important to understand is that bubbles occur with great regularity under similar sets of circumstances. They end in similar fashion, and have ended in similar fashion for thousands of years, though this occurs with greater frequency and impact today. As economic historians press forward with their work, they will find more and more examples of "irrationally exuberant" behavior among even the ancients. Man is essentially an economic being and, human nature being what it is, rarely changes. Thus it is quite likely that all acts of economic exuberance, speculative behavior, and flights of financial folly have been and will remain essentially similar.

If you have any reason to doubt that you will witness another speculative bubble, of some sort, in your lifetime, it may behoove you to examine the cycles that are so prevalent in the financial markets.

Insana Insight: Market historians have done an exhaustive study of the similarities in bubble behavior. An examination of many previous experiences shows how all bubbles, throughout all of recorded history, look exactly the same. These charts track bubbles all the way back to the 1630s and show how all of the patterns are identical.

Dow Jones Industrial Average 1923–1929

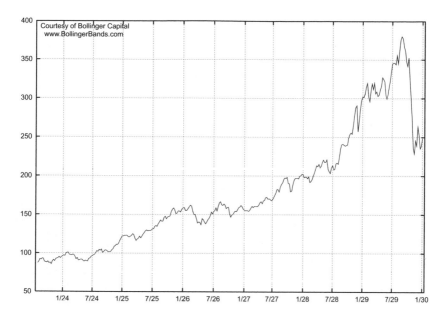

Dow Jones Industrial Average 1961–1969

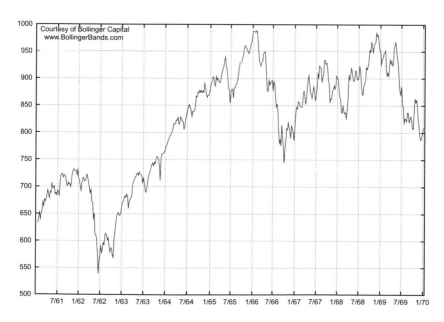

Dow Jones Industrial Average 1971–1974

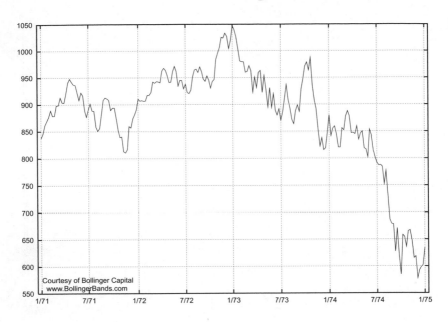

Courtesy of Bollinger Capital
www.BollingerBands.com

Gold Bullion 1971–2002

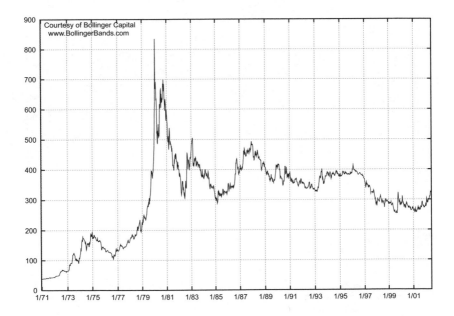

Courtesy of Bollinger Capital
www.BollingerBands.com

Crude Oil 1971–2002

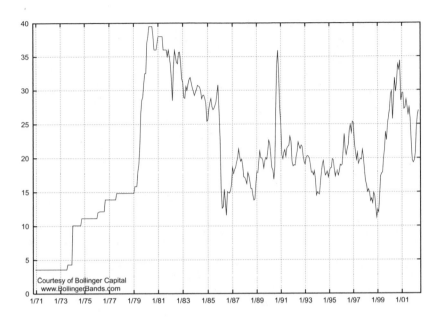

Nikkei-225 1982–2002

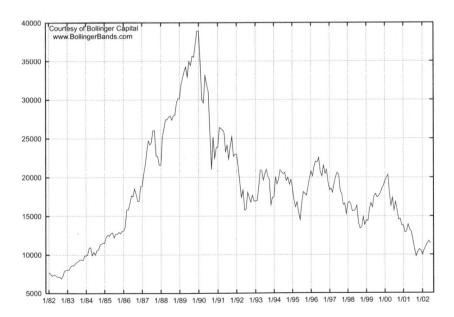

NASDAQ Composite 1991–2002

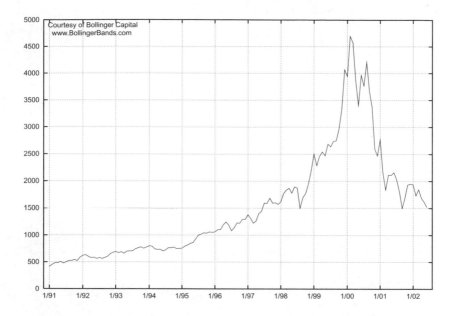

Courtesy of Bollinger Capital
www.BollingerBands.com

From the tulip mania in Holland in the 1630s and Britain's South Sea Bubble in the 1720s to U.S. stocks in the 1920s, Kuwaiti stocks in the early 1980s, Japanese stocks in the late eighties, and finally Internet stocks in the 1990s, the charts of each and every speculative episode are identical. Market historian Jeremy Grantham has suggested in *Barron's* magazine and other publications that in every bubble the declines that follow the rallies wipe out 90 percent of the advances that preceded them! Ninety percent! That means that the majority of investors who participate in the bubble will surrender their profits. It also means that the value of the diminished asset portfolio that an investor holds will have to increase 10 times in value just to break even. (If you buy a stock at $100 and it falls to $10, you need a 10X gain to get back to square one.) In addition, that simple fact does not take into account the opportunity cost associated with waiting for your capital to be returned. Instead of using profits to earn greater returns on your investment dollars, you will have to be suspended in time waiting for an exit point that will allow you to

redeploy your investment dollars. By the way, in most cases of speculative excess, those profitable exit points never come. Stocks that decline 90 percent or more have a greater chance of bankruptcy or
liquidation than they do of returning to peak prices.

REPEAT PERFORMANCES

Repetitive cycles, by the way, are the norm in financial markets. Market analyst and historian Marc Faber, about whom we have already
spoken, has produced a life-cycle chart for emerging markets.

In his seminal work on recurring events, Faber shows how emerging markets, those markets in developing nations that are not yet
mature, undergo very similar stages of development and matura-
tion. Emerging markets, which often are at the center of speculative
episodes themselves, need to be understood in this context if investors
wish to successfully invest their capital in those vehicles. We have, just
in the last several years, witnessed many emerging market bubbles. In
the 1970s, Latin American markets staged fantastic gains, as Western
banks recycled OPEC petrodollars that were sloshing around in their
vaults. The Arab countries, essentially the 13-member OPEC states,
flush with cash from the spike in oil prices, deposited vast sums in
U.S. banks, which, in turn, extended huge amounts of credit to developing Latin American countries. The banks were placing bets on the
vast economic potential of Latin America, in the hope of making billions on their above-market-rate loans to the region. The excess credit
fueled a major economic expansion that eventually collapsed under
the weight of poorly developed political policies and unsound economic policies. (I should note that this process of credit extension
to Latin America dates back over a hundred years. A similar process
took place in the 1870s. In each instance of overzealous lending,
bankers and investors have been disappointed by the lack of economic progress in the region. Argentina's recent currency crisis and
debt default is yet but another example. There is a saying about Latin
America's economy: It has great potential . . . and it always will.)

Latin American markets staged similar advances in the 1990s,
tugged along by an emerging market bubble in Asia that collapsed in

1997. There were emerging market bubbles in Eastern Europe in the late 1980s and early 1990s after the Berlin Wall came down. Poland, Hungary, Czechoslovakia, Romania, and others received a huge influx of capital in the wake of the Soviet Union's dissolution. Western investors expected an immediate capitalist revolution and huge profits from these newly "capitalized" and democratized nations. But as is the case with many emerging markets, the promise of reform was included in the price of the investments long before the reality occurred. Disappointment, fueled by the inevitable setbacks on the road to progress, led to a crash.

The Asian emerging markets bubble of the late 1990s was the most spectacular recent example, since its expansion involved the West very deeply and its collapse had ripple effects that were felt immediately and dramatically around the globe. Part of the cyclical behavior that helps to fuel these repetitive episodes involves the rush to extend credit or capital to investment vehicles or regions that are deemed promising. Once again, in the case of emerging markets, a new generation of investors forgets the mistakes of the old and begins the cycle anew. They believe that these "new" markets hold infinite promise, and are willing to invest, or speculate with, vast sums of money to participate in the coming prosperity. In many cases, they are acting just like the participants in Britain's South Sea Bubble, betting on a new world order that takes far longer to realize than anyone imagines. The hope for quick profit leads to inevitable disappointment and a round of disillusionment that then sucks capital away from the whole enterprise and slows the pace of progress.

Irrational Exuberance

Speculative behavior, whether in emerging markets, new technologies, hard assets, or even collectibles, is all quite the same. The life cycles and chart patterns are remarkably similar, as the work of Jeremy Grantham, another market historian who has done extensive work on repetitive cycles, and Marc Faber prove. The consequences, of course, between a bubble in hard assets and a bubble in technology stocks or in emerging markets can be vastly different.

Asset bubbles tend to cluster around new discoveries, inventions, or frontiers. The discovery and exploration of the New World precipitated the South Sea and Mississippi bubbles almost 300 years ago. Fascination with the Asian tiger economies led to a speculative episode only a few years ago. Bubbles can also involve great discoveries or new inventions, whether it be gold at Sutter's Mill in 1848 or the creation of the first personal computer in Steve Wozniak's garage in 1979. Financial markets greeted each with an unusual amount of glee and irrationality. Manias can also involve trendy business concepts like conglomeration in the 1960s, leveraged buyouts in the 1980s, or the merger mania that was part and parcel of the 1990s experience. Those events tend to be larger, more noticeable, and have a greater impact on the macroeconomy.

But there are tiny bubbles that occur in the markets as well. Some involved the so-called concept stocks of the 1960s. Electronics and hydroponics attracted a great deal of attention then, although we remember little about it today. More recently, "theme restaurants" like Planet Hollywood or the Rainforest Café went through bubbles of their own. While they do not necessarily have the same market or economic impact, these smaller bubbles act in entirely the same manner as their big brothers, following remarkably similar technical formations and going bust in much the same way.

Collectible items experience similar peak moments. We can all remember the days when Cabbage Patch Kids, Furbies, Pokémon cards, or Beanie Babies were the must-have items of the holiday season. People queued up at department stores all over the country, pushing and shoving to be first in line. They paid ever-escalating prices for the goods in question. In the case of Beanie Babies, a hot auction market emerged on eBay. Authentic Beanies commanded prices far in excess of their intrinsic $2 value. What used to be relegated to a bin at the local five-and-dime was suddenly a prized possession. Beanie Babies were actively traded until that market crashed in the late 1990s.

I recall once discussing the exclusive licensee for Pokémon in the United States. It was, and still is, a publicly traded company called 4 Kids Entertainment. The stock exploded in late 1999 to about $95 a share as the Pokémon craze reached its zenith. I questioned the sustainability of the craze. Irate viewers disagreed about the viability of Pokémon and criticized me for not doing my homework. (This, by the way, has happened numerous times in my career.) I wasn't trying to be fashionably contrarian. I was merely attempting to point out that many of these little crazes run their courses in short order. Investors, however, get emotionally attached to these concepts and forget that a child's attention span is not particularly long. Gumby and Pokey were pretty popular when I was a kid, and while they may sell well as nostalgia items today, they are not the must-haves of a generation ago. There have been numerous cycles in which kids' toys have captured the imagination of the little ones, only to be replaced by the next hot item. Pokémon remains a viable business franchise, but, and this is the important part, 4 Kids Entertainment shares have dropped from a high of $95 a share in late 1999 to about $20 a share today. That's a 79 percent decline. This little bubble was no different from any other. All future Pokémon profits were fully discounted at $95 a share. It will take another toy bubble to get 4 Kids back to where it was. Coleco was behind the Cabbage Patch Kids. That, too, was a hot stock. It's gone today.

4 Kids Entertainment

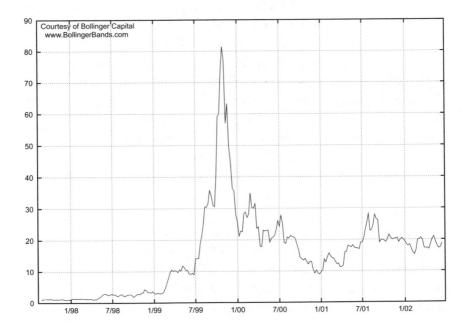

Courtesy of Bollinger Capital
www.BollingerBands.com

I will take a more in-depth look at "tiny bubbles" later on. But I'd like to return my focus to bigger issues that can affect the direction of whole markets and whole economies. Only a few people get burned in these smaller events. Entire populations are affected by true moments of market mania. Before we examine many of those moments in greater detail, I would like to explore the characteristics common to all speculative events, both big and small.

CYCLES AND PSYCHOLOGY

In *Manias, Panics and Crashes,* economist Charles P. Kindleberger discusses the life cycle of these major financial events.

According to the Kindleberger, the five stages of a bubble are "displacement, overtrading, monetary expansion, revulsion and discredit." [2]

Let me break down these concepts so that they are more accessible to the modern reader.

Displacement refers to an event that triggers the initial rush into a particular asset class. In the case of our most recent experience, the technological innovations that led to the development of the Internet set the stage for the boom and bubble. Kindleberger also says that an important monetary or fiscal policy shift can act as the catalyst in the early stages of the bubble as well.

In my own understanding of history, major financial shocks inadvertently create the environment in which bubbles can develop. Whether it was the oil shock in 1973, the Mexican debt crisis in 1982, or the collapse of Long-Term Capital Management in 1998, some form of systemic financial shock can prompt a policy response so strong that it unexpectedly touches off a bubble in a particular asset class. To put a finer point on the matter, some market experts would argue that the Mexican debt crisis in the early 1980s forced the Federal Reserve, then under the competent guidance of Paul A. Volcker, to slash interest rates in an effort to save the U.S. banks that would have been rendered insolvent by a Mexican debt default. Prior to that event, financial assets were caught in an inflationary stranglehold. With inflation at 13 percent and rising, Volcker engineered a dramatic hike in interest rates in the early 1980s. The nation's prime rate vaulted to 20 percent, the economy careened into its deepest recession since the 1930s, and stocks suffered one of their worst bear markets in years. But the threat of a debt default forced Volcker to drastically alter that tight money policy. He began slashing interest rates and expanding the money supply to save the banks. Suddenly the weak economy was awash in money, and stock and bond prices rallied. That moment in time, coupled with the expansionary fiscal policies of the Reagan years, helped create a bubble in the stock market that came to a crashing conclusion on October 19, 1987.

One of the other displacements that occurred in that period involved the introduction and wholesale deployment of innovative, new financial products like stock index futures. These investment vehicles led to some very complicated and dynamic trading strategies that increased market liquidity and volatility in the mid-1980s. (Academics argue that those two items are mutually exclusive, but I don't care . . . I was there. Excuse the digression.)

Dynamic hedging strategies called "portfolio insurance" led to the belief that investors didn't need to worry about a market decline. They needed only to sell stock index futures contracts to protect their portfolios during a downturn. The net effect, of course, was that as the market sped lower in the fall of 1987, large institutional investors all engaged in the same activity, shorting the market through stock index futures as it continued to decline. The piling-on effect was the unintended consequence of this new strategy, and it helped to precipitate the very crisis it had hoped to protect against. Needless to say, the strategy didn't work. As the market crashed, it was impossible for institutions to sell futures fast enough or in quantities great enough to offset the plunge, but that's another story for another day.

The rapid changes in monetary and fiscal policies, when coupled with aggressive financial engineering, provided the displacements to begin and end the boom. Similar developments led to the other bubbles we have been discussing and will discuss throughout the book.

Overtrading is a simpler concept to grasp. As it implies, overtrading involves a higher degree of activity in the market than is the norm. While overtrading can be limited to professional investors, true bubbles form only when the public gets deeply involved in trading the hot commodity. Massive public participation is the hallmark of a true bubble or mania. Overtrading is merely a description of the rapid churning of stock prices, and that, of course, leads to rising share and dollar volumes, not to mention increased interest in the market.

Kindleberger notes that overtrading is driven by the belief that stocks or other asset prices will rise for an extended period of time. Overtrading in his estimation is another name for speculation, that is, the buying and selling of stocks or commodities to resell them at a higher price, not for investment purposes or use.[3] Take, for example, the day-trading frenzy that gripped U.S. investors in 1999 and early 2000. Fresh in my mind are the images of individual investors sitting at computer screens at All-Tek or some other day-trading firm. At those terminals, many day-traders who had given up their day jobs to speculate in stocks, rarely concerned themselves with the fundamentals of the stocks they traded. Instead, they watched charts, looked for repetitive patterns, and tried to profit from the intraday movements of the shares. The feeding frenzy was such that at the market's peak in early 2000, day-traders accounted for as much as 85 percent of NASDAQ volume. They also had an inordinate impact on share prices as the herd thundered from stock to stock, pushing them up and then knocking them down.

The *Wall Street Journal* chronicled the exploits of a Boston-based computer consultant, Charles Molinary, who traded stocks madly on a daily basis. His 600 trades in 1998 netted him a 50 percent gain on a $150,000 portfolio. He was quoted as saying that he bought and sold Yahoo! 50 times. His shortest trade was a seven-minute play on uBid, an on-line auction service. The stock raced 6 points higher in that time, netting him a $600 profit.[4]

That same article noted that Internet investors were the most rapacious traders, shortening their holding periods as the frenzy escalated. In the summer of 1997, it took 58 days for the trading volume of Amazon.com to equal its number of shares outstanding. By December, that churn rate fell to 13 days![5]

The experience, I should note, of day-traders in the 1990s was not unlike the experience of the innocents who were clipped at

Wall Street's "bucket shops" in the 1920s. There, individual investors would walk in off the street, plop down some margin money, and hope the stock they bought, on credit, would go up enough to cover the cost of their margin loan and provide a tidy profit. In those days, bucket-shop proprietors often ginned up a little action in certain stocks to entice the buying public. (That practice was known then and is still known today as "painting the tape.") Once the public got in, the proprietors would drive the stock down, keeping the traders' margin money and then sending them packing. A new group of suckers—oops, customers—would replace the losers in short order.

In the modern version, day-trading firms not only lent money to their clients, but arranged for clients to lend one another money, all in an effort to skirt existing margin requirements. The increase in available "leverage" allowed novice day-traders to traffic in bigger and bigger amounts of stock. In the event of an unexpected market turn, many of these novices were stripped of their funds and wound up on the street. In some cases, traders who were formerly gainfully employed wound up bankrupt. At its worst moment day-trading turned deadly when a busted trader returned to an All-Tek trading facility in Atlanta, Georgia, stepped onto the floor, and opened fire on his former trading mates. Several people were killed in an event that is, unfortunately, not atypical of market manias. (You can see why the word *mania* is frequently used to describe the condition.)

In both the 1920s and 1990s, most traders lost vast sums of money, owing to their own inexperience, lack of knowledge, and the belief that stock trading was an easy way to make a quick buck. In many cases, fraud was perpetrated on the unsuspecting investor as well. Thus overtrading is both a necessary condition and unfortunate symptom of a market bubble.

Monetary expansion refers to an accommodative monetary policy from the central bank. In my mind, it may also refer to the increasingly abundant sources of capital that are often the hallmarks of a bull market in financial assets. As the Fed, for instance, feeds the economy with low interest rates and a growing money supply, stock and bond prices tend to rise. As a consequence, debt becomes less expensive to issue, prompting corporations to borrow more aggressively. Corresponding increases in stock prices make equity a useful currency and allow companies to raise cheap capital in the public market or use their rich currencies to buy other companies. This falling cost of capital allows businesses to expand their operations inexpensively, relatively speaking, and becomes in many ways a self-reinforcing process insofar as monetary and economic conditions don't abruptly change.

At a certain point, the cost of capital becomes so cheap that it may throw the markets and economy into overdrive. That occurs for a variety of reasons. In addition to stimulating business and economic activity, a low cost of capital also helps to fuel more and more speculative activity in the financial markets. Some economists, like Larry Lindsey, who heads George W. Bush's National Economic Council, believe that a cost of capital that is too low—say zero or less in real terms—is the true culprit in a market mania. Lindsey, while still at the Federal Reserve in the 1990s, told me that Japan's stock- and real-estate-market bubbles were exacerbated because true after-tax cost of capital, adjusted for inflation, was less than zero. In other words, money became so cheap in Japan that it paid Japanese companies to borrow or sell stock to the public. The subsequent explosion in available capital led to a frenzy of investment activity. That activity led to overcapacity in many industries. When the Bank of Japan finally tried to prick the bubble by raising interest rates, the markets collapsed and the economy cratered. Suddenly the overinvestment in plant, equipment, and real estate became a drag on economic growth, not a stimulant. Japan remains saddled with these and other problems to this day. (There is, of course, more to it than that, but for the sake of describing the excess of monetary expansion that makes up a speculative episode, I've focused my attention on that factor.)

Revulsion, meanwhile, is a concept increasingly familiar to market participants of recent vintage. The disillusionment that is a hallmark of a burst bubble can be seen on the faces of many investors today. It is reflected in the decreased popularity of the financial media as well. In my personal experience, I have watched CNBC's ratings fall noticeably from their peak in the spring of 2000. Similar effects have been seen at the *Wall Street Journal* and the weekly and monthly financial rags, not to mention the growing disinterest in Web-based financial media like The Motley Fools or theStreet.com.

The revulsion process takes some time to materialize. Investors were not immediately repelled by technology or Internet stocks as soon as they crashed in April of 2000 . . . quite the contrary. They viewed the stunning decline as an opportunity to buy even more shares at bargain-basement prices. That the 25 percent collapse in the NASDAQ in the week of April 14, 2000, should have been taken as a sign of a turning point is now obvious. But back then, it was, in most investors' eyes, a welcome "buying opportunity." Revulsion only occurs when the persistent hope of recovery begins to fade.

Discredit. At that point, a formerly loved asset may very well fall into discredit. Such is the case in Japan today, where stocks are perceived as so risky that they merit no consideration whatsoever. Until quite recently, gold was viewed with similar distaste. Both objects of speculation were, at one time, so attractive that investors could think of nothing but owning them and them alone. Years later, gold, Japanese stocks, and maybe even Internet shares have become so reviled that investors believe they will never again hold any value. It is often at those moments when an asset becomes an attractive investment again, but lessons on contrary investing are best delivered by a more able practitioner.

It has struck me that these market stages are, in some ways, like other behavioral stages experienced by human beings in the wake of irrevocable change. The work of gerontologist Elisabeth Kübler-Ross springs to mind. The UCLA scientist's seminal work, *On Death and Dying,* cataloged the stages that terminally ill patients experience as they contemplate and deal with their approaching mortality.

As I recall the stages, they include shock, anger, denial, bargaining, and acceptance. Investors undergo those emotions in the very same order when their belief in the permanence of a speculative episode is shattered by the inevitable reality that all good things must come to an end. All bubbles, like all lives, are finite. The individual life cycles of bubbles and humans display infinite variety, but are universally limited by an end point. Bubbles, like each member of the human race, recognizably belong to the same species, but are uniquely shaped by time and place. That's what makes each individual bubble so hard to identify as it emerges, just as people often have a difficult time understanding and appreciating the commonalities among different cultures. Variations on the universal themes of human nature make the work of spotting and capitalizing on the similarities, however, all the more rewarding, both in life and in investing.

Since I am discussing the finite nature of human events, let me address an important analytical concept in the world of manias and bubbles, the concept of *terminal value*. It is a theoretical value with which most average investors are unfamiliar. But it is a concept that is especially important in identifying inflection points in a bubble, mania, or secular market move.

Markets or assets hit their terminal values when they have fully discounted all the future profit potential that can be reasonably calculated. That, of course, requires the use of some very fuzzy math. But at the peak of the Internet frenzy, seasoned investors perceived that many technology, Internet, and telecom stocks had fully "priced in" the future income streams or profit potential that could be achieved by the enterprise in the course of its existence. For example, veteran value investor David Dreman, who manages upwards to $12 billion in a manner much like Warren Buffett, concluded that at its peak, America Online's stock price exceeded the value of its future growth by an exponential margin. To justify AOL's peak price, the Internet service provider needed to sign up more than every man, woman, and child on this planet and any other planet that might have men, women, and children inhabiting it. Dreman noted that AOL required 18 billion customers to make its stock price support its stock-market valuation!

In other words, when measured against classic valuation benchmarks, AOL, along with most other Internet or telecommunications stocks of the time, was infinitely overvalued. Realizing that such terminal values had been reached very early in the lives of these publicly traded companies, Dreman and other value investors avoided the investing mistakes made by less disciplined types.

The Radio Corporation of America, RCA, was similarly priced in

1929. Vaulting from $5 a share in 1923 to a split-adjusted high of $600 in 1929, RCA fell back to $5 by 1935. It would not reach its all-time high again until the mid-1960s! The enterprise value of RCA, like AOL, was fully reflected in its share price by 1929. And while RCA would grow and mature as a business over the next 36 years, it would not provide a tradable growth opportunity until the color-TV craze convinced investors that it was again a hot stock.

There will be countless examples of that experience in the aftermath of the Internet bubble just passed. This reality does not, by the way, imply that these businesses will not survive or prosper. Many of the world's greatest, most durable companies have survived numerous speculative events. General Electric, IBM, Coca-Cola, and others have seen their shares prices pushed to extremes both on the upside and the downside, only to thrive in subsequent years.

> **Insana Insight:** But bubbles often force investors to abandon the discipline that governs successful investing. Investors need to recognize that investing involves paying a reasonable price to participate in the future income streams provided by a business enterprise. When that future income is more than adequately factored into the stock price, it is nearly the time to get out. This is not a specific market-timing recommendation. Bubbles can stretch those valuation parameters to a greater degree and for a greater amount of time than seems reasonable. But when, as value investor Mark Boyar pointed out in a letter to clients, stock prices have discounted the hereafter, not just the here and now, the bubble is close to bursting.

7 SIGMA EVENTS

Market historian Jim Bianco, who runs a Chicago-based research boutique that bears his name, points out that these seeming once-in-a-lifetime events are, indeed, happening with ever-increasing frequency. Jim calls these rare episodes "7 Sigma" events. Such events so rare that, statistically, they should occur only once every 24,000 years. For those who remember statistics class, 7 Sigma events were those things that showed up in the far right-hand corner of the bell curve. Sigma is the statistical description of one standard deviation from the norm. To quantify the notion, the concept of 6 Sigma is used as a benchmark in quality studies done by major corporations like General Electric and others. So-called 6 Sigma quality describes a process in which there is only one defective part or process in every million. In other words, 6 Sigma quality is quite rare but worth working toward.

Seven Sigma exists in an entirely different realm. The probability of such a 7 Sigma event is deemed so remote that it falls outside of what statisticians call the normal occurrences that are not only impossible to forecast, but also too improbable to worry about. But as Jim's analysis shows, 7 Sigma events, rare unthinkable events, both in geopolitics and in markets, have occurred every couple of years over the last decade.

When Do Economic Forecasters Miss Big Time?

The <u>absolute</u> difference between first release GNP (before 1992)/GDP (since 1992) and MMS Survey of forecasts – average of current and previous quarters

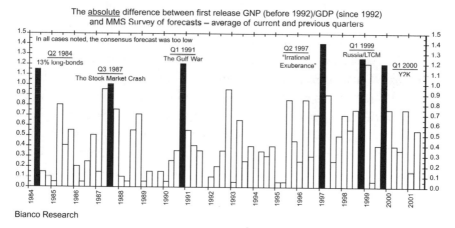

Bianco Research

That means that what was once deemed abnormal is becoming normal. And since it has become normal, it should then become, if not predictable, at least considered possible. If possible, then investors should take proactive steps to protect their portfolios on a more regular basis.

Jim's 7 Sigma events don't apply strictly to market phenomena. Unexpected wars, like the Gulf War or the September 11 terrorist attacks, are included in the analysis since they had such a profound impact on market movements. But even rare market events are less rare than they used to be. Since 1991, investors have lived through a major U.S. banking crisis (1991), a burst bond-market bubble that caused Orange County, California, to go bankrupt, the Mexican debt crisis, and a derivatives debacle that shut down several Wall Street trading firms (1994–1995). Add to that the Asian currency crisis that led to the bursting of an emerging markets bubble, the Russian ruble crisis, and the collapse of Long-Term Capital Management (1997–1998). Each of those events caused unusual and unexpected strains on the global financial system and prompted sizable reactions from economic policy-makers. Those reactions had equally important repercussions for the markets and economies involved. Those events, meanwhile, were not only followed by the technology-Internet-telecom bubble that burst violently only a few short years ago but were, in fact, its precipitating agents. (I will explain more about those relationships shortly.) That's eight major financial episodes in less than a decade! Throw in the stock-market crash of 1987, the bubble in Japan's stock market, the leveraged buyout craze, the bubble in Impressionist art in 1989, not to mention regional real estate bubbles in the United States at that very same time, and there have been 13 major earthshaking financial events in approximately 15 years.

Lest you think they had no impact on your economic life, the bursting of each previous bubble led to a policy response which, in turn, created the next one. In each instance there was a sharp and dangerous break in the stock or bond market which affected the prospects for economic growth. Recall the market-stopping slide in the Dow Jones Industrial Average on October 27, 1997. The 554-point plunge, the largest point drop in market history until the post-9/11 reaction, triggered a market-stopping circuit breaker that day. Similar declines took place less than a year later in the Russia–Long-Term Capital debacle. Exceptional policy responses from the Fed and

U.S. Treasury saved the day each time in recent history, though we had not been so fortunate at previous inflection points. Many economists believe that decidedly poor policy responses to the economic shocks of the 1920s and the 1970s exacerbated the problems wrought by irrationally exuberant markets and subsequent crashes.

The boom/bust cycle that Karl Marx observed in free market, or even quasi–free market, economies is alive and well today thanks, in part, to the speculative excesses that are known to build up in financial markets. (Marx's analytical mistake was to equate boom/bust in capitalist economies with complete collapse and social revolution.) While the threat of an irrevocably damaged system is ever present, it has not happened in a permanent sense yet. But the temporary dislocations, with which we are most concerned, can be frighteningly large even today. That is why it is imperative for all investors to understand the nature of this beast. It will rear its ugly head again in short order.

3

PAST AS PROLOGUE

I'm sure you're beginning to get the point of this exercise. Market manias, however one characterizes them, are repetitive events. They come in different guises, but they occur with serial regularity. And as the world continues to shrink through globalization and technological innovation, bubbles that can greatly affect your own economic future will pop up with increasing speed and potentially more far-reaching consequences. It has long been believed that such periods of financial market excesses occur only once a generation. A new generation of investors makes the same mistakes their fathers did. When it comes to investing, remember it *is* your father's Oldsmobile, to adopt a tag line from an industry in which an entire generation of early-twentieth-century investors speculated. The lack of a historical memory leads to new bouts of unexamined and unchecked euphoria that produce a result very similar to the calamities of days gone by.

You've seen the charts that graphically show how all manias follow the same inevitable course. The slow buildup in excitement—the parabolic arch that represents the manic phase of the bubble, the cresting of that wave, and the inevitable crash. Not only do the markets behave the same way numerically in both price and time, but the historical accounts of each event, at the time it is taking place, read exactly the same as the manias of our own day. In some cases, the parallels are so similar that it is chilling.

The long list of bubbles in the United States alone should be enough to convince investors that these frequent market distortions can cause great trouble in one's portfolio. But each new episode convinces the investing public, as we said, that it is an entirely new phenomenon. Most investors, in fact, fail to recognize that, at best, each new event is only a slight variation on previous themes. Bubbles in the United States are as old as the country itself. On average, there has been some sort of mania or bubble in the United States, albeit in different asset classes, every decade or so. They began in 1792 and have appeared as late as the year 2000. No doubt there will be more.

Now that we've examined the technical features that define bubbles, let's look at some examples that illustrate, in graphic detail, their size, scope, scale, and frequency. We will examine the very first bubble that investors marveled at in modern times and the first mania that touched our economy in the late 1700s as well as touching on later events with which we are more readily familiar. While the stories are fascinating from a historical standpoint, they are extraordinarily useful to anyone wishing to participate in the markets of our own day.

THE PANIC OF 1792

The United States was a very young country when the first initial public offering occurred. While Wall Street was not yet the center of American capitalism, it would play an important role in the country's first speculative episode, its first market crash, and the first attempts at reform. It set the pattern of boom, bust, recrimination, and reform that has persisted until today.

After a great debate about whether or not the United States should have a strong national bank to help facilitate commerce and trade, the Federalists, led by Alexander Hamilton, the nation's first treasury secretary, won the day and established the first Bank of the United States in 1791. The bank, which assumed the Revolutionary War debts of the 13 individual states on behalf of the federal government, was modeled after the Bank of England.[1] Its purpose was manifold: to provide loans in support of trade and industry, to help finance

the activities of the new government, and to provide an income opportunity for the federal government, since the government would
own shares in the new, publicly traded bank. The bank, which was a
controversial creation, was opposed by anti-Federalists and eventually shuttered by Andrew Jackson, but as historian David Cowen
notes in a seminal work on the bank's early days, the impact of the
bank was far-reaching.

In order to finance the bank's operations, it was brought out as a
public company. The U.S. government owned 20 percent of its shares,
while the remaining 80 percent was sold to investors in an IPO on Independence Day, 1791. Twenty-five thousand shares were authorized
at $400 a piece. Five thousand were held by the government, while in-
dividuals could acquire the remainder in 1000-share lots. But the en-
thusiastic reception for the bank's shares forced the government to
restrict the maximum purchase of stock to 30 shares per investor.[2] As
we would witness in later years, the well-heeled gobbled up the offering, putting down $25 and paying the rest of the $400 price on time.
Members of Congress, the secretary of war, merchants, and speculators[3] snapped up the stock, leading to a speculative frenzy in the
shares. The Bank of the United States raised $10 million in capital
and was on its way to becoming an important institution. The general
public missed the boat on this opportunity, though they would be
harmed by a market crash that affected the embryonic U.S. economy
in 1792.

Trading in bank scrip, or the $25 pieces of paper on which the
shares were based, exploded in value. Speculators and ordinary citizens got in on the action, trading the high-yielding bank securities
(the dividend was 12 percent!) at ever-escalating premiums. As
Cowen points out, trading in New York coffeehouses (where the early
action on Wall Street took place) was frenetic. In only a month, bank
scrip jumped from $25 to $250. That meant that a full share of the
bank was worth $625, a gain of 56 1/4 percent in a month![4] The as-
tronomical gains in this first IPO would be repeated time and time
again in other IPOs throughout the history of the United States,
reaching an astounding peak 208 years later.

A few unscrupulous types helped to engineer a ramp in bank scrip in an effort to bull the market ever higher. Again, market manipulation in great bull market runs would remain an enduring feature of the process. The bulls in 1791 would be fought by those in the bear camp, much as they are today. And the bulls overpower the bears while the frenzy is on, only to be washed out when the market tide turns. The bulls often win the battles but lose the wars in these bouts of speculative frenzy.

One such bull was a man of no small repute in postcolonial America. William Duer, about whom I wrote in *Traders' Tales*, was a former assistant treasury secretary under Hamilton who hatched a scheme to corner the market in bank shares. Duer, who had been sanctioned earlier in life for some nefarious financial dealings, always fancied himself a financier of some skill. He had shuttled back and forth between government jobs, often taking advantage of inside information he obtained while in office to profit while in the private sector. He was a well-connected player in both government and finance. He was quite a close associate of Wall Street's first full-time stockbroker, John Pintard, the founder of the New York Historical Society. Pintard, along with a handful of others, would aid and abet Duer's scheme, only to suffer with him when the inevitable crash came. Duer borrowed money from all kinds of local characters. They included shopkeepers, merchants, and even New York City prostitutes. He paid exorbitant rates of interest to his lenders and used the proceeds to finance the purchase of the bank's shares. His aggressive actions helped reinforce the trend, a mad boom in bank shares that represented the first moment of market madness in the history of the U.S. markets.

As Cowen points out, the episode did not go unnoticed in official circles. Cowen compares some cautionary comments from Alexander Hamilton to the "irrational exuberance" warnings of Alan Greenspan in December of 1996. Hamilton, equally concerned by the euphoria that gripped investors in 1792, penned some comments that graphically illustrated his concerns:

> I have learnt with infinite pain the circumstances of a new bank having started up in your city. Its effects cannot [but] be

in every way pernicious. These extravagant sallies of speculation do injury to the government, and to the whole system of
public credit, by disgusting all sober citizens, and giving a
wild air to everything.[5]

Again, a letter from Hamilton's deputy treasury secretary, provided by Cowen, displays an eerily familiar amount of concern about
the madness of the crowd:

> . . . the sudden accumulation of wealth in the hands of indi-
> viduals has introduced a mania which has led in some in-
> stances to an ostentatious display [and] has induced mad
> speculations on the part of the fortunate, and ebullitions [sic]
> of discontent from those who have been disappointed. The
> malignity of one party and pride of the other will probably be
> cured with a few bankruptcies which may be daily expected, I
> had almost said, desired.[6]

Those concerned about the euphoric moment were not unfamiliar
with the impact of recent busts in other parts of the world. The collapse of the South Sea Bubble in Great Britain and the Mississippi
Bubble in France, in 1719 and 1720, had left an indelible impact on
the economies of both nations. In the case of John Law's Mississippi
scheme, the French economy was left in tatters. The bursting of both
bubbles caused large-scale efforts at financial reform that may have
retarded economic growth in the years following.

As Hamilton and others feared, the market suffered a dizzying
collapse the following spring. Hamilton himself may have been the
cause, presumably directing the bank to curtail the widespread lending that helped feed the speculative boom. When the Bank of New
York, the first commercial bank in this country, began to restrain
credit creation, whose ample supply helped to fuel the boom, the market in bank shares collapsed. The Bank of the United States may also
have aggressively reined in its money creation machine as well.[7]

When the market crashed in March of 1792, William Duer's

holdings plunged in value. He, along with other speculators, merchants, and government officials, was severely harmed by the Panic of 1792. Duer, in fact, was ruined. Like any leveraged investor, or one who uses margin to finance trading activity, Duer's stake in the bank was not sufficient to pay back his outstanding loans. Duer threw himself in debtors' prison to avoid the wrath of New Yorkers who would have strung him up in lieu of payment. Duer's role would be reprised by other famous and infamous players in market history whose quick-buck schemes would make them the envy of the population for a time, but then also the villains of the downfall as well.

The above-mentioned bubble and crash is not entirely indicative of a financial market bubble. Owing to the small size of the embryonic U.S. securities market, outright manipulation was the sole province of people as well connected as Duer and his cohorts. Still, the episode contains lessons. Americans are eager to engage in such financial market speculation. We are, by nature, gamblers, speculators, and entrepreneurs. We revel in risk and hope for reward. This is an American trait that has, as you can see, existed since the nation's early moments. In addition, this early speculative episode was financed by an aggressively easy monetary policy, a key topic we will turn to again and again throughout this book. Although the Duer episode has not been widely discussed or studied among market historians, its discussion here serves to set the stage for later, more manic action. Indeed, in the true spirit of America, it didn't take long for investors to embark on another wild ride.

Insana Insight: Personality, good business and family connections, charisma, style, and good looks are no substitute for investing acumen and integrity. Such charming personal qualities cannot save speculators from ruin, nor, sadly, from taking their less famous, well-bred, and charismatic followers with them.

THE CANAL CRAZE AND OTHER ANCESTORS
OF THE INFORMATION SUPERHIGHWAY

I mentioned briefly the beginnings of the canal mania that took hold of the U.S. markets in the early 19th century. It was the first time a genuine innovation prompted a bubble in U.S. stock prices. Canals and turnpikes (turnpikes were toll roads controlled by gates or "pikes") were the first "infrastructure" plays to excite domestic investors, but certainly not the last. But for a nationwide infrastructure system to have a dramatic impact, the early states had to take steps that ultimately allowed a much freer flow of goods and services across state borders than was possible in the years immediately after the Revolutionary War. As you'll recall from your seventh-grade history class, the ill-fated Articles of Confederation did little to foster a national economy. The Articles established loose economic links among European countries that bound the Common Market together until that was superseded by the Maastricht Accord in 1991. The Articles represented an accord among sovereign states to work closely together but not to integrate completely. The founding fathers were reluctant to create a monolith like the one they had so recently fought so hard to escape. The Articles did not harmonize fiscal or monetary policies among the original states, making interstate commerce difficult for exporters of goods and services. Most disruptive were the tariff policies that differed wildly from state to state. The varied tariffs hardly greased the skids of commerce and made it nearly impossible for entrepreneurs to benefit from their fast-growing, newly independent country.

But once early America overcame those challenges and incorporated, if you will, under the new Constitution, a nationwide system of transportation venues became possible. Despite deep misgivings among the best and brightest of the founding fathers, like Thomas Jefferson, the Erie Canal was successfully built. So was the Cumberland Trail. Canals and turnpikes made it possible for the thirteen states to shrink the distances, metaphorically speaking, that separated their residents and integrate their economies much more efficiently. The building of those new information highways—literally dirt roads and water channels—touched off an economic boom and a market mania as well. Each innovation in transportation infrastructure required significant investment, public and private, and promised significant profits. The promises were not often kept. Take, for instance, Great Britain, which witnessed a massive run-up in canal shares between 1767 and 1793.[8] Edward Chancellor's classic book on bubbles, *Devil Take the Hindmost,* shows how the early speculation in canals provided investors with spectacular returns, running in the neighborhood of 50 percent. By the time the canal craze broke in 1793, however, thanks to an economic crisis caused by the French Revolution, those returns dwindled to only 5 percent.[9] Canal prices crashed and it would take more than two decades for the British to engage in another speculative episode, this time in rail stocks.

You might be wondering why infrastructure projects like these command the attention that they do and captivate investors as they have done repeatedly for nearly 200 years. It is quite simple: infrastructure improvements, particularly those undertaken on a grand scale—be they canals, turnpikes, plank roads, railroads, highways, the auto, or the Internet—greatly expand trade, increase the size of the economy, enhance productivity, and create new profit opportunities for businesses. In addition, the type of growth that emerges from the deployment of these innovations tends to be high quality. Inflationary pressures are held in check during more productive times, the pace of commerce quickens, and living standards tend to rise rapidly and broadly as geographical areas become smaller, and the sense of community becomes larger. The delivery of goods and services thus becomes cheaper, more affordable, and more widely dispersed with each innovation. Over water is quicker than over land. By rail is quicker than by water. By air quicker than by rail. And by Internet is quickest of all.

As a consequence, these innovations in infrastructure have most often led to the greatest bouts of irrational exuberance in American markets. And so it began with canals and moved on to turnpikes as the nation grew and prospered in its early days.

Turnpike corporations, rather than canal companies, were the leading type of business formed in the northeast United States between 1800 and 1830.[10] But by as early as 1810, turnpike companies had developed a terrible reputation for delivering a return on invested capital. American turnpikes were plagued by expensive maintenance, and the widespread practice of "shun-piking": travelers would simply walk or ride around the tollgates, so often, in fact, that new paths appeared in adjacent fields, circumventing the only means turnpike companies had for collecting revenue. American turnpikes never achieved the type of mythic status that they were accorded in Britain a few decades before.[11] Instead, American investors saved their interest and cash for a bubble that would form a few years later, though its explicit intent would be to pave the way for a new America, much like canals and turnpikes offered to do contemporaneously. This pattern of infrastructure development and the associated excitement in the markets is a recurrent one in American economic history. It is a persistent preoccupation of American capitalists who view new frontiers in the context of expanding trade, increased efficiency, and, most important, greater profitability for the companies involved. Infrastructure development has been championed by politicians and businessmen alike. In 1955, for example, Al Gore Sr. pushed Congress and the White House to build a nationwide system of highways to connect one coast to the other and speed the development of the national economy. Thirty-six years later to the day, his son, the vice president of the United States, Al Gore Jr., called for the development of the "information superhighway." Linking distant communities to speed commerce has been the goal of this nation's visionaries for the entire history of the country. Al Gore's information superhighway speech echoed both the recent and the distant past.

Canals and turnpikes are fairly well-known examples of infrastructure manias predating railroads, and there is something in the very scale of these projects that makes it easy for us, even now, to understand their appeal to investors. Let's examine an infrastructure bubble less well known than turnpikes and canals, although contemporaneous with those phenomena, based on a mundane technological improvement: wooden plank roads. The simple idea of putting wooden planks on dirt roads sparked a decade of investment mania in the United States.

In a fascinating piece of historical sleuthing, two University of California professors uncovered one of the earliest full-blown infrastructure bubbles in early American history. "Plank road fever" is what they call it, a mania for companies that built wooden plank roads designed to connect villages to the centers of their towns. While turnpikes and canals were used for long distances, plank roads had a utility value that was regional. It was like the difference between the Internet itself and local area networks. The tale of plank road fever, and its associated hype, reads remarkably like the literature of our own day, in which the information superhighway would, at long last, create a borderless global village that offered a sense of community, renewed vigor in business and commerce, and, of course, vast riches to those who participated. The authors of the book quote a wonderful passage from *New York History,* a New York State Historical Association publication that describes, in quite familiar terms, the madness of the day.

> Plank Roads are emphatically the *people* roads; they can use them regularly to fit their own convenience, they promote social intercourse among neighbors, afford ready dispatch for medical relief in case of sickness by abridging distance, and remove all occasion for excuse to attend religious worship in bad weather. Every improvement in locomotion benefits society morally, and intellectually, and not only tends to expedite interchanges in the various productions of the soil and of the arts, but increases intercourse and removes the local and provincial prejudices, and thus links together the social fabric with stronger and more lasting bonds.[12]

Insana Insight: The notions of increasingly speedy commerce, greater social interaction, and lifestyle improvements are not unique to the Internet promoters of our time. Consider Vice President Gore's information superhighway speech in July of 1990. Notice the similarities in both style and substance:

> If we had the information superhighway we need, a child could plug into the Library of Congress every afternoon and explore a universe of knowledge ... A doctor in Carthage, Tennessee, could consult with experts at the Mayo Clinic on a patient's CAT scan in the middle of an emergency. Teams of scientists and engineers working on the same problem in different geographic locations could work in a "co-laboratory" if their super-computers were linked ... We are witnessing the emergence of a truly global civilization based on shared knowledge in the form of digital code.[13]

Manic Marketing

Indeed, the notion that a single technological improvement could radically alter the fate of mankind has been the premier marketing tool associated with all sorts of bubbles and manias, including the as-yet-undeveloped perpetual motion machine. Remarkably, all bubbles arising from infrastructure improvements have made these claims. In the long run, the claims prove true. In the short run, the overhyped promise of radical social change proves disastrous. The world changes at its own speed, waiting sometimes for years if not decades to embrace the visions of prophets, hucksters, and wild-eyed self-promoters.

In the case of plank roads, there was a remarkably vigorous interest in this transportation innovation, despite the lack of hard evidence that such roads were viable in the long term. Plank roads are, as they sound, roads made of wooden planks, instead of gravel or dirt, which were popular in the early days of this country. A Russian innovation, plank roads were used more aggressively in Canada and then copied here in the United States.[14]

Plank-road-company securities promised returns or dividends of anywhere from 10 to 40 percent per annum, according to the literature of the day.[15] Very few, the authors point out, ever even paid 10 percent. And yet, between 1847 and 1857, some 1388 plank road companies incorporated in the 17 states; 340 alone were incorporated in New York.[16] In New York, those companies built 3000 miles of plank roads. And "at least 1,000 plank roads were chartered nationwide."[17]

They went public by the hundreds, with few prospects for profitability. As was the case with both plank road companies and Internet firms, profitability, or lack thereof, was no impediment to enticing investors. The effort was helped by aggressive pamphleteering on the part of self-styled plank road promoters, who made dubious claims about a number of attributes of their projects. They claimed that plank roads had unusual durability, 10 to 15 years, as opposed to their real shelf lives, if you will, which was closer to 4.[18] They overestimated rates of return on invested capital and overhyped the roads' utilitarian values, often leaving out such niggling concerns as the fact that horses riding over the planks would sometimes slip through the planking and break their legs, a rather substantial deterrent to use among horse owners who either rode them or used them to pull wagons or carriages.[19]

As has been the case in all bubbles, the plank road fever broke badly. Since the planking didn't last as long as promised, repair work came quickly and at a hefty cost. Many companies did not generate sufficient profits to replank their roads. Many plank road companies folded, despite legislative relief aimed at easing their cost burdens.[20] The authors summarize the whole affair quite succinctly with an investor's tale of woe:

John Taylor, a prominent businessman in the Albany area, typified the plight of investors. In 1850, Taylor invested $900 in three local plank roads. Over the twelve year period his combined dividends totaled less than $80. In 1856, he unloaded $250 worth of stock in the Albany and Rensselaerville

Plank Road Company for the rock-bottom price of $25. His investment in the Albany and Hunter Plank Road was especially disastrous. Taylor scribbled in his account book that, "This road worn out and burst out without paying dividends, leaving heavy debts." By 1865, the vast majority of plank roads that had been constructed had been either abandoned or connected to turnpikes of earth and gravel.[21]

The turnpike, canal, and plank road crazes would soon give way to the wild action in railroad stocks and bonds. The mania for railroad securities began in Britain and was as spectacular an episode as one can imagine.

> **Insana Insight:** Infrastructural innovations lend a dangerous glamour to even the most ordinary and incremental of improvements, like putting wooden planks on dirt roads. Investors should be particularly skeptical of the time lines claimed by promoters and analysts (often one and the same) for the transformation of the world as we know it by a particular innovation. Such radical change may indeed occur, but many years after the projected payback.

RAILROADED

Only a few years after plank road fever reached its peak, the railroad craze was in full swing. The new bubble would last for nearly 50 years. It would prove intermittent as an influence on the financial markets. But by the time it had gathered a full head of steam, if you'll pardon the pun, the railroad bubble would qualify as one of the biggest speculative bubbles in U.S. history.

The great railroad boom in the United States took a while to reach a crescendo. In fact, a railroad boom in Great Britain was fully under way just as the U.S. boom began. The British bubble burst in the 1840s. The British collapse had little impact on the formation of the mania that grew in the United States to epic proportions.

It started rather inauspiciously in the summer of 1831. The Mohawk and Hudson Railroad began its Albany and Schenectady service in an unexpectedly smoky manner. Art Cashin points out that the passengers on the first rocky ride were deluged with smoke and ash from the engine up front because there were no windows to let in fresh air. Despite its discomfort, the journey successfully promoted the railroad and led to many many more trips before the transcontinental railroad was completed in 1869. The Mohawk and Hudson was listed on the New York Stock Exchange that year. Many railroads would follow until a full-blown mania in railroad securities took hold. In a speech given during the height of the Internet craze, Art Cashin drew some very telling parallels between the development of the Internet and the development of the information superhighway of the 1800s, the railroads:

> Through virtually all of human history man's universe was the small community in which he lived. Someone once suggested that such a limited universe was defined by the sound of the church bell.
>
> What you ate was probably grown within the sound of that bell. What you wore or used was made within the sound of that bell. You would have found your spouse, your doctor and your education all within the sound of that bell. And . . . if *you* made things . . . your customers were likely to be within the sound of that church bell.
>
> But the emergence of the railroads changed all that. Now things could be made or grown far away—where land or labor or power was cheaper or more plentiful—then it could be shipped back to where the customers were. Suddenly regional brands and even national brands were possible.
>
> Just as the Internet would later, the railroads held the promise (or threat) of changing the way business had been done and the way people lived for century after century.

Railroads, like canals, plank roads, and turnpikes before them, promised to change the American way of life. Not only is that promise familiar, but, as Cashin explains, so is the terminology underlying the way those changes would occur. Art noted that according to railroad business models:

> The first thing they needed was traffic (does that sound familiar?). They offered services *free* to draw traffic. They went to Ireland, Poland, Germany and elsewhere offering cheap passage and free land to anyone who would set up a farm or a business along their route.
>
> (Do you know why the capital of North Dakota is named Bismarck—it was because the Northern Pacific thought it would help them attract German farm immigrants—it did!)
>
> Railroads also needed *access* (a phrase we also hear today in the technology group). The railroad access was to ports, supplies, cities, whatever. This led the railroads to pay exceptional prices for small competitors who provided them with a "connection" (another thing we see again).
>
> There were even roads that concentrated on what we now call "B-to-B"—supplying steel companies, coal companies, etc. There were even attempts to assure "content" (things that would induce the "clients" to use the route).

Despite the clear historical analogues between the Internet and the railroad, even such technology visionaries as Intel's former CEO Andrew Grove failed to see or admit to seeing the links to the past. In an interview with the *Wall Street Journal*'s David Hamilton, Grove made the following observation: "the development of anything Internet is proceeding in a completely different environment than any other technological development in my professional lifetime that I've encountered."[22] Ironically, Grove's comments were made at the peak of the Internet frenzy. Art Cashin disagrees with Grove to an extent. Maybe while the Internet was unique in Grove's professional experience, its development was hardly unique in history:

> I could go on with the analogies between the railroads and the e-world but you're probably wondering what about the

stocks. Well, hard to believe but they were volatile—even without earnings.

In a few weeks in 1863, the New York and Harlem RR shot up 110 percent, dropped 50 percent, then shot up 60 percent.

Railroad stocks, like Internet stocks in the 1990s, came to dominate the stock market far out of proportion to their actual importance to the national economy. And it's difficult to overstate their importance to the development of the economy. Still, as we would see again later, the influence on the stock market exceeded, for quite some time, the impact on the economy. Art details that domination:

> In 1835, there were three railroads listed on the NYSE. Five years later, there were ten. By 1860, railroads accounted for 40 percent of the total capitalization of all listed stocks. The IPOs were heavily hyped and often oversubscribed. (Ironically, by some measurements the tech bubble hit 40 percent of the total cap just as the bubble burst.)
>
> Over the years as the railroads moved to the ultimate heavy consolidation, they contributed to great volatility, several major corrections, at least one panic, and a few booms.

Economist Robert Sobel wrote that the mania for railroad stocks and bonds was not confined to U.S. investors. When it was in full bloom after the Civil War, foreign investors bought up all the railroad stocks they could handle, even those who were burned in the British bust in the 1840s. Foreign investment in railroad securities totaled $52 million in 1853. By 1869, it had ballooned to $243 million. Half of the shares of the Central Pacific, Louisville and Nashville, and Norfolk and Western were held by overseas interests.[23] But like the infrastructure plays of more recent vintage, investors, domestic or foreign, had little regard for the economic fundamentals critical to successful investing. Small investors didn't know about or ignored construction of unnecessary, often purposely redundant roads, misspent government subsidies, widespread corruption, and chronic stock-price manipulations. Sobel explains:

Because of the manipulation by insiders, the small stockholders did not share in the successes of most roads, but their money helped the managers to over expand operations, construct unneeded roads, and practice corruption on a gigantic scale . . . some roads did show remarkable progress, and this encouraged those who held shares in new enterprises. The Union Pacific and Central Pacific, completed in 1869, showed net earnings that year of over $2 million. This figure doubled within less than 2 years, with no end in sight. Little wonder that the prices skyrocketed, dragging in their wake securities of questionable value. Even companies that had never shown profits, and had little hope of recovery, were sought after by investors. The magic word was rails, and the Street's heroes were congressmen who voted new appropriations, presidents of favored lines, and foreign investors. The beneficiary was the small shareholder, who saw the bids rise almost daily. The price for this apparently limitless prosperity was to be a crash and the worst depression up to that time." [24]

The parallels between the railroad mania and the Internet infrastructure craze are striking. In real economic terms, the building of regional and transcontinental lines had a profound impact on the U.S. economy, boosting productivity and allowing individuals to travel relatively cheaply and over great distances. In addition, the railroads sped the pace of communications, creating the early precursor of a national information superhighway. But the marketplace behavior fully anticipated the impact of the rails long before the reality set in. And the speculative mania that accompanied the phenomenon was not without its manipulative games, as we would later see in the Internet days.

Here, Charles Geisst delivers a typical tale of greed and deception:

[Russell Sage and Jay Gould] teamed up to seize control of the Union Pacific Railroad. Shortly thereafter, their immediate target became the Kansas and Pacific Railroad, which had a virtual monopoly on land grants and right-of-way in its area.

They claimed they were about to open a competitive line in Colorado, which forced down the price of Kansas and Pacific on the stock exchange. Secretly, they began to buy up shares in a cornering operation when the stock became extremely depressed. They then sold the Kansas and Pacific to the Union Pacific for an enormous profit of $40 million. The competing line was abandoned as soon as it had served its purpose. Gould did the same to the Union Pacific in 1883. After stripping it of its assets he sold off his interests when the press and Congress again began to show interests in his actions.[25]

Some market watchers believe that many of the fiber-optics companies that laid all that cable were engaging in a similar form of speculation. Build a network and hope a major communications company buys you out. Qwest was the only firm able to achieve a merger with a major local phone company, US West. The rest have run into serious trouble. Qwest, by the way, like Global Crossing, became the subject of an SEC investigation into its accounting practices. We will deal with the unseemly side of a bubble at the end of this book. But the variation on that railroad theme was not a resounding success this time around, except, of course, for the founders of the firms who sold their stock holdings before the inevitable crash came. The founders and original investors at Global Crossing sold over a billion dollars' worth of stock before the firm careened into Chapter 11.

Insana Insight: Notice how repetitive the game actually is. There is a fitting historical analogue for every mania or bubble visited upon the investing public. Professional investors spend hours, days, and sometimes weeks searching out these important parallels. The time spent examining the patterns of the past saves, or even makes, them money. Individual investors should behave no differently. There is no shortage of high-quality work on financial market history. Some of it actually makes for exciting and entertaining reading. For more on that, see the bibliography at the end of this book.

THE BUSINESS CYCLE

Of course, as the twentieth century began and the industrial age dawned, technological innovations came faster and had greater impact than ever before in human history. Great strides in transportation, technology, and telecommunications were made. Wireless communication was made possible. Electricity was harnessed for both business and residential use. The telephone was developed and deployed. The automobile was mass-produced. Radio became a national communications medium, and experiments with television caused a great stir not two full decades into the century. Each new innovation not only changed the face and pace of American life but also caused breathtaking gains in share prices for the public companies involved. Investors, flush with the promise of a new era, subscribed completely to the notion that a new economic paradigm was being made possible by rapid technological innovation and that life, as it was then known, was about to change dramatically. That sentiment, which still echoed from the railroad days, would reverberate down the corridors of Wall Street many times in the ensuing decades.

Between the railroads and the automobile there was another craze that capitalized on an innovation in transportation that was quite personal . . . the bicycle. In a fascinating tale about the rise and fall of the Schwinn Bicycle Company, Judith Crown and Glenn Coleman (who, in the interests of full disclosure, is my editor at *Money* magazine), chronicle a bicycle bubble that inflated wildly in America in the 1890s.

The explosion in bicycle firms at the end of the 19th century was truly mind-boggling and certainly mirrored the type of activity and behavior associated with bubbles in the financial markets, although bicycle mania did not involve public company stocks. Again, the technology took quite a long time to perfect. The authors note that bicycle sketches were found in Leonardo da Vinci's folios as early as 1493, though the authorship of the sketches remains unclear.[26] The first bicycle, they point out, was developed by the Marquis de Sivrac, who invented "an adult version of a hobby horse," known as a *velocifère,* French for "fast carry." [27] The simple bike was refined and reworked in both Britain and the United States over the course of the next 100 years, until Stephen Crane, author of *The Red Badge of Courage*, wrote, "Everything is Bicycle" in the *New York Sun* in 1896.[28]

Crane's observations, recorded in the book, concerned a two-wheel craze on Broadway that altered New York's landscape rather noticeably in the days of horse and buggy: "On these gorgeous spring days they appear in thousands. All mankind is a-wheel apparently and a person on nothing but legs feels like a strange animal. A mighty army of wheels streams from the brick wilderness below Central Park and speeds over the asphalt. In the cool of the evening it returns with swaying and flashing of myriad lamps."[29]

The picture is reminiscent as well of turn-of-the-century Paris, where the bicycle got its start and where artists like Toulouse-Lautrec and Manet captured those Parisian street scenes with such color and verve. But the mania for bicycles became an American phenomenon that both created and destroyed personal fortunes among those who attempted to harness the two-wheeled beats for profit rather than fun.

Consider some of the statistics that Crown and Coleman gathered on the bike craze:

- There were an estimated 10 million cyclists nationwide by 1899.

- 300 firms mass-produced bicycles in the decade, spawning a $60 million industry.

- By the end of the decade, bicycle production reached 1 million units.

- Piano sales plunged 50 percent as bicycling became the rage.

- The supply of horses declined by 7 million between 1894 and 1898 owing to the bike and electric streetcar. [By the way, autos would have the same impact on railcar production by the 1930s.]

- Cyclists waited months for bikes to be delivered at the peak of the craze.

- Bike prices averaged $40 to $100 in a decade where the average annual income was about $1000.[30]

The crash, the authors report, came in 1905 as the auto rose quickly in popularity. Annual bike production plunged by three-quarters in 1905 while business collapsed. Only 12 manufacturers remained when the shake-out was completed.[31] The publication *The Wheel* made the following observation about the swift and severe bust: "Many fortunes have been wrecked, many business reputations blasted or sorely wounded. The great green public . . . has been led to believe that the manufacture of bicycles was an El Dorado or Klondike, and in some respect it does not differ from those famous gold fields: It has been fraught with disaster and disappointment." [32]

> **Insana Insight:** Notice how the sentiments are identical in both boom and bust, with each experience being chronicled. The innovation, invention, or feat of financial engineering is always the most important, most profit-making enterprise known to man. When it ends, it is "fraught with disaster and disappointment," each and every time.

AUTO NATION AND RADIO DAZE

Two of the biggest bubbles of the industrial age involved transportation and telecommunications, and these again, were not unlike many previous episodes. But autos and radio caused an excitement that was reminiscent of the railroad craze and certainly foreshadowed the popularity of other transformational industries. Bicycles were a transitional rather than a transformational industry, which explains, possibly, the lack of a public market fascination with the two-wheelers. A much greater and broader excitement would take hold with truly transformational industries like autos and radio. Of course, there was also great investor enthusiasm that centered on the telephone, electrical utilities, and other industrial-age developments, but autos and radio were represented in the marketplace much the same way as other hot new investments were in earlier times and would again be in subsequent years.

The American fascination with the auto did not begin and end with the cars themselves. Investors were particularly enamored of auto investments as well, leading to a large number of car companies going public. Between 1903 and 1924, some 181 companies were created to build and sell automobiles.[33] Though the figure may have been somewhat higher when all start-ups were included, the number of companies actually making cars early in the 1900s is breathtaking.

Auto Eroticism

As in the case of the Internet, the failure rate among auto companies was quite high. According to author Ralph C. Bernstein, who studied the formative years of the American auto industry, 137 of the first 181 companies failed by 1927. Of course, less than a handful of auto manufacturers remain today anywhere in the world, let alone the United States. On May 10, 1998, Ed Kerschner, chief market strategist at UBS PaineWebber, was among the few analysts who recognized the similarities between the Internet craze and previous periods of market insanity. Kerschner, citing a study from the time, noted that between 1900 and 1908, 485 auto and auto-related companies entered the industry. Only 262 survived until the latter date.[34] And like Bernstein, Kerschner noted that of those companies that went public, few survived, despite their popularity as investment vehicles. The high failure rate was also akin to the Internet since long-term profitability was extraordinarily difficult to achieve. In the short run, and this is much unlike the Internet experience, successful auto companies raked in the dough. Ford, for instance, began with capital of $28,000 and within 15 months "produced a profit amounting to ten times that sum."[35] Still, long-run profits were as elusive for auto companies as they would prove to be for airlines or Internet firms. But investors remained undeterred. In the midst of the Internet frenzy, Kerschner noted that "even though [automobiles were] a lucrative business with explosive growth, many individual companies proved to be poor investments."[36] By the time the bubble burst, Internet stocks would turn out exactly like the automotive group of the early 1900s. That view was supported by other works of market history written during a previous boom time . . . the late 1960s. Author John Brooks wrote,

"Automobile stocks were to the stock market of the 1920s what electronics would be to that of the 1950s; by the time the really big market advances of the period were underway, General Motors, Fisher body, Du Pont and Yellow Cab were called the Four Horsemen of the boom, and it was a standard Wall Street joke to speak of the market collectively as a 'product of General Motors.' "[37] The anecdote is reminiscent of the Four Horsemen of the NASDAQ—Microsoft, Dell Computer, Cisco Systems, and Oracle Corporation—whose saddles modern investors rode.

Unlike most dot-coms, however, automobile companies were true growth vehicles (if you'll pardon the pun). Auto production rose steadily throughout the period in which the stocks were hot. Installment loans to consumers, a novel payment mechanism, facilitated the purchase of a car. Auto production rose 225 percent in the 1920s.[38] From 1921 to 1925, production jumped more than 100 percent, from 1.5 million units to 3.6 million.[39] The auto business became a multi-billion-dollar enterprise in short order. With the exception of 1924, auto production rose every year in the decade until the Great Depression slammed on the brakes. The 1920s were, in some ways, an innovative period similar to the 1990s. Rapid technological progress, the spread of capitalism around the globe, rising international trade, and other such beneficent forces drove the greatest bull market in American history. The confluence of favorable influences would lead to a massive bubble in equity prices, with particular emphasis on those industries whose rapid growth had paced the change.

Radio Activity
Radio also held a particular fascination for investors in the Roaring Twenties. Radio, like many other new forms of communication, offered limitless promise. Developed to allow two-way communication for both commercial and military applications, it also quickly became a medium for an entirely new form of entertainment. The development of radio, or wireless, technology took years to perfect, but once the bugs were worked out, the radio industry grew rapidly. So did the original radio companies. General Electric's RCA unit and Westinghouse are two of the most notable firms that prospered from their

forays into wireless. Economist Robert Sobel notes that some of the hot radio IPOs of the 1920s—Philco, Zenith, CBS—are still around today. Atwater-Kent, Crossley, Grebe, GrigsbyGrunow, Freed-Eisemann, and Fada, however, are now listed under that fine old Latin phrase, *sic transit gloria mundi.*

RCA was, in fact, the stock most emblematic of the times. From a low of just over a dollar, the stock would soar to nearly $600 by 1929.

RCA 1926–1933

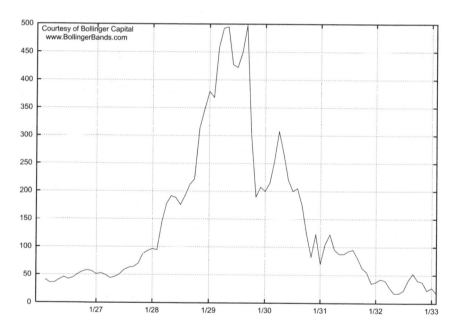

Courtesy of Bollinger Capital
www.BollingerBands.com

RCA's archrival in radio, Westinghouse, vaulted from $92 to $313 between March of 1928 and September of 1929 as the market peaked.[40] The action in even the most staid industrial companies was equally explosive, but the fascination with radio and its promising new technology drove the share prices to extremes that were notable even by the standards of those wild days.

Like the entire market, RCA shares would crash that year and revisit their lows in the middle of the following decade. RCA's split-
adjusted high would not be hit again until the mid-1960s when it
benefited from the color-television craze that was emblematic of the
1960s bull market boom.

Radio, like autos and unlike the Internet, however, produced
profits in relatively short order. That the valuations on radio stocks
would reach stratospheric levels is not surprising since they were
among the most active shares in that great bull market period. But as
we have seen in other similar periods, the terminal value of RCA's
profit stream was aggressively discounted in the company's 1929
stock price, a valuation problem that would be revisited time and
time again in market history. The late economics historian Robert
Sobel notes that RCA's revenues from radio jumped from $1.5 million
in 1921 to $11.3 million the following year![41] Industry sales exploded
113 percent in the same period, while from 1921 to 1926, radio sales
vaulted from $12.2 million to $206.7 million.[42]

You can see why investors were so enamored of the new technology and of the companies involved. But as Internet entrepreneurs later
found out with companies like AOL and Yahoo!, businesses mature
and the rapid, wild, and uncontrolled pace of growth that defines the
early days of any viable new industry gives way to predictable growth
rates. AOL is finding that out today. After delivering service to over
40 million subscribers by the year 2002, its core Internet service operation has seen its growth rate slow dramatically, forcing a shake-up in
AOL Time Warner's internal management structure and calls for a
spin-off of the underperforming AOL unit. In less than two years
after AOL and Time Warner merged in the biggest media deal in history, valued at the time at $110 billion, observers would be calling for
the media company to split from the unit whose lofty stock price
would allow an upstart Internet company to buy one of the most
prized media assets in the world! In the first quarter of 2002, AOL
Time Warner wrote off some $50 billion in goodwill values associated
with the depreciated value of the assets acquired when AOL and Time
Warner merged. AOL Time Warner shares lost a staggering $140 bil-

lion in market value since the deal was announced and consummated. In the era of radio, RCA and GE parted company as well. General Electric eventually jettisoned its RCA unit only to buy it back in 1986 and reunite with the NBC broadcast networks that were the hallmark of radio's halcyon days. The more things change, the more they stay the same.

Past and Prologue

Later innovations like the personal computer and advances in biotechnology prompted bubbles of their own. While the PC and biotech bubbles were not part of a larger, secular bubble in stock prices, they both formed in the early years of an emerging bubble in stocks, 1982 and 1991, respectively.

Again, the analysis of UBS PaineWebber's Ed Kerschner proves helpful. In his comparison of several transformative industries to the Internet, he and his associates pointed out that the PC bubble was begun with the coming of Apple Computer to Wall Street in 1980. The brainchild of innovators Steve Jobs and Steve Wozniak, Apple Computer touched off a frenzy in PC stocks that, while relatively short-lived, was dramatic nonetheless. By 1983, Kerschner's research shows that 150 companies were selling personal computers.[43] That only a handful remained in the next decade was reminiscent of the action in autos. Eight PC companies went public in the first half of 1983, Kerschner notes, the peak year of the PC frenzy, which by Internet standards, I might add, was a relatively paltry number. And also foreshadowing the trend that would later emerge in the Internet shakeout, many of the companies plunged in value, by upward of 50 percent by 1984. Other names like Atari, Commodore, and Eagle Computers would disappear altogether. Like every other frenzy, the PC mania's ending was punctuated with a scandal. That, too, is a characteristic of the end stages of a mania, something we will explore in greater detail in later chapters.

The biotech mania that took hold in the late 1980s and early 1990s was even more intense, in some ways, than the industry bubbles that occurred before it, but it had the requisite characteristics of a true bubble. One of its most important features was the complexity of the science involved. One interesting feature of most bubbles that are based on innovation is the degree of difficulty we find in analyzing the prospects of the new technology involved. The science of biotechnology is so complex that few investors, or analysts for that matter, were able to accurately assess the true viability of each of the companies in question. (The complicity of analysts in selling questionable ideas to the investing public would become an even hotter issue when the Internet bubble burst nearly 10 years later.) But the promise of disease-curing, life-span-extending technologies was compelling to investors and regular folk as well. The excitement generated by the new advances promised by biotech caught Wall Street by storm in 1991.

PaineWebber's Kerschner notes that 30 biotech companies went public in 1991. Riding the wave of Amgen's success in bioengineering two successful drugs, investors backed any company that had a scientific-sounding name. PaineWebber's biopharmaceutical stock index rose 189 percent in 1991. *Business Week* noted at the time that "if in January 1991 you had invested in one of the six companies with 'immune' in its name—Immunex, Immulogic, ImmunoGen, Immunomedics, MedImmune or Immune Response—you'd have a 60–1,200% gain by December."[44] Sounds quite similar to the dotcom frenzy that followed, doesn't it? As the following table shows, biotech stocks suffered a bear market that punished unthinking and uncritical investors over the subsequent six years.

A Tale of 35 Biotech Stocks

COMPANY	12/91 PRICE	1992 LOW PRICE	5/5/98 PRICE	OR DATE ACQUIRED
Affymax	$28.500	$14.000	$30.000	3/95
Alliance Phar	29.250	9.250	7.375	
Alteon	30.000	8.250	4.313	
Amgen[1]	37.875	24.625	59.813	

COMPANY	12/91 PRICE	1992 LOW PRICE	5/5/98 PRICE	OR DATE ACQUIRED
Applied Bioscience	14.250	8.375	10.844	9/96
Athena Neurosci [1,2]	14.625	6.625	8.462	7/96
Biochem Phar	9.813	5.313	25.125	
Biogen [1]	20.000	9.125	44.500	
Centocor [1]	53.500	9.500	41.125	
Chiron [1]	17.438	8.688	19.688	
Collagen	21.750	13.250	18.750	
Cygnus [1,2]	22.750	8.000	11.125	
Cytogen	18.500	13.375	1.313	
Diagnostic Products	36.750	20.125	28.938	
Enzon	14.125	5.875	5.875	
Genentech [3]	32.250	25.750	68.813	
Genetics Institute	38.000	38.000	39.250	1/92
Gensia Sicor [1]	34.667	18.250	5.063	
Genzyme [1,2]	28.519	15.777	31.438	
ICOS [1,2]	11.500	5.250	15.000	
Immune Response	39.250	12.250	12.750	
Immunex [1]	59.250	22.500	72.250	
Immunomedics	8.625	5.500	5.125	
Life Technologies	11.667	10.500	35.625	
Liposome Co	14.125	7.375	5.906	
Medimmune	43.750	12.500	53.125	
Molecular Biosystems	36.500	17.000	9.938	
Regeneron Phar	18.125	7.750	10.000	
Scios	22.500	6.250	12.750	
Sequus Phar [1]	18.500	6.875	12.063	
Somatogen	43.000	13.000	9.438	
Synergen	68.500	32.250	9.250	12/94
SyStemix	54.750	18.250	19.500	2/97
US Bioscience	78.000	12.250	9.063	
Xoma [1]	21.000	8.750	5.125	

Source: PaineWebber

The innovators made millions of dollars in all these cases, in part by taking the risk of starting a new business, but also by selling a portion of their stock to the investing public while their companies' share prices were selling at peak valuations. That would be true of auto company assemblers, PC builders, biotech businessmen, and Internet entrepreneurs.

Early innovators like Thomas Edison, George Westinghouse, Alexander Graham Bell, Samuel Insull, Henry Ford, and Billie Durant would get rich in each successive wave of advancement. That was true in every era from plank roads to railroads to autos, radio, and beyond. The financiers who supplied the capital for each new project would also benefit handsomely. The elder J. P. Morgan and his contemporaries would not only finance much of the expansion, but would ultimately control a sizable number of the assets as well.

The technological innovations that took place at the start of the industrial age were as revolutionary as the advent and arrival of the information age. There were some very big winners who were the business idols of their day. There were big losers when the bust finally came. And there were villains who, right or wrong, paid a large price for being the poster children for the excesses of the moment. We will compare those characters later in the book, but for every Ken Lay, Gary Winnik, or Dennis Kozlowski, you can find a Samuel Insull, Charles Mitchell, or Richard Whitney.

Insana Insight: One of the ancillary lessons to be learned in this exercise is that the early investors, though they may not see the inevitable crash coming, still manage to cash out their winnings before all the trouble begins. That has been true in plank roads, railroads, radio, and the Internet. While I am not suggesting a conspiracy of any sort, still, in all bubbles some obvious frauds are perpetrated. But even the most optimistic entrepreneur takes some profits off the table, if nothing else to diversify some of his or her assets that have grown in value. Karlheinz Muhr, a Wall Street professional who specializes in managing risk in large portfolios, teaches clients that they need to protect their portfolios when their investments are highly concentrated in a particular asset class. And while he believes that you cannot get wealthy through diversification, you can maintain wealth by spreading the profits from a concentrated position over a variety of asset classes once your investment has reached critical mass. That insight is often lost on investors who have accumulated great sums of money during the inflation phase of an asset bubble. Rather than taking profits and accumulating wealth, many simply let the profits ride for far too long in the hope of achieving still greater returns. That moment of mass delusion, when most investors do just that, led to one of the oldest maxims on Wall Street: "Bulls make money. Bears make money. Pigs get slaughtered."

4

——— ——— ——— ——— ——— ——— ———

TINY BUBBLES

There are physicists, theologians, sociologists, and market analysts who have long sought a grand unifying theory to explain the various phenomena they study. In the case of physicists, the so-called grand unifying theory will tidy up all the loose ends that quantum theory has yet to explain and answer the last questions we have about the origin, behavior, and life cycle of our universe. In theology, the questions about the nature of man and the meaning of life still defy explanation despite advances in science. In sociology, experts look for behavioral patterns that will allow them to predict how crowds will react in certain circumstances. Market specialists also examine behavior, crowd psychology, and the patterns that repeat themselves throughout market history.

Boom and bust cycles describe the economic environment in capitalist societies. Cyclical patterns show themselves in stock-, bond-, and commodity-market history. Bubbles are a feature of that cyclical behavior and, quite remarkably, share the same characteristics whether we are discussing mammoth secular market trends or small fads that occur within larger cyclical phenomena.

Closed-End Fun

Sometimes, smaller bubbles can occur apart from a generalized trend in the stock market. Case in point, the bubble in closed-end country funds that took place in the mid-to-late 1980s. Hyping the benefits of Europe's plan to integrate economically, mutual-fund marketers sold shares in mutual funds that became proxies for the markets of Europe. Eventually, the funds included other geographies as well, but in the late 1980s, Europe was the center of the action.

Before we examine the phenomenon itself, a little background on why Europe was such a fertile area in which to invest as the 1980s drew to a close. While the U.S. markets languished in the wake of the 1987 stock-market crash, Europe was making enormous plans to put an end, once and for all, to the policy clashes that kept the members of the European Common Market from operating as a cohesive economic force. Despite the Treaty of Rome, which in 1957 set the parameters for an integrated and eventually united Europe, the culturally different countries of the EC only infrequently harmonized their political and economic policies to the good of the entire continent. But as the U.S. and Japanese economies grew strong in subsequent decades, European officials who shared a vision of a fully integrated continent began the process of creating a single economic power bloc, complete with synchronized fiscal, monetary, and tax policies and a single currency. It was a herculean undertaking that was completed successfully at the start of the new millennium. But investors began to capitalize on the planned cooperation as the decade of the eighties came to a close.

Forecasting a more efficient, leaner, meaner, and productive Europe, Wall Street investment houses began peddling "closed-end country funds." These vehicles were closed-end mutual funds that purchased a basket of stocks representative of the equities in a specific European market. Closed-end funds, unlike open-end funds, limit the number of units created and sold to investors, so like stocks, there is a scarcity value associated with them as well as with the underlying securities that make up their investments. Because of the scarcity value, there are times when the price of each fund unit can trade at a premium to the value of the underlying assets. Or, conversely, sometimes the fund units trade at a discount to their asset values. Hence the volatility in closed-end funds can be quite a bit greater than their open-end counterparts, where more and more units are created as investor demand dictates.

The hyperbolic way in which the prospects for an integrated Europe were marketed gave rise to a bubble in these funds that exhibited exactly the same characteristics we would expect in bigger bubbles. Shares of these funds soared in value, peaking dramatically in 1989. The Germany Fund, the New Germany Fund, the Italy, Spain, and Portugal Funds were the darlings of their day. The added kicker, by the way, that drove the hottest action in closed-end country funds came as the Soviet Union was dissolving, the Berlin Wall was falling, and the so-called peace dividend was being created.

Suddenly the funds began trading at significant premiums to their underlying asset values. It was not unusual for the funds to be priced at 150 percent of the value of the assets in the portfolio. Again, the presumed scarcity value of these investment vehicles made them much-sought-after commodities. Sophisticated, well-heeled investors could easily buy European stocks in their home markets, but individual investors were limited to more costly options. The country funds gave everyone equal access to foreign markets without the bother of having to travel to far-flung places or engage in any serious study of overseas politics and economics. The frenzy was on. Despite warnings from experts not to overpay for closed-end funds, which should normally be bought at a discount, not a premium to the underlying asset values, investors bid up the shares. They scoured the world for new funds in exotic markets like Thailand, Malaysia, and Indonesia. The Russia Fund was a late favorite that burst onto the scene as the former Soviet Union inched toward replacing its state-run economy with an embryonic capitalist system. One of my personal favorites was the Cuba Fund, which was a closed-end country fund that expected to invest in Cuban securities. Since it was illegal for Americans to invest in Cuba, not to mention difficult since there wasn't anything in which to invest, the Cuba Fund invested some of its money in Florida-based or Caribbean-based companies that stood to profit from doing business with Cuba when and if that ever happened. A lot of the Cuba Fund was invested in T-bills or other cash equivalents, sitting idle but waiting for the day when Cuba would be ready and willing to take American investment dollars. Such was the craze that the Cuba Fund was actively bid up.

Germany Fund

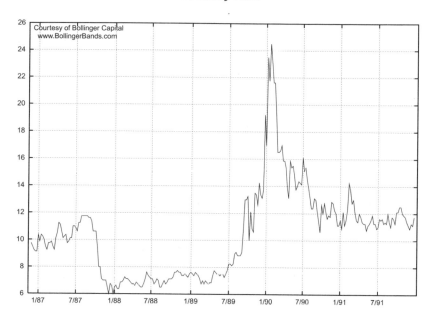

Austria Fund

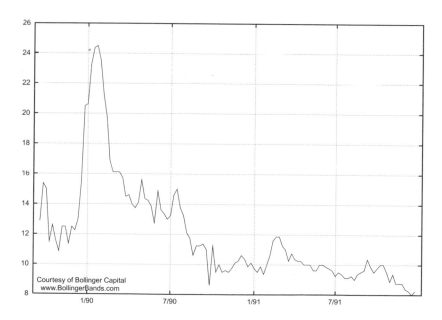

Spain Fund

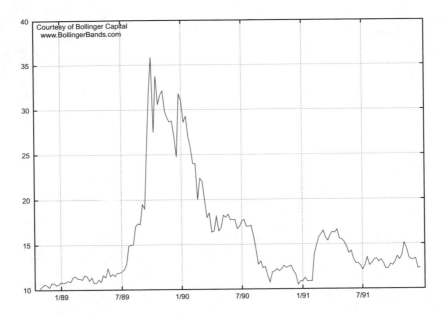

Italy Fund

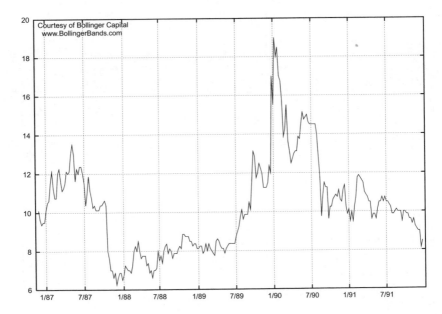

Thai Fund

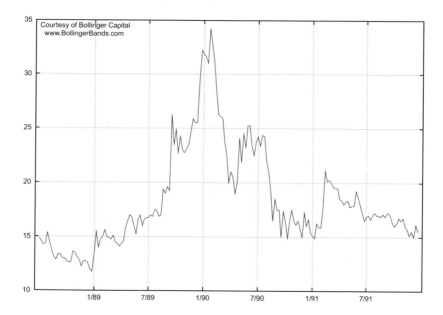

Courtesy of Bollinger Capital
www.BollingerBands.com

Interest in those countries would be dwarfed by the emerging mar ket bubble that expanded in the middle of the next decade, only to crash with world-class force in 1997. Still, as the U.S. market crested in the autumn of 1987, single-country, closed-end funds were still growing in popularity and would continue to do so for another two years. Part of the action was driven by U.S. investors looking to diversify their stock holdings away from American assets, which by that time had gone up an astronomical amount. But Japanese investors, flush with cash from their rip-roaring bull market, truly exploited the asset class. Japanese investors had a large appetite for all kinds of investments as their market was reaching its historic peak in the fall and winter of 1989. Not only did their hot money push the closed-end country funds to ridiculous prices and valuations, it also poured into Impressionist art, U.S. real estate (remember Rockefeller Center?), golf courses (remember Pebble Beach?), American cattle ranches, and expensive jewelry.

As early as 1987, the Taiwan Fund sold at a 270 percent premium to its net asset value.[1] At the peak of the single-country, closed-end fund mania, investors in the Spain Fund could have bought all 50 stocks in the fund's portfolio, in Spain itself, "at well below half the price of the Spain Fund!"[2] As I suggested earlier, however, foreign investors were usually prohibited at the time from buying shares in the markets of Europe or Asia directly, hence the need for a proxy like these. The forbidden fruit of foreign markets was much too appealing for many to resist, despite the high costs and high volatility that were the dominant feature of closed-end funds at the time.

Wall Street firms met the rising demand with a proliferation of mutual funds and other investment vehicles designed to offer investors from all over the world a chance to go global. A total of 50 country funds were already trading or registered to be listed by the autumn of 1989, with tens of billions of dollars invested in them. Brokerage firms introduced variations on the theme with warrants on various overseas markets. So-called Kingdom of Denmark warrants on the Japanese market became useful proxies for Japan's benchmark Nikkei. I recall that as the Nikkei began to crack in the early days of 1990, savvy American investors used the warrants as an easy way to short the Japanese market. Some made quite a killing thanks to the emergence of the foreign market surrogates. However, closed-end country funds were essentially one-way bets on the markets of the world. Until the crash came, the only way to play was to the upside.

Submerging Markets

By 1989, closed-end funds were the rage on Wall Street, with the European markets as the focus. Emerging market funds tagged along for the ride. But once again, what passed for research and analysis proved to be only marketing savvy and promotional hype. True, Europe would unite economically in the year 2000, with a single currency and improved prospects for growth. But investors and analysts failed to anticipate the problems and costs associated with that planned integration. The fall of the Berlin Wall allowed West and East Germany to reunite as a prelude to a wider European union. But the cost of bringing Berlin back to the fatherland was astronomical. West

Germany, under Chancellor Helmut Schmidt, essentially bought out East Germany and, very simply, overpaid. The price of integration threw Germany's finances into turmoil, fed inflation, and pushed domestic interest rates higher than they would otherwise have been. Higher inflation was a feature of the global economy, causing many central banks to tighten policy and leading to slower growth around the world. The Japanese market peaked out, eventually siphoning off all the available capital, or hot money, that was used to inflate the bubble in closed-end country funds and other speculative vehicles. When the Gulf War came a little over a year later, the entire world was in recession, a factor not anticipated by the country-fund enthusiasts.

The road to pan-European union was difficult as well. Denmark, neighbor to the 1991 Maastricht Accord that set the stage for the creation of the new single currency, the euro, took several extra years to opt in. Great Britain stayed out of the union in 1992 amid the collapse of its currency, the pound sterling; it severed its link to Europe's currency regime at the time, deciding to float the British pound against all other currencies and avoid the difficulties of harmonizing its economic policies with those of the Continent. Other countries failed to opt in, threatening the planned merger.

The funds crashed as those cracks in Europe's newfound unity began to appear. They have yet to reemerge as investment darlings and have been replaced by other vehicles that allow investors to reap rewards in foreign markets through more direct means. Some funds, like those directly focused on Europe, collapsed, never to regain their former stature. The emerging market country funds came back to life when emerging market bubbles in Asia and elsewhere renewed interest in these investments. Sadly, they crashed again in 1997 and have stayed in single digits ever since.

These smaller bubbles recur with even greater frequency than the kind that affect entire markets or whole economies. They all share the same characteristics of the bigger brethren, but they do not cause as much overall damage. The emergence of an integrated pan-European trading zone was a displacing event that triggered the burst of action. Hot money, flowing into country funds, provided the fuel. Speculative fervor about the promise of a reinvigorated Europe created the hyper-trading activity that drove fund unit prices well above intrinsic values. And the failure of the integration process to deliver immediate and measurable benefits, coupled with rising global interest rates, popped the bubble, causing a crash in country-fund shares. It was classic bubble behavior writ small.

Country funds are not the only area of the investment world that experiences these tinier bubbles. A host of fads have gripped investors periodically, from oil-and-gas limited partnerships to solar-panel investments to theme restaurants to collectibles. The patterns are always the same, driven by the belief that somehow, someway, the rules of investing are being rewritten. Each event, as we have stated, drives the prices and valuations of the new, new thing to ever-greater heights, only to collapse by the requisite 70 to 90 percent.

Costly Collectibles

In the case of one category of "investment," for lack of a better description, sometimes the action is so out of line with underlying value that it merits special attention. We all have stories of the comic books, trading cards, and school lunch boxes we once owned but gave away and are now worth a small fortune. Everyone we know claims to have owned Hank Aaron's rookie card, the very first copy of *Superman,* or a *Star Trek* lunch box that is today highly coveted. And indeed, in some cases those nostalgic old items are worth countless thousands of dollars. But such rarities cannot be purchased and stored with the foresight that one day they will be worth significantly more than the price for which they were paid. No one could have guessed that Hank Aaron would hit 714 home runs, or that *Superman* would be among the first multimedia hits of modern times, or that *Star Trek* would even survive its first ratings-challenged season.

But that never stopped the successful marketing of instant collectibles that formed their own bubbles as soon as they were introduced to the market. I mentioned Pokémon earlier in the book with specific reference to the mania for shares in 4 Kids Entertainment, the licensor of Pokémon products in the mid-1990s. 4 Kids benefited handsomely from the Pokémon trading cards, toys, and television shows that sprang from the original Japanese hit items. While the trading frenzy in 4 Kids shares was irrationally exuberant, it was the product of a successful toy line and, as such, was not entirely without merit. The valuation extremes seen in the company's stock price hit absurd levels, and as mentioned, investors believed that the Pokémon craze would not only last forever but grow exponentially forever as well. That's where the problem often lies. It's not that the product's or service's popularity won't grow forever—it's that products or services, regardless of their utility value, simply cannot grow exponentially forever, thanks to a finite consumer base and the law of large numbers.

Kid Stuff

The extraordinary run-up in the prices for Beanie Babies, however, put the Pokémon action to shame. The cute, bean-filled toys cost little to produce and were by no means unique. True, the original Beanie Babies carried with them "certificates of authenticity," separating them from Beanie Baby wanna-bes, but that was about it. Regardless of the questionable intrinsic value of Beanie Baby dolls, consumers were taken with these little stuffed toys and, at the height of the frenzy, bid them up to astronomical prices. The price-to-intrinsic-value gap was in some cases far wider than ever seen in financial market bubbles of similar intensity.

Ty Warner's marketing of Beanie Baby dolls exploited collectible psychology brilliantly. The billionaire marketing whiz would retire many of the Beanie Baby models he produced each year, making their scarcity value on the secondary market shoot quickly skyward. By limiting the production of old-model Beanies, Warner helped create demand for newly issued characters as well, a tactic that drove the manic pace of sales for quite a bit longer than anyone would have ever predicted. Internet stock promoters used a similar tactic when selling tech shares to the public. Internet firms going public through IPOs often restricted the offering size to about 20 percent of the company's outstanding shares. The limited supply of stock in a market where the demand for Internet shares was insatiable not only helped to propel new issues to stratospheric levels, but also solidly supported the after-market behavior of the issues.

Warner manipulated Beanies' scarcity with large-scale giveaways, a combination that bordered on genius. Product tie-ins with McDonald's and Beanie Baby "giveaway days" at ball games and the like often drove attendance at these events considerably higher. The *Montreal Gazette* reported in 1998 that ballpark attendance rose as much as 25 percent when the little dolls were handed out for free.[3] Not only did Warner create excess demand through shrewd marketing deals, he also limited supplies through even more cunning strategies.

Perhaps Warner's most cunning ploy was to announce that he would cease production of all dolls at the end of the 20th century, seven years after their introduction. That announcement sent buyers, for whom the notion that Beanie Babies might one day no longer be produced was unthinkable, into a panic. Prices exploded on the secondary market, often the on-line auction market on eBay.

Cabbage Patch Kids may have caused queues at stores around the country and the occasional trampling of customers who were caught in the last-minute Christmas rush to buy them in December 1983, but Beanie Babies represented a true bubble. The so-called hang-tags and tush-tags that authenticated the Beanie had to be in perfect condition for a baby to bring full price in the secondary, or trading, market. Wrinkles, creases, or tears pushed Beanie prices down as much as 60 percent.[4] In September of 1998, the *Wall Street Journal*'s Richard Gibson wrote of a man who had lost a considerable sum of money in the stock market (the market had plunged in late August, early September) and decided to take all of his remaining cash and plow it into Beanie Babies. In a month and a half, he claimed he had regained all his lost wealth.[5] Some 43,000 Beanie Baby web sites emerged by the end of 1999. *Mary Beth's Beanie World* magazine boasted 1 million readers in the United States at that time. When Ty Warner threatened to cease production, Ty Inc.'s web site received 3.44 billion visits.[6]

Today, Beanie Baby prices have come back down to realistic levels. They have, in short, crashed. There is, of course, no telling whether in 20, 30, or 50 years Beanie Babies will be the type of collectible toys that have enduring value. That is an impossible forecast to make. But when any asset sells at over 1000 times its face value, someone has overpaid. That someone is usually the one holding it with the hope that someone else will pay 2000 times its face value . . . a forlorn hope, even in Beanie Baby land.

In 2002, only a few of the Beanie Babies offered on eBay's auction site managed to stay above their purchase prices. And even those that commanded premiums were still far below what the true believers expected over the long haul. Beanie Babies, Cabbage Patch Kids, Furbies, and Pokémon are not the types of crazes that cause wild dislocations in the nation's major financial markets or in the overall economy. But the behavior among participants is exactly the same as in larger events. These bubbles do not require massive infusions of liquidity or need to be socially or economically significant. Instead, simply the appearance of a toy like this is enough to lead to a mania. Once the new "must-have" item makes the scene, the hype, overtrading, and speculative excesses that mark a mania arrive in full flower. The inevitable crash comes either when prices move too far above the intrinsic value of the toy or another object of interest comes along to take its place. To borrow from Gertrude Stein, "a craze is a craze is a craze," regardless of size.

THE BIGGEST BUBBLE OF THEM ALL

The great bull market of the 1990s began on October 11, 1990. The bull move had a rather inauspicious start. It began in the throes of a global conflict in which the forces of Saddam Hussein had overrun Kuwait and were threatening the borders of Saudi Arabia, the world's biggest exporter of oil. The president of the United States, George Herbert Walker Bush, made it clear that Saddam Hussein's incursion "would not stand." His plan to liberate Kuwait and protect Western oil interests was hatched in the months immediately following Saddam's August 2 invasion.

As I discussed in *The Message of the Markets*, the financial markets behaved strangely in the autumn of that year. Stocks began to rally in October despite obvious worries around the world that a war between coalition partners and the battle-hardened Iraqi army could prove bloody and quite costly. World oil supplies were at risk. Destruction of Kuwaiti and Saudi oil fields meant $100-a-barrel oil, global recession, and a militarily destabilized world. Such was the thinking of the time. But instead of realizing that doomsday scenario, the Allies won a quick and decisive victory. Oil prices plunged as a consequence and financial markets rallied in anticipation of an economic recovery rather than a debilitating and deepening recession.

The stock market hit its bear market lows in October and never looked back. In fact, on the day war broke out between the Allies and

Iraq, the Dow Jones Industrial Average jumped a surprising 107 points, celebrating a victory that, while certain in retrospect, was far from assured at the time. (Such are the powers of the markets to discount future events, but that is the subject of a previous book.) The rally, which would last a record nine and a half years, would be the longest, most powerful, and most durable bull market in U.S. history. It would also evolve into the biggest speculative episode, or bubble, in financial market history.

By the time the market peaked in March of 2000, the percentage of household assets invested in equities exceeded that of real estate, a first in this country's history. Nearly 50 percent of all American households owned stock, another record. Somewhere between 80 and 100 million Americans had either direct or indirect exposure to the stock market, through burgeoning 401(k) plans, pension funds, or through their wildly speculative day-trading activities. At the height of the 1920s bull market, there were only 6 million active brokerage accounts in the United States out of a population of 120 million! And they thought *that* bull market was wild.

In addition to the orgy of speculation, as it would come to be described by some observers, the old rules of market valuation were shattered. Standard gauges of the stock market's absolute and relative values rose to untold highs. Price-to-earnings, price-to-book, and price-to-dividend ratios all reached extremes not seen in this or any other country's economic history. Relative valuations compared with bonds or precious metals also widened to new levels. More millionaires and billionaires were minted, and at a faster pace, than at any time since the Gilded Age. The Internet's biggest star, Jeff Bezos, founder of on-line bookseller Amazon.com, was named *Time* magazine's Person of the Year in 1999. The peak value of his stake in Amazon reached $10 billion. And that mind-numbing figure was built in the space of only a few years. Internet CEOs became celebrities, as did Wall Street analysts and CEOs of Fortune 500 firms. Last but not least, business journalists became almost as recognizable as their mainstream counterparts. Such was the interest in anything related to business.

The ancillary effects of this bubble created inflated values in other areas of the economy as well. The bubble in tech boosted home values in certain areas of the country to astronomical heights. In Silicon Valley and Silicon Alley, home prices soared. Restaurants in both areas were the beneficiaries of the momentary largesse of Internet entrepreneurs and investment bankers who routinely spent thousands of dollars on client dinners.

I should note, however, that unlike previous bubbles, a companion bubble in real estate everywhere did not occur—rather surprisingly, I might add. Still, the McMansions built by those newly minted stock-market millionaires got great press in lifestyle sections of the nation's newspapers and magazines. In less than 40 years, the size of the average house in America doubled from 2000 to 4000 square feet. Eight-thousand-square-foot homes in New York's luxurious Hamptons community were the prize possessions of the investment banking elite. The colossal homes of the likes of Bill Gates, Larry Ellison, and Jay Walker were the envy of even the wealthiest on Wall Street.

Gilded Age

It was a heady time, quite unlike any other in recent memory. An entire nation of investors and entrepreneurs was destined to be rich. And it all began quietly, without notice, in a world at war nearly 10 years prior. Few predicted the eventual outcome. But by its end, almost everyone thought that prosperity would last forever and that a comfortable retirement was only a few short years away. Few, if any, predicted the market's collapse or the economy's future troubles. But at both the beginning and the end of the run, some elements of the changes were in fact predictable. All great bull markets, bubbles, and manias start and end with similar ingredients. They are fueled by similar events and punctuated by remarkably similar stories of wealth, greed, and hubris. They are, like human nature, quite repetitive, but for some reason, this is rarely recognized.

That all appears quite obvious now, but the seeds of this speculative event were sown in the early days of the 1990s, as stocks emerged from a 12-month bear market and the economy tentatively emerged from recession. In many ways, the early days of the 1990s bull market are unremarkable compared with its very last days. While growth was powerful and steady, stocks at the beginning of the bull market did not see the heart-stopping gains that occurred between 1995 and 2000, though there were definitely some speculative elements at work. Between 1990 and 1995, a mutual-fund mania gripped investors. As they took on more and more responsibility for their own retirement savings plan, as mandated by the shift from defined benefit to defined contribution savings plans, individual investors snapped up mutual-fund shares like they were going out of style. In many ways, however, that shift in savings and investing habits was hardly irrational. Tax-advantaged savings accounts like the 401(k), IRA, and Keogh were a cut above the defined benefit plans that had, for so long, been used by employers to provide retirement security. The so-called defined benefits were often not so clearly defined. And in the case of financial difficulties or, God forbid, bankruptcy, defined benefits could ultimately be defined with the number zero. So the wholesale shift into a new class of investment vehicle was essential in order for a new generation of workers to save for the golden years.

Assets of stock-market mutual funds, which were puny throughout the great bull market of the 1980s, exploded to $1.1 trillion by 1998. Between 1996 and 2000, even more money entered the market—a total of $1.1 trillion was invested in mutual funds in that four-year stretch alone. In early 1998, investors threw $21 billion a month into equity mutual funds.[1] Those records were eclipsed in 1999 and 2000. Many observers (me included) fretted that the rush to mutual funds resembled the type of pooled investing madness that dominated the 1920s and 1960s and helped to bring about the market's eventual troubles in both those periods. Bank deposits plunged to about a quarter of household assets, a 50-year low, while stocks grew to 57.6 percent of household financial holdings, an all-time high.[2]

The concept behind that massive shift from bank deposits and CDs turned out to be a winner for most of the decade, but it was not without risk, both in the middle of the period and, disastrously, at the end. Stocks and bonds suffered important setbacks in 1994, at the height of our concerns. Some market analysts describe 1994 as a bear market year for stocks. The return on the S&P 500 was nil. Bonds, most assuredly, experienced the worst year in 70 years, suffering record-setting losses at the time and posting negative returns for the year. We will examine the bubble in the bond market in the early 1990s later in this book. The savage bear market that mauled bond-market investors was the predictable outcome of a yet another bubble, financed by easy money from the Fed and the Bank of Japan, but at the moment, that is a digression from our story. The setback in the stock market, however, only served to set the stage for more exuberant and volatile times. There would be bigger and scarier stock-market declines in 1997 and 1998 before the NASDAQ crash came in April 2000.

Still, the mutual-fund mania of the time was spectacular in its own way. As assets invested grew exponentially, the number of funds proliferated. In 1987, there were hundreds of funds dedicated to investing in stocks. By 1995, that number jumped to several thousand. And by the end of the decade, there were more stock-market mutual funds than there were stocks in which to invest!

Equity Mutual Funds Versus NYSE Stocks

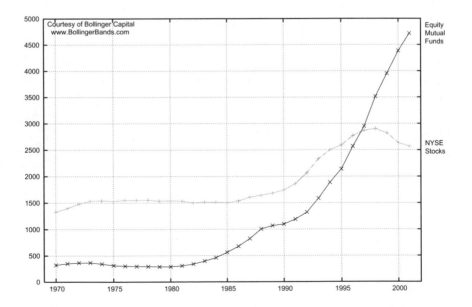

Courtesy of Bollinger Capital
www.BollingerBands.com

That immense imbalance in the supply and demand for stocks certainly helped to sustain and exacerbate the gains enjoyed by the equity market in the latter half of the 1990s.

Common Characteristics

Like any newly forming bubble, the ingredients for a new and massive bull market in stocks were evident. Falling interest rates and energy prices were instrumental in setting the stage for renewed economic growth that would be aggressively discounted by the stock market before a recovery became apparent to the general population. And, as we will see time and time again, a major crisis, this time in the U.S. banking community, sparked an aggressive move by the Federal Reserve to lower interest rates and expand the money supply to allow the nation's most troubled lenders to recapitalize themselves and help lead the economy out of its slump. In the 1990s, each financial crisis set the stage for a new and bigger bubble to emerge from the debris of the previous one. While some academics and monetary-policy officials might disagree, the monetary-policy response to each significant crisis of the nineties—the banking crisis in 1991 (remember when both Congressman John Dingell and presidential candidate H. Ross Perot publicly declared Citicorp insolvent?), the Mexican debt crisis in 1995, the Asian currency crisis in 1997, the collapse of Long-Term Capital in 1998—contributed to the next wave of market euphoria.

This idea is not new. As I noted before, market historian Marc Faber cites the work of Frederich Hayek and Irving Fisher, who, many years ago, observed that monetary policy is integral to the development of market manias. The entire decade was chock-full of the ingredients needed to create, extend, and fully inflate the bubble until it was bigger than any other bubble in financial market history. And indeed, by the time it reached its full size, the bubble in technology and Internet stocks, as measured by the NASDAQ Composite or the S&P 500, was the biggest bubble of all time.

"NASDAQ MANIA"

In the wake of the September 11 terrorist attacks on the World Trade Center and the Pentagon, it is almost impossible to accurately recall the ebullience of the previous decade. There was, in the year 2000, a general sense that anything was possible. New technologies promised to make our lives simpler, more efficient, more enjoyable, and far longer than anyone ever before imagined. Internet technology, broadband service, biotechnology, and genomics all promised the types of scientific breakthroughs that had once been the realm of science fiction. "Virtual reality" was going to allow us to transport ourselves quickly along the information superhighway of life, telecommuting to work, shopping in cyberspace, messaging our friends instantly, while the mapping of the human genome would extend our life span by years if not decades. New and implantable body parts would allow us to run like a sophisticated airplane, flying at ever higher altitudes in life as long as we maintained the fuselage, replaced worn-out parts, and added a memory chip here or there to aid the medical community in understanding our personal medical histories. It was a brave new world.

That brave new world had some brave new heroes as well. Jeff Bezos opened a public library that had any book we could imagine we wanted. He sold it to us at a discount, while Jay Walker gave us cheap airfares to any destination, as long as we purchased our tickets on the Net. John Chambers promised us an unending stream of broadband capacity that would deliver new and exciting services to our homes, while Bill Gates became the richest man in the world, by a factor of two, supplying the software that powered the gateways to cyberspace. Everything we thought or did would be different from anything we had thought or done in the decades and centuries before. We were creating a new human form, an elevated being that would not be bounded by the limitations of time or space. Such was the euphoria that gripped the nation at the start of the millennium.

That euphoria, of course, was inextricably linked to the behavior of financial markets. Because of the economy's new paradigm, a paradigm shift had taken place in the stock market as well. Bear markets were a thing of the past. Stocks had only one way to go, and that was up. The normal constraints of valuation and the vagaries of the business cycle had been repealed. Eternally rising rates of productivity and never-ending noninflationary growth were now the norm. Because of the massive shift in the underlying composition of the economy, prosperity would become a permanent feature of economic life. It was only a matter of time before poverty, first in America and later in the rest of the wired world, would become a vestige of the "old economy."

Recall, as well, the frenzy over the so-called B-to-B companies, like Ariba and others. Their new Internet marketplaces allowed companies to buy and sell goods and services to one another over the Net. The intense and intimate customer/supplier relationship was about to become frictionless. Gone would be the middleman, who extracted a pound or two of flesh from the sales process. Business costs would plunge and profits would grow by leaps and bounds. True, entire groups of people employed in the middle would be driven out of work, but that transitional unemployment would be more than compensated for by the dramatic efficiencies that accrued to the corporate entity. The company, flush with profits, would seek out new and bigger opportunities and hire workers anew. These dynamic and hyper-efficient business enterprises would be the envy of the world as they deployed capital more effectively and to greater productive use than ever before.

I say these things not derisively, but only in an effort to describe the environment in which the most recent bubble inflated and expanded to its record size. In point of fact, many of these early promises are coming true. However, the realities that we are beginning to appreciate were reflected in the prices of many New Age stocks long before the bubble burst. Hence, as many intelligent pundits observed at the time, the bubble stocks reached their terminal values when the market peaked, but the industries that they represented would not mature, in some cases, for years, if not decades. That was true in many new paradigm periods of the past as well; whether it was in the railroad era, radio era, or computer and electronics era, this type of thinking and behavior accompanied each and every bubble.

Al Gore's thoughts on the Internet, again, merely echoed the past when he quoted a prominent scientist: "Supercomputers break these barriers to understanding. They, in effect, shrink oceans, zoom in on molecules, slow down physics and fast forward climates." [3]

Pax Americana II

Interestingly, these lofty ideals were established in what most believed to be an unprecedented time of peace and prosperity. The 1990s were home to the longest economic expansion in American history. And the decade-long "Pax Americana" had led some to declare the end of history, where history was defined as a consequence of armed struggle among competing national interests. In fact, proponents of the new paradigm envisioned a world without national borders and without boundaries of any sort, a true global village that was democratic and egalitarian, where information was distributed immediately, accurately, and equitably among the citizens of the world. There had been no other moment in history like this one. Or so some thought. Comparisons to previous bouts of such euphoria were deemed inapplicable and shortsighted. *Luddite* was a common description for those who dared compared the Internet to the radio, the auto, or the railroad. Other nicknames, unprintable in a family publication, were applied to those of us who suggested that the mania in technology and Internet stocks was just another example of a market pushed to extremes by the hope and hype of "true believers."

I should take a moment to note that while many observers, myself included, were skeptical about the Internet's true profit potential, it didn't stop us from contemplating joining or starting our own Internet enterprises. As a professional journalist, I was making quite a good salary both at the beginning and at the height of the bubble in stocks. But I, along with many of my colleagues, was quite envious of several of our friends and acquaintances who had become instant millionaires at dot-com firms. Jim Cramer, founder of theStreet.com, had a stake in the firm valued, I believe, at $300 million the first day theStreet.com became a public company. David Kansas, a young journalist like us, had left the *Wall Street Journal* to become theStreet's managing editor and was worth an instant $9 million that day as well. Needless to say, many of us looked for ways to hitch our own wagons to the information superhighway. Luckily, I stayed put, collected my salary, and avoided losing the equity I had gained from nearly a decade with CNBC and its parent company, General Electric. No doubt, our equity value has declined in recent years, but it remains mostly intact, despite its fallen price. Sometimes it's best to be bound contractually to a firm as others venture out into riskier territory. While you give away some of the upside, you are protected rather nicely from the downside. In the case of theStreet.com (and this is not a knock against either the site or Jim Cramer), the stock plunged from an all-time high of over $70 a share to less than $2.50 a share today. And as was the case with many instant millionaires—and instant billionaires, for that matter—it's not that easy to keep the money when it comes that quickly. Indeed, of *Forbes* magazine's ranking of the world's billionaires, 87 fell of their perches in 2002 . . . talk about easy come, easy go!

Nouveau Riche

But still a lot of new wealth was created during the tech boom. Those who benefited most thought it would go on forever. Economist John Kenneth Galbraith wrote in his classic work *The Great Crash of 1929* that similar feelings gripped the public in the 1920s. Then, investors speculated wildly not only in stocks but in real estate. The Florida real estate market was the hottest in the country at the time. Of it Galbraith wrote, "The Florida land boom was the first indication of the mood of the twenties and the conviction that God intended the middle class to be rich."[4]

It was against a very similar backdrop that stocks soared to unprecedented heights in the 1990s and that the average investor, from technology company employees to vagrants on the street, found a deep and abiding interest in the ways of Wall Street. In *The Message of the Markets,* I shared a story about a homeless man who asked a New York Stock Exchange floor trader about an Internet stock in late December of 1999. I do not mean to condescend to even the least financially secure among us, but when the homeless are trading Internet stocks, it's obvious to me that the last buyers have entered the market and the only thing for the savvy investor to do is to sell. The tale is reminiscent of Bernard Baruch's story about how, when he was asked for a stock tip by a shoeshine boy in 1929, he promptly went to his office and sold all his stocks. He survived the crash. The shoeshine boy probably didn't.

Broken Barriers

On March 10, 2000, the NASDAQ Composite hit its all-time high of 5048. As recently as the autumn of 1998, it had traded as low as 1400 or so, in the depths of the Russia/Long-Term Capital crisis. The ensuing 250 percent gain included a rally of 85 percent in 1999, a record advance for any major market average in the history of the world! The bull market in stocks between 1995 and 2000 shattered every record scored in previous bull runs. Length, size, valuations, and a host of other benchmarks were eclipsed in that five-year period. The three main stock-market gauges in the United States advanced 20 percent per year for an unprecedented five-year period. The performance skewed all the information on the average rate of return from equities going back 20 years. Suddenly, from 1985 to 2000, the average annual return on the S&P 500 jumped to 15 percent from the 10.6 percent annual gain that the market had delivered since 1926.

But while the overall stock-market performance was astonishing in those five years, the performance of NASDAQ stocks was simply breathtaking. Volatility in individual NASDAQ stocks shattered the old volatility records scored in the late 1920s. It was not unusual for NASDAQ-listed IPOs to score triple-digit percentage gains in the first day of trading. Big-name Internet stocks routinely jumped 20 percent or better in a single session. At its all-time high, the price-to-earnings ratio of NASDAQ, a key measure of valuation, exceed 200, an all-time high for any market.

As David Sylvester pointed out in the *San Jose Mercury News* in March of 2001, the NASDAQ's price-to-earnings ratio exploded to nearly 246 at its peak, up from an average of 41 between 1986 and 1989. In other words, "investors paid $41 a share for every $1 a share earned by NASDAQ companies" for 13 years, before that valuation benchmark expanded by a factor of six as the bubble became fully inflated.[5]

The NASDAQ 100, or top 100 NASDAQ companies, had a P/E of 3666 when the five largest companies were excluded. In other words, most NASDAQ companies were essentially selling at nearly infinite multiples of their expected profits. Veteran professional investors and naive individual investors showed blatant disregard for the valuation parameters that have always governed stock-market investing. While both absolute and relative valuation benchmarks can change slightly under different interest-rate, inflation, and growth scenarios, there were no scenarios that could have justified the extreme valuations witnessed at the NASDAQ's top in March of 2000.

Internet Insanity

Consider a brief recap of just how wild these gunslinging days of the Internet mania truly were. Here is a sampling of news items that illustrate just how frothy the market became as trading activity advanced and stock prices raced ever higher:

• By October of 1999, the combined market value of 199 Internet companies tracked by Morgan Stanley Internet analyst Mary Meeker reached an eye-popping $450 billion. Revenues totaled $21 billion. The companies have lost a combined $6.2 billion in the most recent 12-month period![6]

• America Online alone, by April of 1999, had a market value of $150 billion, equal to that of Coca-Cola. It sold at 600 times trailing 12-month earnings. At its peak during the 1920s. The Goldman Sachs Trading Company, one of the darlings of Wall Street in the 1920s, sold at 108 times earnings, while the likes of Polaroid or other so-called Nifty Fifty stocks of the early 1970s bubble sold at between 95 and 100 times earnings.[7]

• When it came to overvaluation extremes, Hal Varian of the New York Times found this gem in the work of newsletter writer Arnold Kling: "Yahoo!'s stock price valuation at that time (March

2000) could be justified only if it eventually received 24 billion page views a day, which meant that every man, woman and child would have to go to it each and every day."[8] I should add that each man, woman, and child would have to go to it four times a day to make the math work!

Other classic valuation benchmarks were violated in similar fashion. The so-called dividend yield on stocks plunged to levels never before seen on Wall Street. This yield, which is simply computed by dividing a company's annual dividend by its stock price, has been an accurate gauge of value for a century. Stocks appear to be cheap when the dividend yield is high, say 6 percent or so. And stocks have been historically considered richly priced when the dividend yield fell below 3 percent. The stock market's dividend yield fell below 2 percent at the peak in early 2000. For some industries, the yield fell below 1 percent, or, in the case of many new-era technology firms, was nonexistent since they didn't pay dividends at all.

Nasdaq Composite Index with 200-Day Moving Average

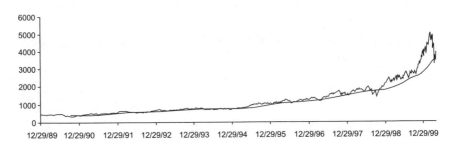

The NASDAQ Composite, at its all-time high, reached a new technical level compared with other major market peaks. Technical analyst John Roque, who analyzes stock-market charts for the Wall Street firm Arnold & S. Bleichroder, pointed out in early 2000 that the NAS-DAQ Comp traded at four standard deviations above its 200-day moving average. This is a rather arcane measure of a market's overextension, to be sure. But according to technical analyst John Roque, no other market average, in the history of the world, ever climbed so far above such an important trend line, anytime or anywhere! Here's an easier measure of overvaluation to comprehend. In normal times, the value of all publicly traded stocks trades between 40 and 60 percent of this nation's gross domestic product. If GDP is a trillion dollars, the value of the stock market—or market cap, as it is commonly called on Wall Street—would be between $400 billion and $600 billion. Market analyst Marc Faber points out that when the stock market reached its zenith in early 2000, the market cap of U.S. stocks reached 184 percent of GDP. In 1929, the market cap to GDP ratio was only 81 percent. That was a record at the time as well. Even more striking, Faber notes, is the fact that dollar trading volume in the U.S. market peaked at 288 percent of GDP in 2000, compared with 140 percent in 1929. Faber adds that dollar trading volume between 1930 and 1980 never exceeded 15 percent of GDP!

Hard to Believe

Some of my favorite stories, however, involve stocks whose Internet-related run-ups were absurd beyond belief. K-Tel International, which I have long described as a telephone marketing company that sells bad 1970s music, went from about $3 a share to $34 a share when it announced it would sell bad seventies music on the Internet. It trades at about 17 cents today.

Zapata Corporation, a maker of fish- and bonemeal, shot straight up on the day it announced it would deemphasize fish- and bonemeal and instead become an Internet holding company. Quite frankly, investors did not care if the planned restructuring made sense, as long as Zapata was turning itself into Zapata.com. The company, however, never made good on its promise to recast itself as a profitable Internet enterprise; instead, it became another also-ran of the Internet frenzy.

But such is the nature of the bubble beast. Each new mania, in some ways, exceeds the extremes of the prior experience. Japanese stocks were valued more richly than any other market in history, far surpassing the extremes set in the United States in 1987 or 1929. It

K-Tel 1995–2002

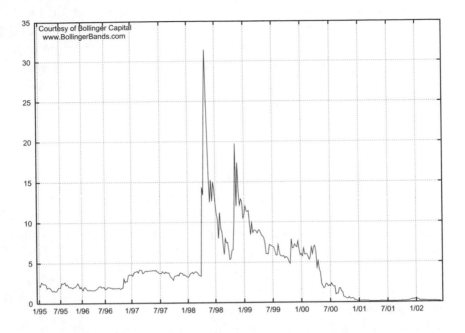

took less than a generation, albeit a generation of unrelated investors, to forget the lessons of Japan.

Lesson Lost

In that experience, the world at large believed that Japan had perfected an economic model that far surpassed Western-style capitalism. Tokyo's unique blend of mercantilism, capitalism, paternalism, and, to an extent, socialism became the standard by which the world measured itself in the 1980s. The Japanese markets, which were the direct beneficiaries of that excitement, were inflated to such an extent that the world's previous bubbles paled in comparison. That bubble, like our own, started with little fanfare. It collapsed into an economic black hole from which the Japanese economy has yet to extricate itself. But again, the belief at the top was that "it was different this time" and that the old rules of economics simply didn't apply. The bubble in the NASDAQ ended the same way. The NASDAQ, while significantly above its postcrash lows, remains nearly 60 percent below its all-time high. As of this writing, the NASDAQ Composite (unlike the Dow or S&P, I should note) needs to advance nearly 200 percent to return to its record high.

Like many bubbles of this magnitude, the bubble in NASDAQ and technology issues began with a technological innovation. Again think turnpike, railroad, automobile, electricity, radio, and computers for the appropriate historical links. It is in the mind of a great inventor, in the lab or on the factory floor, that we can find the origins of a bubble, and this time . . . it was no different.

Internet Inception

The true birthplace of this bubble is found in academia, where, decades ago, university professor/scientists were trying to find a way to communicate with one another via computer. Using the big mainframes that were the innovations of their era, they constructed a communications network that allowed them to "chat" with one another in a relatively convenient way. But like the experiments that long-preceded the advent of radio and television, this early version of the Internet remained a well-kept secret for many years.

The government and military also had something to do with the development of the computer network that would one day be known as the Internet. But it was not until CompuServe was formed that the commercial applications of such a service were truly explored.

You might be surprised to learn that CompuServe was actually a small start-up firm founded by Jeffrey M. Wilkins in Columbus, Ohio, at the tail end of the 1960s technology boom. It was described in the press as a data retrieval company as late as 1985 in a *New York Times* article that focused on a battle for control of the firm between its founder and its eventual buyer, H&R Block, the tax-preparation company.[9] According to the article, Wilkins was fighting to buy his company back, which he took public in 1979, because H&R Block didn't believe it appropriate for the company's management, including the founder, to retain an equity stake in the firm.[10] Even in those early days, Internet entrepreneurs wanted a piece of the action. Wilkins had sold his firm to H&R Block in 1980 in an effort to raise more capital. Their relationship would end in a feud over stock options, foreshadowing a much bigger debate about Internet riches that was still almost 20 years away.

The whole idea of electronic commerce had relatively humble beginnings. Exactly 20 years before the Internet bubble was fully inflated, both CompuServe and a rival firm, The Source, started "electronic information services for personal computer owners." [11] The budding on-line services offered several features that are only today being fully deployed in the Internet world, like electronic mail, "home shopping, electronic 'bulletin boards,' up-to-the-minute news, travel information, encyclopedias and much more." [12] The Source was started by the Reader's Digest Corporation. It would be followed in 1984 by Trintex, a joint venture among IBM, Sears, and CBS. Trintex, which in 1988 decided to offer videotext, would be renamed Prodigy. Like CompuServe, the venture between the nation's biggest computer company and biggest retailer (at that time) would attempt to capitalize on the emerging market for home shopping services and electronic information services. Anyone who recalls the on-line services of the day remembers the painfully long waits to download information, the awful printer quality (remember the dot-matrix printers?), and the relatively cumbersome nature of the entire process. It was a rather inauspicious start for an industry that would, within a decade, become the hottest investment idea in over a generation.

Unoriginal Origins

Venture capitalist Roger McNamee suggests that all bubbles begin in this manner, particularly those that involve great leaps in technology and new infrastructure build-outs. McNamee says that at first, a lot goes on under the radar screen of the general public. The "early adopters" experiment with form and function. Great strides are made with the enabling technologies that allow the new industry to develop. We witnessed that with canals, turnpikes, railroads, radio, and the automobile, not to mention television and the computer. It is only after those stages that competitors proliferate and demand for the new services begins to accelerate.

CompuServe, Prodigy, and The Source launched the Internet revolution, but they did not survive it intact. Just as IBM abandoned the market for personal computers and personal computing software, they would walk away from being a major player among Internet service providers, allowing more aggressive upstart companies to refine the early work and turn it into a commercial success. The company that managed to market Internet services aggressively and actually produce profits from that endeavor today owns the biggest media company in the world, AOL. But AOL also began humbly at the start of the information age.

In May of 1985, a small company called Quantum Computer Services incorporated in the state of Delaware. Over the next four years it would offer on-line services like Q-Link, PC-Link, America Online, and Promenade for various computer companies. The services, which rivaled the pioneers of the Internet, Prodigy and CompuServe, would, within a few years, become the leading providers of Internet access, with 34 million members around the world today, though that success was far from assured or envisioned at the time. In 1991, Quantum changed its name to America Online. On March 19, 1992, AOL sold a portion of its stock to the public at $11.50 a share, listing on the NASDAQ under the symbol AMER. In many ways, the greatest stock-market bubble of all time began at that very moment. Despite the fact that the development of the Internet had been going on for over 30 years, the greatest strides in its deployment came in the 1990s. The tiny firm itself had been experimenting with Internet access for seven years, largely unnoticed by the population at large. But in the minds of many observers, the IPO of AOL was a watershed moment that would give rise to an entire nation's fascination with Internet and technology investing.

AOL's aggressive pricing, branding, and marketing campaigns fostered rapid growth for dial-up Internet access, allowing other applications to flourish as well. It essentially proved that the Internet and its graphic companion, the World Wide Web, had great mass-market appeal, despite the skepticism of even those who helped to invent it. As a result, names like Yahoo!, Amazon.com, and eBay burst onto the Internet scene. And the companies that supported the build-out of Internet infrastructure—like Cisco, Oracle, Sun, and JDS Uniphase—became household names as the stock market created a new wave of Gilded Age entrepreneurs. Each new innovation in Internet technology led to a new frenzy in related stocks. Each climbed faster than the group before it. From ISPs to B-to-C, to B-to-B, individual investors salivated, in Pavlovian fashion, as Wall Street introduced each new acronym.

Yahoo!, for instance, made its way into the S&P 500 faster than any other company in U.S. market history. Its peak market capitalization, at $250 billion, was greater than that of either the American auto or airline industries at the time. The fascination with the Internet is now legend, but we have, it seems, already forgotten the extent to which investors willingly took risks to pay higher and higher prices in the hopes that a future set of investors would pay still more. That belief, by the way, is known as "the greater-fool theory"—the notion suggests that there will always be a greater fool to buy from you what you yourself purchased at far too high a price. Alas, at market tops, as we recently pointed out, all the fools have bought, so there's no new fool to bail them out.

Yahoo! was one of the hot stocks of its day, an Internet service provider that not only served as the door to the Internet for its growing subscriber base, but also provided a host of services, communities, on-line chat rooms, and research tools. It also sold advertising to those companies that wanted their presence felt on the Net. Yahoo!, along with AOL, EarthLink, Mindspring, and Microsoft's MSN, constituted the first set of Internet darlings on Wall Street. The dot-coms, as they were known, were as good as gold on Wall Street. Wall Street analysts and money managers, unable to measure the growth of these businesses by using standard benchmarks like revenue and profit growth, turned to newly invented gauges like *page views* and *unique users* to track the growth of interest in a particular site. And everyone thought the new valuation yardsticks were novel and fresh. But in many ways, they were just new ways of expressing old concepts that in previous bull market manias had been phrased just a little differently.

Insana Insight: K-Tel was one of the first companies to use television and telephones to sell its products. In the 1990s, it added *dot com* to its name, but its products were still hopelessly dated. This was a glaring example of how investors lost sight of exactly how an impressive new technology would be used. The Internet could not make K-Tel's products sell any better than they already had, given the limited appetite among consumers for those goods. In a bubble, investors care only about the innovation but are rarely discerning when it comes to application.

HOT STOCKS

While the gains in stock-market averages were breathtaking in the mid-to-late 1990s, the volatility in individual stocks reached record proportions. Even the immense gains in individual share prices in the 1920s paled in comparison to the explosive advances scored in the late 1990s. It was not unusual for newly traded stocks to jump 50 percent or more on their first days as public enterprises. The San Francisco Federal Reserve, while studying the wealth effect from hot California Internet stocks, found that in 1998 and 1999, the peak years of the frenzy, first-day returns on IPOs exceeded 50 percent, while in 1999 alone, one-quarter of all IPOs doubled on their first day of trading.[13] In the prior eight years, first-day trading gains averaged only 10 to 20 percent.[14] What was even more telling about the peak experience was that when examined one year later, many of the gains had stuck. An index of new companies tracked by the San Francisco Fed was up 250 percent over the 12-month period, an astonishing gain for new companies. Of those companies, 323 were domiciled in California. Their total market capitalization at the peak of the Internet bubble reached $676 billion! Wall Street brokerage firms earned billions of dollars in underwriting fees by bringing these firms public, while Wall Street performance pay—bonuses really—topped $13 billion in 2000, up from a record $12 billion in 1999, according to the Securities Industry Association.

The numbers from that peak moment were at the time and remain unbelievable. There have been immense gains in previous market bubbles, lofty valuations, and unusually high rates of return. But this experience topped them all. And the gains in individual issues were, as we said, even more remarkable.

Eye-popping IPOs

Economist Robert Samuelson recently wrote that of the 456 initial public offerings issued in 1999, a full 77 percent were for companies that had no profits. Quoting University of Florida economist Jay Ritter, Samuelson noted that the staggering number of new public companies losing money was a huge contrast with previous periods.[15] Ritter's work showed that in 1994, fully 75 percent of new public companies actually had profits! Investing had gone from a sober and businesslike environment to a true casino in only five short years.

Two stocks in particular made headlines for their opening-day performances: theglobe.com and VA Linux. Theglobe.com was a so-called Internet community targeting young people, run by two entrepreneurs who at age twenty-four became instant millionaires. On November 12, 1998, theglobe.com went public, scoring an initial gain of 606 percent. It would be eclipsed by VA Linux, a maker of so-called open-system software, which would soar 698 percent in late 1999. Both shares would plummet in the ensuing bear market. By April 2001, theglobe.com was selling for less than 25 cents.

Theglobe.com ended up the subject of both press and regulatory scrutiny since many mom-and-pop investors bought shares on the very first day of trading, which produced the stock's all-time high. While insiders were making a bundle selling out in the offering, retail investors got hammered, paying peak prices for a stock that spent the next several years heading straight down. Individual investors believed they were buying the stock at its offering price of $9 a share. Many retail clients paid upward of $80 a share as the stock zoomed skyward. Investors put in so-called market orders, which instruct their broker to buy the stock at the market price. Since theglobe never traded at its IPO price of $9, investors paid whatever the prevailing price was that day. So they paid many times the offering price and got badly burned in the process. Many sued their brokers or the brokerage firms they did business with. Settlements were reached among various parties to help mitigate the losses.

Many observers, including Greg Ip, then the markets reporter for the *Wall Street Journal,* noted that a raging bull market turned into a bubble on the day theglobe.com went public.[16]

The *Wall Street Journal*'s "Dairy of a Bubble" shows in graphic terms how that bull market inflated into a bubble.

Diary of a Bubble

Dow Jones Internet Index, daily close

Settlement talks collapse in Microsoft antitrust case

Accountants question Drkoop.com's ability to remain 'going concern.'

AOL announces merger with Time Warner

VA Linus IPO sets new record for first-day price gain at 698%

FreeMarkets almost triples filing range on its IPO to $40-$42

SEC Chairman Arthur Levitt criticizes on-line brokers' ads

eToys' IPO

Henry Blodget puts $400 price target on Amazon.com

Theglobe.com IPO sets then-record for first-day price gain at 606%

Higher-than-expected inflation number released

Theglobe.com postpones its IPO because of market turmoil

Lehman credit analyst questions Amazon's viability

Drkoop.com goes public

Ebay's IPO

E*Trade's new TV campaign begins

600
500
400
300
200
100

1998   1999   2000

Courtesy of *The Wall Street Journal*

Silly-con Valley

Many, of course, compared the Internet days to the gold rush or the
railroad boom, both of which touched off major bull and bear markets in stocks and bonds. But if one looks into the recent past, one can
find an even more direct ancestor. Consider the following passages
from two pieces describing the electronics mania that gripped Wall
Street in the late 1950s and early 1960s.

> Much to the surprise of many, the electronics issues took Wall
> Street by storm [in 1959]. The district seemed to be talking of
> nothing but space travel, micro-circuits, transistors, klystron
> tubes, and other esoteric things . . . By March, the industrial
> index had crossed the 600 mark; 3 months later it was just
> below 650 . . . At mid-year a rash of new companies ap-
> peared, with such names as Astron, Dutron, Transitron, and a
> host of other "trons" and "electros," and they were taken up
> quickly by a science-crazed public.[17]

> A well known broker at the time, Jack Dreyfus of Dreyfus
> and Co., humorously describes in the *New York Times* "tron
> mania" and how to value the stock of a company that partic-
> ipates in a technology no one understands: "Take a nice little
> company that's been making shoelaces for 40 years and sells
> at a respectable 6 times earnings ratio. Change the name from
> Shoelaces, Inc. to Electronics and Silicon Furth-Burners. In
> today's market, the words "electronics" and "silicon" are
> worth 15 times earnings. However, the real play comes in the
> word "furth-burners," which no one understands. A word
> that no one understands entitles you to double your entire
> score. Therefore, we have 6 times earnings for the shoelace
> business and 15 times earnings for the electronics and silicon,
> or a total of 21 times earnings. Multiply this by the 2 for the
> furth-burners and we now have a score of 42 times earnings
> for the new company."[18]

Sound familiar? Furth-burners may have been the most recent
forerunner of dot-com or any other bit of jargon that got modern in-

vestors all too excited about the prospects for certain companies and industries.

The author of the book from which those two quotes come goes on to make the distinction between higher- and lower-quality speculations, something that is reminiscent of our latest experiences:

Bad trons (early sixties) versus good trons (late fifties):

> There was an important difference . . . between the star performers of the 1st Eisenhower administration, and those of the early 60s . . . many of the electronics—stocks like Litton Industries, Texas Instruments, and Fairchild Camera—were substantial companies. On the other hand, most of the glamour issues of the late 60s had few assets, meager earnings and often deficits, and questionable hopes for the future. The speculative fever of 1960–62 was based on strange-sounding firms, esoteric commodities, shrewd promotions, and gullible customers. The key issues of this phase were low-priced electronics stocks which were usually traded over-the-counter or on the American Stock Exchange . . . In late 1960 and early 1961, there was a mad scramble of customers and orders each time a new issue was marketed. By then almost any new stock could be counted upon to show a 20–50% rise in price on the first day of trading, and then level off before either rising once more or falling.[19]

In the telecom world, companies like Lucent, Cisco, and others, makers of Internet connection devices like routers, hubs, and switches, presented equally fascinating and esoteric-sounding possibilities to the investing public. At its peak, Cisco Systems sold at 137 times earnings. Investors paid handsomely for Cisco's consistent 30 to 50 percent growth rate, which at the time appeared rational. When Cisco's growth rate stalled in 2000, the stock plunged from a high of $84 a share to a low of $12. No one really knew what routers and switches were, nor did they care. As long as they owned stock in companies that made routers, switches, or furth-burners, investors were happy and secure in their financial futures.

Fiber-works!

The final stage of the 1990s tech mania centered on fiber optics. That, too, was reminiscent of previous waves. Corning, the once-proud maker of oven-safe glassware, reinvented itself as a maker of fiber-optic cable. Global Crossing, now bankrupt, raised tens of billions of dollars of capital via the stock market to lay cable across oceans in an effort to wire the entire world with broadband capacity. A host of fiber companies from JDS Uniphase to Corning were bid to astronomical levels, even as a money-sucking glut of fiber-optic capacity was being put in place. To this day, the fiber glut remains. Nearly four times as much fiber as is needed is in the ground, much of it unlit, much of it causing huge capital drains on the involved companies. Worse still is the fact that the glut of capacity is holding down the prices that fiber companies can charge for their services. With these prices plunging and no end to the glut in sight, many fiber firms face bankruptcy or liquidation.

It's interesting to note, as a sidebar, that in the days of the great railroad mania that began in the mid-19th century in the United States and continued for decades, overcapacity was also an issue. Many enterprising railroad entrepreneurs built or threatened to build new track to compete with dominant carriers in a particular region of the country. Their hope, I am told, was not to build a successful railroad, but to scare the existing carriers into buying the redundant track and either using it or shutting it down. The builder of the excess capacity was paid a premium simply to go away. In fact, so rampant was the overbuilding of railroad track at the time that of the first 70,000 miles of track laid, 40,000 went unused. Many of the track builders went bust.

As I mentioned, there have frequently been financial market bubbles built around so-called infrastructure plays. As venture capitalist Roger McNamee has pointed out, infrastructure development and deployment is a highly capital-intensive undertaking. Whether it's building turnpikes, digging canals, laying track, paving highways, or laying fiber, the process of creating vast national or international networks takes time, labor, and huge amounts of money. Not surprisingly, there were bubbles associated with turnpikes, canals, railroads, electricity, radio, computerization, and the Internet. Each, of course, reflected the character and characters of its day, but each is remarkably similar in size, scope, and conclusion. In the case of railroads and other infrastructure development programs, the government played a leading role. Whether it provided funds for construction, land grants for the transcontinental railroad, or both in the case of the national highway system, the government's largesse played a large role in the development of those new productivity-enhancing networks. It did the same, to a degree, with the development of the Internet. By its declaration of a moratorium on the sales tax, at least one aspect of the information superhighway was allowed to grow without facing profit-retarding taxes. In addition, the expansion of the world's fiber-optic network capacity was enhanced by a little tax-avoidance scheme that allowed Global Crossing, for instance, not to pay taxes. By incorporating in Bermuda, Global Crossing significantly cut its tax bill, laying fiber in a most aggressive fashion. Those tax loopholes are currently being investigated by Congress for the appearance, if not reality, of impropriety. As modern as it may seem, even the highly complex attempt at laying fiber across vast oceans had its corollary nearly 200 years in the past in the days of the canal mania. I will examine historical analogues to the most recent bubble in subsequent pages, but a quick discussion of the first infrastructure play in the United States will help put the telecommunications bubble in some perspective.

The first mania for canals and their financing vehicles, canal bonds, began in 1825 with the proposal of the Erie Canal. Market trader and historian Art Cashin explains in his book *A View of Wall Street from the Seventh Floor* how speculative an enterprise the canal was. Its development was very much like that of the Internet since it would "require tools not even invented yet. And its structure needed material that science said couldn't be developed (like cement that could be poured and cured under 4 feet of water)."[20] The 400 miles of canal, cut through mountains, swamps, and forests, cost the then-sizable sum of $7 million. Cashin notes how Thomas Jefferson referred to the project as "sheer madness." But the effort proved quite successful, helping to enhance New York City's status as a center of commerce. Bondholders who had financed this "sheer madness" were fully repaid in 11 years, according to Cashin. The success of this issue led to a wave of speculation in canal building, which like every other bubble before it, and every bubble after, crashed and cost investors a great deal of money. The ebullience created by this endeavor led to one of the early bouts of market euphoria in the United States.

Insana Insight: It doesn't matter if you're investing in canals or fiber-optic cable. Manias all begin in similar fashion and end in exactly the same way. Of course, it's hard to recall those past examples or recognize the uniformity of behavior because each event looks slightly different from the one just passed. But it is critical for investors to appreciate manias and bubbles as a form of temporary insanity so that they can objectively address the issues pertinent to such economic conditions. And it is the investor with a memory who has the best chance of avoiding the incapacitating delusions that will keep him or her from making money when the next big bubble comes around. In any flight of fancy or temporary delusion, the rules that govern reality are suspended for a time. But there is always a return to normality. In finance, it's called regression to the mean. In life, it's called coming to your senses.

THE NASDAQ CRASH

The crash in NASDAQ stocks that came in April of 2000 should not have taken investors by surprise. It came after an unprecedented run in technology stocks that catapulted the NASDAQ 85 percent higher in 1999 and an additional 25 percent in the first two and a third months of the new year. On the final day of 1999, I delivered a piece on CNBC warning investors of a "blow-off" top in the NASDAQ. In fact, media observer Howard Kurtz of the *Washington Post* captured my point of view on the era in his bestselling book when he said that the Internet craze was "either a transforming moment in history or the greatest run of Wall Street bullshit that anyone had ever seen."[21]

The blow-off began in earnest right at the start of the new millennium. A blow-off occurs when a market average or individual stock spikes higher in what technical analysts call a "parabolic" move. To understand the style of ascendancy, just think of the near-final scene in *The Perfect Storm*. George Clooney's fishing boat, in its last attempt to weather the storm, is driven directly into a monstrous wall of water. The boat travels up the face of the massive, storm-induced wave, briefly touching its crest, and is then hurled back down into the sea. The NASDAQ followed a similar trajectory in its last rally attempt, exhausting itself at the crest and then collapsing under the weight of rising interest rates, extraordinary valuations, and the irrational belief that the tsunami could be successfully ridden into a new tidal wave of prosperity.

NASDAQ Composite 1995–2002

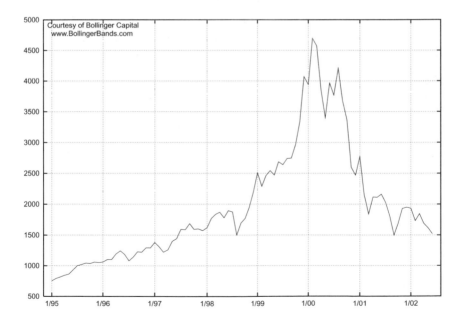

Courtesy of Bollinger Capital
www.BollingerBands.com

In April of 2000, only one month after hitting its all-time high, the NASDAQ plunged 25 percent in a single week. Well-respected traders that I knew recognized the sell-off for what it was . . . a crash. Admittedly, many of us in the financial media were somewhat reluctant to use the C word in fear of throwing gasoline on a raging fire, but ultimately we did, and the characterization was accurate, despite our reservations and the despite the criticism leveled against us by those who viewed the break as the ultimate buying opportunity.

It took a full week to do what the Dow had done in a single day back in October of 1987, but it was still a crash. It not only resembled other great market breaks in history, it also ushered in a long-term decline in technology stocks that represented the bursting of the bubble. Within the space of a year, the NASDAQ would decline by a whopping 60 percent. Before it reached its final decline, it would fall by nearly 75 percent. Over $3 trillion in market value was erased in the first year of the drop alone. In the two years after the peak, some $6 trillion of market value was wiped out, a third of the stock market's entire value.[22]

Many of the bubble's hottest stocks—Internet service providers, e-tailers, so-called B-to-B enterprises—would implode by 90 percent or more. The decline fit market historian Jeremy Grantham's prophetic model exactly. Grantham pointed out that all bubbles, once they burst, decline 70 to 90 percent from their highs before they finally hit bottom. It is a decline from which many of Wall Street's darlings have yet to recover.

Massive Internet bankruptcies followed in relatively short order. In 2000, more than 200 Internet and technology firms went belly-up. In 2001, that total ballooned to 537. As stated, the bust was entirely reminiscent of what happened to auto stocks in the early days of the previous century. Of the hundreds of firms that followed Henry Ford's lead in mass-producing automobiles, some were acquired, many went bankrupt. Less than a handful still exist today.

The gold rush and the boom in railroad shares ended in a spectacular bust known as the Blizzard of 1857. It mirrored the collapse of the Internet stocks in more than one way. The gold rush and railroad mania created a nearly insatiable appetite for shares in both those endeavors. Of course, investment houses and the firms themselves were more than willing to accommodate the demand. Banks also got in on the act, following the path of miners into the Western states. The banks, according to historian Charles Geisst, issued a steady supply of notes, reflecting the ever-increasing supply of gold. The printing of paper money, which was not controlled by a national central bank at that time, caused inflation, which "created the appearance of even more prosperity." [23] As is often the case, excessive credit finances uneconomic ventures that, in turn, go bust when credit conditions tighten or economic condition deteriorate. A case in point is the failure of the Ohio Insurance and Trust Company in 1857, whose collapse touched off a panic in American financial markets that ended the speculative interest in gold and rail shares.

Pattern Recognition

Indeed, not only are the formative periods for bubbles remarkably similar, so are the crashes. In the worst-case scenarios, entire markets can decline by as much as 90 percent. The Dow Jones Industrial Average plummeted 87 percent from its high of 381 in September of 1929 to its low of 41 in the summer of 1932. If we examine more recent examples, the great break in the so-called Nifty Fifty stocks of the early 1970s produced a bear market decline of 50 percent in the Dow between 1973 and 1974.

Japan's Nikkei plunged more than 74 percent from its high on December 31, 1989, to its most recent low of about 9,800 in early 2002. That bear market is one of the most vicious ever recorded, lasting over 12 years. Even the 1930s break in the Dow reached its nadir within 8 years, though it took 25 years for the blue chips to revisit the lofty levels recorded in late 1929.

For technical analysts, who analyze stock charts, the similarities among the Dow in 1929 and the Nikkei in 1989 were too dramatic to ignore. My colleague John Bollinger, with whom I worked at the Financial News Network, called the top in the Nikkei based on such pattern recognition well before the high was reached.

Dow Jones Industrial Average 1923–1929 (lower)
Nikkei 225 1981–1989 (upper)

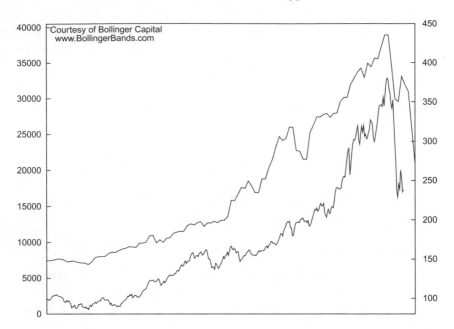

Courtesy of Bollinger Capital
www.BollingerBands.com

The patterns traced out by both big bull markets were compared to produce an eerily familiar trajectory. Equally interesting is that both declines were extraordinarily alike in terms both of magnitude and, for much of the bear market period, of duration. The Nikkei's bear market, as I pointed out, has lasted considerably longer. Those same analysts compared the Nikkei with the NASDAQ, and again, the charts proved quite useful in foretelling the future course the NASDAQ would take. Don Hays, a well-respected technical analyst who now works independently but worked for decades at Wall Street firms, noticed the striking similarities between the Nikkei and NAS-DAQ and found the comparison quite useful in determining the expected magnitude and duration of the NASDAQ's first important decline.

NASDAQ Composite 1991–2002 (lower)
Nikkei 225 1981–1990 (upper)

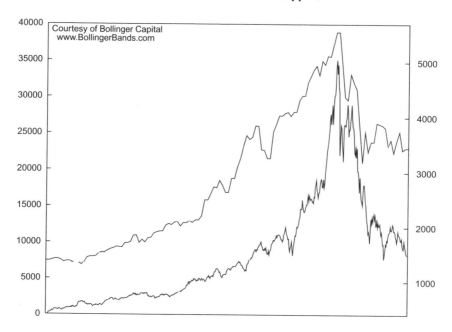

However, as the charts began to diverge, Hays grew more bullish about the near-term prospects for the NASDAQ in 2002, a mere two years after the bear market began. He was among the first analysts on Wall Street to suggest that the decline was reaching an important turning point, separating him from the rest of the pack. Unfortunately, by the summer of 2002, the NASDAQ was on course to follow, rather than diverge from, the Nikkei's sickening slide.

Still, the speed with which the NASDAQ plunged after hitting a frenzied high in 2000 is notable and, most certainly, memorable. That the crash came and went (thus far) without creating a great, national economic catastrophe is, as I've noted before, testimony to smart monetary and fiscal policies adopted by Washington in the aftermath of the crisis.

Technology in Tatters

But while the statistics on the NASDAQ's decline are eye-popping in themselves, even those dramatic numbers belie the devastating impact the decline had on the growth of the technology industry. The collapse of the NASDAQ had several unanticipated consequences for technology companies, not the least of which had to do with the currencies of these companies being rendered entirely useless.

Let me explain. As the bull market in technology stocks rambled on, rising equity values allowed technology companies to grow aggressively through acquisitions. Their ever-rising stock prices gave them a vehicle through which they could buy out competitors and collaborators alike, adding to their earnings growth with little impact on their balance sheets. Since buying additional profit growth through acquisition was relatively cheap and made quite attractive by the rich equity valuations that technology companies enjoyed, tech firms went on a buyout binge in the late 1990s. It was true, I should add, for almost any industry whose public stocks participated in the great bull run. Merger and acquisition activity swelled to a record $1.4 trillion in the United States in 1999 and held relatively steady at $1.2 trillion the following year. Global M&A activity peaked at nearly $2 trillion in the same period. The bull market fueled the "strategic mergers" that brought about an unusually rapid pace of consolidation in many industries by the end of the 1990s. In no other industry did such aggregation take place as aggressively as in technology.

To put it simply, rising stock prices pushed down the companies' cost of capital to nearly zero, giving them quite a dramatic incentive to expand aggressively. Companies could expand essentially for free, resulting in a tempting, if not entirely irresistible, condition in which to promote buyout binges! While some of the acquisitions were dilutive to near-term profit prospects, investors shrugged off the implications because they believed the buyouts were an inexpensive way to generate future long-term growth. (Put simply, *dilutive* means that an acquisition will depress earnings per share, a key profit measurement, for a number of years to come.) But because of some pretty complicated accounting tricks, many of those buyouts also allowed tech companies to play games with their books and inflate profits, which also helped to justify their acquisition appetites.

As the NASDAQ crashed, such advantages were completely wiped out, bringing merger and acquisition activity to a virtual standstill within a year. M&A volumes collapsed even more dramatically than they did in the last big buyout bust at the end of the 1980s. The death of deal-making resulted in a high number of pink slips being issued to Wall Street investment bankers who had grown more accustomed to getting other types of paper, particularly the green kind.

But that was not the only negative effect the fall of the NASDAQ had on technology companies. Many firms were unable to replenish their capital bases as the market fell. Initial public offerings dried up as the market careened lower, shutting the door on those venture-stage firms that hoped to raise capital in the public equity markets. In addition, existing public companies could not raise money through secondary offerings since "unfavorable market conditions" meant they could not get attractive prices for their newly issued shares. The closing of the financing window forced many start-up firms into bankruptcy as their sales and profits grew too slowly for them to fund their ambitious expansion plans. Hence the massive number of bankruptcies witnessed in 2000 and 2001.

The seizing up of the money markets had disastrous consequences for new public companies, particularly when one considered the expansion strategies employed in the world of e-commerce. Recall the business model of many Internet firms that were trying to build their brand names, even before they had fully built their businesses. Many of the companies used the bulk of the proceeds they received from public investors to launch flashy ad campaigns in an effort to sidestep the normal course of business building. In the traditional model, firms take advantage of the demand for new goods and services by creating and marketing products that satisfy a demonstrated need in the marketplace. As their customer bases grow and the products become more and more popular, profits begin to appear. The profits are normally reinvested in projects that will provide new sources of revenue and income. A portion of the profits are retained to build brand value, which can be created through a variety of techniques, not the least of which is aggressive, savvy promotion and advertising.

Unattractive Models

The dot-com world threw that business model completely on its head. Instead of waiting to reach profitability, Internet firms spent most of their newly raised capital on flashy, expensive advertising and marketing campaigns. The sock puppet that became the recognizable mascot for Pets.com remains a vivid image of the Internet's heady days. In the fourth quarter of 1999, Internet companies spent billions of dollars on ads on radio, television, newspapers, and magazines. The ad explosion, not coincidentally, reached its peak just as the NASDAQ was topping out. Many firms raced to buy ad time during the extraordinarily pricey Super Bowl telecast, hoping to create a successful national brand in the early days of the firm's existence. Some, like CMGI, the faltering Internet incubator now trading for pennies a share, decided to skip commercials during the Super Bowl and just turn the actual stadium where the game was played into a corporate monument. In 2000, CMGI agreed to pay $114 million over 15 years to call the new home of the New England Patriots "CMGI Field." Catchy, isn't it? Such a strategy put the cart before the horse, but in the Internet glory days the brand was deemed more important than the business!*

There, was, however an enormous flaw in that "branding" approach to growing and operating an enterprise. It assumed that the financial markets would unceasingly finance the cost of advertising and promotion while investors waited for demonstrated growth in both the top and bottom lines. The crack in the NASDAQ, which occurred for a variety of reasons, stopped the perpetual money machine dead in its tracks. Those companies which had, essentially, blown their

---

*Naming a stadium, by the way, became a corporate curse in the late 1990s. Many companies that paid hundreds of millions of dollars to brand a stadium— PSINet, CMGI, Enron—went bust shortly after they announced their deals. Stadium naming became another one of those great anecdotal indicators that warned of an impending top in stock prices!

cash wads on advertising were left with shockingly little cash with which to fund the normal course of business. Many Internet firms had what they call on Wall Street extraordinarily high "burn rates." Most Main Street folks would say that Internet companies spent money like it was going out of style, or more appropriately, money burned a hole in their pockets. Not only did these firms fail to save for a rainy day, they didn't even have enough capital left to survive the sunny ones.

Faced with few financing options, the firms began slashing their burn rates in an attempt to meet their lofty profitability targets. Their stocks plunged because without rapid growth, those targets became increasingly impossible to meet. Layoffs ensued. Expansion plans were trimmed and brand building became more and more difficult. Internet stocks dropped like rocks because they had priced in rapid growth, eventual profitability, and the creation of enterprise values that were suddenly called into question in the absence of marketing and promotion budgets. Many Internet firms, particularly the so-called e-tailers like Pets.com or WebVan, ran out of cash before they made a profit. Amid mounting losses, the firms folded.

Almost immediately, the bankruptcies began to pile up, much as they did with railroad and auto companies that tried to make it through the early and most capital-intensive phases of the industry's development. While those firms didn't spend as much money, initially, on advertising and promotion, they were similarly capital-intensive businesses. Cash drains were equally onerous and presented remarkably similar problems. Well-capitalized firms that used their cash prudently thrived. Those that didn't were either acquired at bargain-basement prices or went out of business. Such was the case in the Internet days as well.

The Incubus

Another failing of the Internet mania that was laid bare by the crash was the faulty business models some of the most popular enterprises of the era employed. The one most reminiscent of failed schemes in past bubbles involves the "Internet incubators." Those firms, which included David Wetherell's CMGI, Internet Capital Group, or Bill Gross's Idea Lab, were Internet holding companies that made money by supplying capital to Internet start-ups and then taking them public. These firms became, in essence, public venture-capital funds whose entire investment portfolios were concentrated in Web-based firms. Now, there's nothing inherently wrong with publicly traded venture-capital firms, since, unlike traditional VC businesses, they allow the average investor to participate in the financing of new companies and then profit from their growth, an option rarely open to anyone but the moneyed class. The problem with the Internet incubators was first and foremost the assumption on which they were based and the structures of the holding companies themselves.

The assumption was, quite obviously, that each of the many portfolio companies in the CMGI family would continue to grow exponentially and feed the growth of the other firms in the matrix. From Lycos to Raging.Bull.com, the CMGI family of firms drove page views in each of the other sites. The various relationships among the CMGI companies prompted a viewer of one site to visit other sites within the group in an effort to stimulate traffic and push up the measurement benchmarks used to determine growth. As each of the services pushed users to other sites, the portfolio companies were able to inflate the "hit" counts and show above-average rates of growth. That made their stock prices rally every time a new threshold was crossed. CMGI, which owned controlling stakes in all the portfolio companies, rose along with each of its holdings.

The CMGI model was, as we know now, predicated entirely on an eternal bull market in Internet stocks. As long as the stocks of its portfolio companies rallied, so did shares of CMGI. As CMGI spiraled higher, it was able to use its stock to buy more and more fledgling Internet firms and spin a portion of those shares out to the public. The daisy chain of investments made founder David Wetherell a nearly instant billionaire.

I recall speaking to David at a Fidelity Investments seminar at which we both spoke. Seated together at lunch, I asked him how his life had changed as a consequence not only of being billed as the Internet's first true visionary but also of being one of its first billionaires. He said his newfound wealth allowed him a number of conveniences that made life and work more compatible. Buying a new plane, for example, afforded him the luxury of bringing his wife on business trips rather than spending his entire working day separated from his family. Warren Buffett told me that one of the best ways to tell that a company is about to be in trouble is to check which executive recently canceled the lease on a corporate jet! If investors shorted the stocks of those companies with which leases had recently been canceled, they could make a bundle! (Buffett's Berkshire Hathaway, by the way, controls NetJet, a firm that leases time shares in private jets to businessmen.)

CMGI 1997–2002

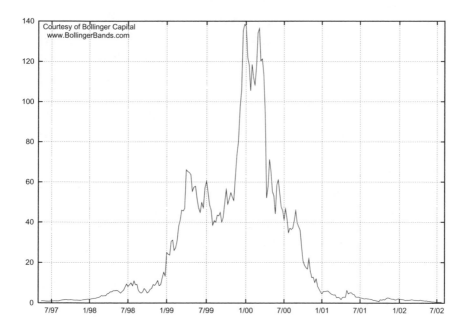

Courtesy of Bollinger Capital
www.BollingerBands.com

The CMGI model, like the Internet bubble, was reminiscent of some flawed concepts in previous market manias. CMGI, Internet Capital Group, and Idea Lab were like the investments trusts of the 1920s or the interlocking shareholdings of Japanese companies in the 1990s. They worked quite well as the market moved higher, but they imploded as the market dropped in value.

Incubator or Investment Trust?

In the 1920s, the Goldman Trading Company, a spin-off of the vener-able brokerage and investment banking firm, was one of the hottest vehicles around. The trading company was an investment trust—a company that bought shares in other publicly traded investment com-panies. Through a series of mergers and investments, Goldman had leveraged itself by buying into the forerunner of the modern mutual-fund company. Each of Goldman's investments, in turn, invested in other investment firms. And as each of those stocks rallied with the great bull market, Goldman shares went higher in tandem. Economist John Kenneth Galbraith wrote of the wild orgy or speculation that occurred in Goldman shares. They went public on December 4, 1928, at $104 apiece. By February 7, 1929, Goldman reached a high of $225.50 a share. At that price, the Goldman Sachs Trading shares were worth double the value of the assets held in the trust. Such was the interest in investing in companies that invested in common stocks.[24] Galbraith points out that in the wake of the crash, a Gold-man principal, one Mr. Sachs, was testifying before Congress about the role of investment trusts, some of which were fraudulent and all of which had collapsed in value. He was asked to state the price of Goldman Sachs Trading Corporation shares several years after the crash. They had fallen from a peak of over $225 a share in 1929 to a low of $1.75.[25] CMGI would re-create that pattern 70 years later.

To assume that modern investors would remember that lesson of so long ago may be far too optimistic. But the Japanese engaged in ex-actly the same type of thing in the 1980s. Their investment trusts were disguised as the world's biggest and most impressive banks! These highly capitalized lenders were among the most aggressive speculators in the Japanese markets, but the speculation was disguised as strategic investing in critical areas of their economy.

Interlocking Investments, Part II

Japanese banks owned stakes in many domestic manufacturing, ex-port, and real estate companies. For instance, Mitsubishi Bank owned shares in Mitsubishi Heavy Industries, Mitsubishi Motors, and other members of the Mitsubishi family. In exchange for a large percentage of their progenies' business, the banks provided low-interest loans to help the firms expand, both domestically and globally. Their cross-holdings in their subsidiaries' firms also involved "interlocking directorships" in which the related firms held stock in one another. These interlocking directorships, known as *keiretsu,* provided a kind of glue among the companies and cemented their financial futures together. It also meant that as Japanese stock and real estate prices skyrocketed, Japan's banks grew ever more valuable as a consequence of their ownership interests in the hottest areas of the Japanese markets. Both stock and real estate values were part of the Japanese bubble, which provided twice the inflationary power of a single-asset episode. Bank capital expanded dramatically as the twin bubbles inflated, allowing the banks to expand more and more aggressively. And, in an even wilder turn than occurred in the 1920s or in the Internet bubble, Japanese banks were allowed to count their stock-market holdings as so-called tier-one capital on the balance sheets. That meant Japanese banks became among the largest and, at least temporarily, best-capitalized institutions in the world. For a time, U.S. legislators considered relaxing domestic rules that prevented U.S. banks from owning commercial enterprises so they could better compete with the Japanese behemoths.

Fortunately, smart regulators like former Federal Reserve chairman Paul Volcker opposed such a relaxation of the rules. That kept U.S. banks out of the trouble that befell Japan's banks and still troubles them today. Indeed, when the Nikkei-225 crashed in 1990 and headed lower in the course of the next 12 years, banks suffered an enormous loss of capital. As the value of their stock and real estate holdings imploded, so did the size of their capital bases and the share prices of their own stocks. The recession that crippled the Japanese economy turned low-interest loans to family companies into high-cost liabilities that will likely never be fully repaid. The consequence of the leverage that banks enjoyed as the markets moved higher, but suffered from as the markets subsequently collapsed, has been extreme. Each year that the Nikkei declines further means that Japanese banks are dangerously close to running afoul of international regulations that mandate a certain amount of capital for world-class banks. Nonperforming loans continue to hobble the banks as the economy weakens further. It is a self-reinforcing death spiral that is the direct inverse of the virtuous circle that made the banks so attractive during Japan's great bubble.

Insana Insight: All of these models worked well while bull markets were in full swing. But when the crashes came, the holding companies, whether they were investment trusts, banks, or Internet incubators, spiraled down in value. The leverage that had worked so well on the upside had catastrophic consequences on the downside. In the early examples, the economic implications were dire. The collapse of investment trusts helped to hamstring U.S. equity markets for decades just as the collapse of Japan's banks hamstrings that country's markets. In the case of the Internet incubators, the problem is merely symptomatic of the problems associated with the Internet mania. The declines, however, are very real for those Internet visionaries who were once billionaires.

6

TRENDWATCHING

Bubbles, manias, and even brief fads follow the same arc or pattern and end in very similar fashion. Kindleberger, the author of *Manias, Crashes and Panics,* described the various stages of a mania. Grantham and Faber and others graphically illustrated the technical patterns that they follow. The parabolic arc is the technical "sentence" of a bubble or manic moment, the crash its exclamation point. Few observers have, in a comprehensive manner, married the fundamental and technical characteristics of these ever-increasing events to present investors with a clear picture of what bubbles are and how they live and die. That is the aim of this section of the book—to give you the tools with which to identify manias or bubbles *as they happen,* not after the fact. Only by recognizing the early ingredients and hallmarks of a bubble, secular trend, or even temporary fad can you hope to ride the wave successfully. And while there is absolutely no perfect strategy for timing one's entry into and exit from the market, using one's knowledge of big and small cycles can help you get in early and get out while the getting is good. There is no doubt that identifying a bubble while it's occurring will force you out of the market before the peak. That way you get to keep most of your hard-earned profits in the bank, waiting patiently for another market opportunity to emerge.

As I mentioned before, those who exited the market as early as

1998 and banked their profits outperformed those who remained invested through the peak in early 2000 and then suffered through the major declines that followed. But for some unknown reason, and despite examples almost too numerous to detail, investors keep on believing that each new cycle is separate and unique, that each new fad, trend, mania, or bubble is somehow exempt from the rules that govern all market cycles. Whether it is stocks, bonds, art, real estate, precious metals, or other commodities, all assets have a certain intrinsic value. That value has been determined by hundreds, in some cases thousands, of years of price history. Valuation parameters have been used successfully in that time. They cannot simply be discarded because a new generation rewrites the rules of investing. It does not work that way. Values, of course, are both absolute and relative. Valuations can stretch under some circumstances and contract under entirely different conditions. But the broad benchmarks that define historical valuation parameters are useful in and of themselves in determining the entry and exit points for all kinds of investments.

But in addition to valuation parameters, the characteristics common to all big market moves are also worth knowing. They will help you identify emerging trends, play them, and then help you identify the endpoints in a particular cycle.

In some ways, I agree with Kindleberger about the various aspects of a bubble. But I also think the common characteristics require more specificity than offered in his book. Similarly, the terminal points need clarification and amplification to be useful as tools rather than merely observations of large market cycles. I would like to add some specificity and some historical examples to buttress Kindleberger's arguments. Displacement, for instance, comes in a variety of guises, each of which requires comment. So, too, monetary influences, which can either occur as official rate cuts from a central bank, money creation from the Treasury, or excess credit availability provided by financial intermediaries. We have seen, and will continue to see, historical examples of each. While they all have the same net effect, it is important to identify how each differs and how each manifests itself in the marketplace if one hopes to accurately gauge the prevailing environment. In the same manner, bubbles burst when conditions change. Money and credit can become scarcer, but not always through the same mechanism. An invention or discovery can fail or prove ineffective in a number of ways. But as bubbles burst, tighter credit and the failure of a new invention to live up to its hype are usually the root causes for the troubles. Understanding the manner in which both those problems begin is integral to successfully exiting an asset class before the real problems cause a crash.

Five ingredients and characteristics occur at the beginning and during the inflating of all bubbles. When the first three exist simultaneously, a bubble will inevitably emerge, and in the discussion that follows, we'll focus on these.

- Eureka! New discovery or invention

- Easy money: low-cost or highly available money and credit

- Government largesse: favorable fiscal conditions and tax incentives

- Auspicious economic conditions

- External stimulants

What Kindleberger calls displacement, I would identify as discovery or invention. Displacement assumes that an external factor—or "exogenous event," as economists like to call them—must occur to get the ball rolling. In my mind, exogenous events are separate and apart from discoveries and inventions. The ending of a war and its impact on fiscal and monetary policy, which Kindleberger holds out as an example, is not, by itself, the type of event that can be forecast or analyzed in advance. Those are external or exogenous events. And while it's true the end of both world wars in the 20th century ignited strong markets and economies, only one preceded a bubble. Postwar prosperity is not always unhealthy and, indeed, can frequently lead to a healthy reordering of priorities, not merely to rampant speculation. The type of bubbles and manias I am exploring deal more with factors that are intrinsic to markets and economics rather than to geopolitics.

I agree with venture capitalist Roger McNamee, who believes the biggest and most important bubbles occur as a result of the displacement that comes from invention and discovery. McNamee devoted a great deal of time to studying the impact of invention-based bubbles, in terms not only of their market consequences but of their long-run economic impact as well. McNamee found that the biggest bubbles appear to center on infrastructure developments, like turnpikes, canals, railroads, autos, telephone, radio, computers, and the Internet.

I would also part company with the Kindleberger model in saying that monetary expansion does not *follow* speculation, monetary expansion *finances* it. In its most recent incarnation, the true moment of intense overtrading occurred after more than 100 central banks around the world lowered interest rates in the wake of the Russian debt crisis and the collapse of Long-Term Capital Management. That global infusion of liquidity turned a roaring bull market into a moment of sheer madness. The overtrading, or speculation, could not have occurred without those emergency rate cuts. Overtrading, of course, pushed equity values inexorably higher and, in a way, made capital still cheaper, but that was an effect not a cause of the environment in which it occurred.

Insana Insight: My nearly 20 years of observing market behavior has taught me that speculation is not possible until money is either cheap, available, or both. And while new inventions or discoveries can surface in tight money environments, without an easy money policy, it is highly unlikely that a general market bubble or mania can occur around them, despite the enthusiasm with which that new invention or discovery might be greeted. Easy money, therefore, is the most necessary precondition for a bubble, though, of course, it is not the only one. I know of no examples of manias or bubbles in all economic history that were not, at least in part, predicated on some form of easy money. Again, it can result from a dramatic lowering of interest rates, excessive money or credit creation, cheap foreign funds (so-called hot money) entering an economy or market, or new equity issuance. In some periods, like the mid-1980s, high-cost junk bonds were used to fuel a great leveraged buyout bubble. While interest rates paid on the bonds were extraordinarily high, usually in the low-to-mid teens, the bonds were readily available and easy to float. So great was the mania that RJR Nabisco's $25-billion buyout was financed almost entirely with junk debt in a deal that was the largest of its kind ever recorded. So intense was the mania to take companies private at their "fair market values" that analysts wrote pieces on how to take IBM or General Motors private in an LBO. Both firms would have had a price tag, or "private market value," that topped $100 billion. But the hubris of the time was such that no firm was too big to be bought out.

More Than Money

Easy money is not the only thing that inflates a bubble. As economist John Kenneth Galbraith noted in his work on the 1929 stock-market crash, "it takes more to start a speculation than the general ability to borrow money."[1] But the availability of money or credit and a relatively low cost of financing are, in my mind, the ever-present features of an asset bubble. It was no doubt true in an Athenian property bubble in 333 B.C.E. and has been true ever since. Excessive use of credit—or "leverage," as market experts call it—contributed to tulip-o-mania in Holland in the 1630s. The South Sea and Mississippi bubbles in 18th-century Britain and France were almost purely a function of overextended credit. Of course, the sales pitch in both cases centered on great discoveries in the New World, principally of gold, though as discussed earlier there was much more to it than that. The lure of invention and discovery precipitates investors' interest. Easy money facilitates their participation. A recent article in *Forbes ASAP* notes that at its peak, shares of the Mississippi Company were worth more "than all the gold and silver in France." French speculators were so enamored of the possibility of owning all the gold in the New World that they paid a price in excess of the gold and silver available to them. They leveraged themselves well beyond their ability to repay their speculative bets.[2] Indeed, the amount of debt behind these two great schemes was astronomical and, in fact, destructive to the British and French economies once those bubbles burst.

Technological Innovation

I plan to spend a considerable amount of space and time discussing how easy money, low interest rates, and high availability of credit inflate all types of bubbles. The biggest bubbles, which we have already discussed, emerge from important technological innovations or new discoveries. Canals, turnpikes, plank roads, railroads, autos, radio, computers, and the Internet created the biggest bubbles in market history and underpinned some of the strongest periods of economic growth in our history. But the bubbles themselves could not have occurred without the assistance of an easy money environment. Many periods that produced technological innovation also benefited from low rates and ample credit. Those conditions were abundant even in this country's early days.

Easy Money

The very first stock-market mania in our own country was set off when the first Bank of the United States "within months of opening its doors . . . flooded the market with notes and credit."[3] David Cowen, who analyzed the balance sheet of the first bank, demonstrated that the largesse of the bank's policies helped to finance a major run-up in bond prices, which was exploited by speculators like William Duer. Additionally, Duer employed a great deal of leverage himself, borrowing funds from anyone who would lend in an effort to corner the market in U.S. government bonds. From late 1791 to early 1792, securities prices soared until a more restrictive bank curtailed credit and brought the market to a crashing halt. As Cowen points out, the bank, and possibly Treasury Secretary Hamilton, were so worried about the speculative excesses in the market that they choked off credit and turned a bubble into a panic.[4]

By the way, the first market crash in the United States so unnerved brokers, dealers, and investors that new rules were put in place to ensure orderly and liquid markets for U.S. securities. On May 2, 1792, 24 stockbrokers gathered under a buttonwood tree on Wall Street in lower Manhattan and signed the Buttonwood Accord. The pact brought the New York Stock & Exchange into existence. The brokers, devastated by the Panic of 1792, wanted to do business only with reliable and creditworthy customers. So the 24 who remained after the panic established the Exchange. The institution is over 210 years old and still going strong. Money and credit would play central roles in all future episodes in both the United States and elsewhere, wherever bubbles grew.

Another speculative episode followed that panic almost immediately. John Kenneth Galbraith writes of a real estate bubble that grew wildly in the years after the War of 1812. State chartered banks, with few assets to back their aggressive note printing, made credit cheap and plentiful. The banks were housed in "churches, taverns or blacksmith shops."[5] In fact, they were set up in any place that was large enough to do business. The credit boom led to a major bull market in property. The second Bank of the United States, chartered in 1816, added a little monetary fuel to the fire. The property bubble burst in 1819, causing great trouble for the economy, one of the first major boom/bust cycles in the U.S. economy.[6]

The canal, turnpike, and railroad bubbles were financed with cheap and ample credit. So were the great land booms that captured investors' attention in Florida in the 1920s, California in the 1980s, and Silicon Valley in the 1990s. It is altogether possible that another real estate bubble is forming in the United States even as this book goes to press. One bubble often develops from the policies designed to mitigate the effects of a previous bubble's collapse, the rubble from one used to build the foundation of the next speculative episode. In the wake of the bursting of the technology bubble immediately following the September 11 terrorist attacks, the U.S. Federal Reserve, along with many other central banks, dramatically lowered interest rates to prevent an economic catastrophe. Rates were pushed to levels not seen since 1961. Short-term interest rates fell as low as 1¾ percent, pushing mortgage interest rates down accordingly, at least for several months. The low rate environment created a wave of mortgage refinancings and, more important, pushed new home purchases to record levels in 2001 and early 2002. As *The Economist* noted in April of 2002, low interest rates in the United States and around the world supported not only home buying but also home prices. The gains in home prices, which averaged 9 percent in 2001, well above the inflation rate, helped to offset the loss of wealth from two years of falling stock prices. If home prices extend those gains for a number of years, as they did in the 1970s and 1980s in the United States, a bubble could very well form.

Personal Experience

I recall from my days living in Southern California the intensity of the real estate bubble that grew there. Homes became commodities, like any other, purchased only with the notion of reselling at higher prices. Homes were not places to hang one's hat but places to simply hang around until they were worth sufficiently more than they cost to buy. New home developments just north of Los Angeles drew hundreds of prospective buyers. People would queue up early in the morning in areas like Santa Clarita to apply for a new home purchase. Young people, short of cash, borrowed 100 percent of the money needed to get in on the action. A common practice of the time was to borrow the 10 percent down-payment money from a family member or friend. Lenders generally looked the other way as first-time buyers put absolutely no equity into the home.

On the Financial News Network in the spring of 1989, one of the San Fernando Valley's hottest young real estate entrepreneurs, Mike Glickman, made a bold proclamation that Southern California real estate values would never fall. Glickman, who at age 15 delivered real estate tear sheets for a local broker, became one of the most successful real estate agents by the time he was in his early twenties. By age 30, he owned the fastest-growing real estate brokerage in the region. He was frequently billed as one of the best young entrepreneurs in Los Angeles. He paid above-average commissions, gave generous perks and bonuses, and expanded his operations with a speed unheard of in the real estate business. In March of 1989, when he made his bold assertion that the market would never go down, he was riding the wave of a 15-year bull market in real estate. The bubble had been inflating with great vigor for at least the preceding five years. His comments marked the top of the cycle. When interest rates started to go up in 1989, leveraged transactions in the stock market and the real estate market were hit hard. Within a year, Glickman's operations were severely constrained. He eventually went personally and professionally bankrupt, the victim of overexpansion and the undying belief that prices only go in one direction . . . up. Real estate prices in Southern California crashed. Those who bought at the top watched the value of their homes plunge by 25 percent or more. The bear market in real estate would last close to eight years. It would be a decade before prices returned to their precrash levels. The entire real estate bubble, while driven by the changing demographics of the region and a huge population influx, was financed by very easy money. The implosion of that bubble, along with a huge bear market in commercial real estate, would saddle the nation's biggest banks with uncollectible debt. The subsequent banking crisis in 1990 and 1991 led the Federal Reserve to embark on another dramatic lowering of interest rates. That repetitive cycle led to the new bull market in stocks and, ultimately, a new bubble in financial assets.

If individuals grow enamored of their homes as alternative investments, a bubble, repetitive phenomenon that it is, may begin to grow again in real estate. Wall Street economist and market strategist Ed Yardeni believes that the next bubble will occur in residential real estate. You'll read more about coming bubbles later in the book. But once again, easy money may provide the gas to inflate the bubble.

Easy Does It

Easy money comes in many forms, from very low-cost capital to very high-cost capital that is unusually abundant. Economists have long studied the root causes of big market swings and unusually large shifts in economic growth rates. Most often, monetary policy is a key determinant in both the direction of the stock market and the growth of the economy. There is, however, a vigorous debate still raging on the role of monetary policy in several key speculative episodes that gripped this nation over the course of the last century, not the least of which centers on the 1920s bull market and the subsequent Great Depression.

Economists Milton Freidman, Alan Meltzer, and others have taken great pains to prove that excessive monetary stringency by the Federal Reserve, beginning in 1928, turned a garden-variety business recession into the woeful period we all know as the Great Depression. They appear, at least in some of their work, to be less concerned with monetary policy as fuel for the great bull market that preceded the Depression, but other economists argue that an overly aggressive and easy policy in the years prior to 1928 provided the liquidity, or fuel, that drove the stock market to astronomical heights by the autumn of 1929. Economist John Kenneth Galbraith implies, in his work on the Great Crash, that the stingy credit policies of the Federal Reserve might have been supplanted by the aggressive lending practices of both the New York banks and the big brokerage houses. In 1928, the Fed set short-term interest rates at roughly 5 percent, but lenders were charging investors call money rates (for buying stock on margin) of 12 percent at the same time. Quite naturally, margin lending exploded as member banks borrowed from the Fed at 5 percent and relent the money at 12 percent, creating what Galbraith calls "possibly the most profitable arbitrage operation of all time."[7] So, despite a relatively tight monetary policy from the Fed, other lenders stepped into the breach and made credit available to investors, which, in turn, provided the cash for investors to bid up stock prices.

Margin buying of U.S. stocks surged to record levels in the 1920s, despite the relatively small number of active accounts. Plentiful credit and ever-rising stock prices proved an incendiary combination. Coupled with the important technological innovations of the day, most notably autos and radio, and the ingredients for a major bubble in stock prices were evident in the 1920s.

The easy money pattern would repeat itself with serial regularity throughout the remainder of the century, not just at home but abroad as well. Numerous bubbles grew out of the excessive availability of credit that sprang up in the United States, Kuwait, Latin America, Asia, and elsewhere.

In the early 1970s, a most unlikely bubble occurred around a group of stocks called the Nifty Fifty, a glamorous group that promised eternal growth during an unusually erratic period in this nation's economic history. Born in a period of rapid technological advancement, companies like IBM, Polaroid, and Xerox, stodgy household names to us now, were at the forefront of exciting innovations. Their stocks, far from the staid blue chips they are now, functioned as speculative investment vehicles.

Easy Money + Fiscal Stimulus

In the "Roaring Eighties," the massive mania for stocks was the product of many of the ingredients that highlighted previous episodes. But it was one of the few periods in market history in which *every* form of stimulus helped to create and perpetuate a stock-market move of epic proportions. From its low of 774 in the summer of 1982 to its high of 2722.15 in the summer of 1987, the Dow Jones Industrial Average soared 252 percent, just shy of the gains witnessed in the Roaring Twenties. The bull market of the 1980s was breathtaking in its magnitude and duration. Although it was a purely "professional" play, with individual investors not participating in the same manner as they would do in the 1990s, the bull market in the "decade of greed" was a sight to behold.

The bull market that commenced in August of 1982 was born of crisis, as many bull markets are. The U.S. economy was hobbled by the worst recession since the 1930s, consumed by a condition known as "stagflation," where inflation, unemployment, and interest rates were all in double digits. The banking industry was reeling from soured loans to troubled Latin American nations, and a malaise gripped the nation that was nearly unshakable. Unemployment and inflation rates topped 13 percent. The nation's prime lending rate exceeded 20 percent! Home and car purchases collapsed under the unusually heavy financing burden. Gold and oil prices soared, drawing money away from financial assets. Indeed, U.S. Treasury bonds were nicknamed "certificates of confiscation" since their yields failed to keep pace with the soaring inflation rate. Financial instruments were universally loathed, leading *Business Week* magazine to declare "the death of equities" in the summer of '82.

But just as the entire investing population began to believe that stocks and bonds would go down forever, and gold and oil would soar, a strange phenomenon occurred. Latin American nations, specifically Mexico, threatened to declare a moratorium on the tens of billions of dollars in debt they owed to struggling U.S. banks. The default scare nearly turned a terrible recession into another Great Depression. In order to prevent a wholesale financial catastrophe, the Federal Reserve promised to backstop the banks, providing billions of dollars in bailout assistance. The Fed slashed interest rates and turned on the monetary spigot, ballooning the nation's money supply in an effort to "reliquefy" the banking system and stimulate the stagnant economy.

The trick worked marvelously well. The stock market shot up in late 1982. Bond prices rallied while interest rates plunged. Pent-up consumer demand was unleashed as more affordable financing rates led to new home and car purchases. Existing homeowners were able to refinance their mortgages and boost their disposable incomes greatly in the process.

At the same time, the federal government, under President Ronald Reagan's direction, cut tax rates aggressively, again boosting the purchasing power of needy consumers. Government spending also increased dramatically on defense programs (which created countless jobs) and on a whole host of programs that stimulated state, local, and national economic activity. The trillion-dollar defense buildup, a variety of make-work, pork-barrel projects, along with huge increases in entitlement spending, "primed the pump," as economist John Maynard Keynes liked to say. That added gas to an economy that was already being fueled by the Fed's new easy money policies.

Consider the dramatic stimulus that hit the economy at that time. From 1982 through April 1986, bond-market interest rates fell from a high of 14 percent to a low of just over 6 percent.

30-Year U.S. Treasury Bond Yield

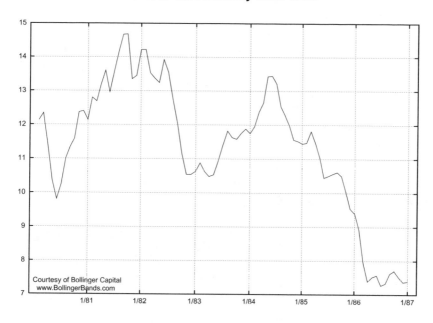

U.S. Money Supply-M1 1980–1987

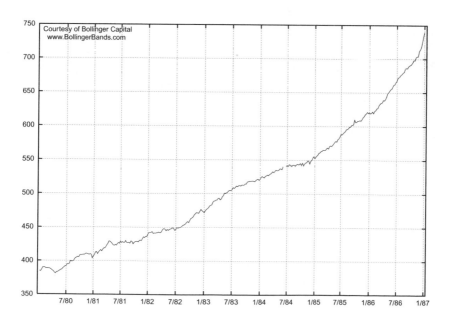

The nation's money supply grew rapidly each year, while government spending was rising so rapidly that deficits climbed to over $200 billion a year. The national debt more than doubled in the period. Other tax breaks, like the deductibility of junk-bond debt, helped to fuel a corporate buyout boom that was part and parcel of the general bubble that occurred on Wall Street. We'll discuss the buyout boom in greater detail later in this section.

Crude Analogy

Other developments aided consumers and businesses as well. An unexpected decline in crude-oil and gasoline prices acted like yet another tax cut for consumers.

Crude Oil 1980–1986

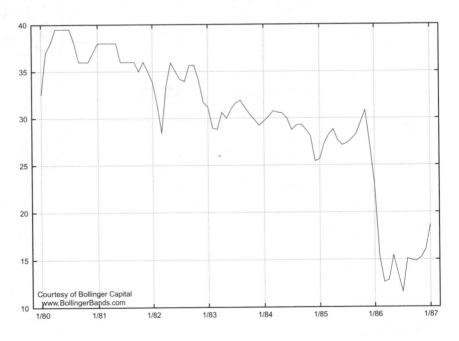

Courtesy of Bollinger Capital
www.BollingerBands.com

As gasoline prices fell, consumers got back more and more disposable income, allowing them to spend less on driving and more on other goods and services for the first time in several years. A big drop

Deze fyne Modele Kaarten worden gemaakt te Schothanenburg by Law= rens Bombarst inde vroetende droom goud-myn graver

Aas

Daar is maar een weg ter geluk gewis Zoek 't licht schuuw d' Actien der duisternis.

The Mississippi Bubble was one of the largest financial manias of all time. The central character was a crafty financier by the name of John Law. So widespread was the craze that playing cards emerged at the height of the euphoria. These two cards represent the popular interest in the Mississippi Bubble in 1720.

The first Bank of the United States was the institution central to the first mini-bubble and first panic in U.S. securities markets. This check, signed by the nation's first Treasury Secretary, Alexander Hamilton, dates to a few years after the first U.S. market panic.

Another check from the Bank of the United States, $200, payable to one Matthew Carrey, May 1795.

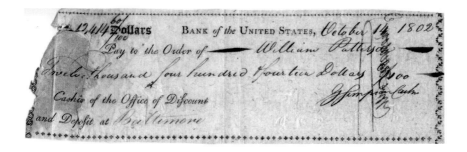

A Bank of United States check payable to William Patterson for $12,400 in October 1802. The first Bank would not last much longer.

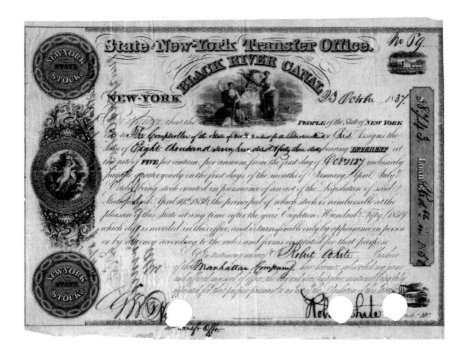

The canal craze was the first large-scale financial bubble in the United States of America. This Black River canal bond was issued by the State of New York Transfer Office for the Black River Canal, October 23, 1837.

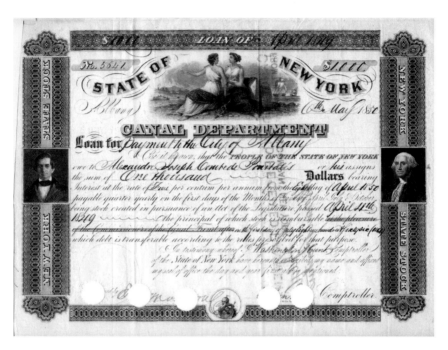

Canals remained in vogue for a number of years after the peak of the craze. This canal department bond, with a face value of $1,000, was issued by the State of New York Canal Department, May 1850.

The auto craze produced several hundred publicly traded companies, many of which went bust when the bubble burst. Rickenbacker Motor Company was one of the many auto stocks from the Roaring Twenties. This certificate is for 50 shares, dated September 3, 1928.

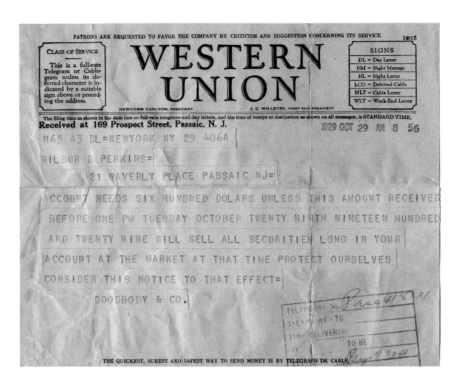

This Western Union telegram is the modern equivalent of a margin call on stocks, dated October 28, 1929 (Black Monday). The telegram, issued during the darkest moments of the great crash, reads: "Account needs six hundred dollars unless this amount received before one pm Tuesday October 29, 1929 will sell all securities long in your account at the market at that time protect ourselves. Consider this notice to that effect. Goodbody & Co."

Remember the Stutz Bearcat? Stutz was another of the great early players in the booming auto business of the 1920s. This is a certificate for 100 shares of Stutz Motor Company issued to the Orvis Brothers on April 21, 1937. Stutz survived through much of the depression but no longer exists today.

Emerging markets experienced bubbles in the late 1980s and the mid-1990s. The brochure from the Scudder Pacific Opportunities Fund and the India Growth Fund are reminders of how recently investors were carried off to exotic markets, only to lose their money.

in oil and gasoline prices, economists say, is the functional equivalent of a tax cut, or simply put, another form of easy money.

As a consequence of the highly simulative actions, the economy began to grow, and to grow rapidly. The stock market began to deliver rates of return that were far above normal, inviting more and more investors to take advantage of the newfound strength in equities.

Other Factors

Advances in computer technology were also viewed as a positive catalyst for growth and productivity. Personal computing at work and at home brought labor-saving efficiency, thanks to innovations from Microsoft, IBM, Digital Equipment, Hewlett-Packard, Apple Computer, and others.

Globalization helped to boost international trade while the creation of new and exotic financial instruments made markets seemingly more efficient and more able to facilitate the movement of capital instantaneously around the world. The final stimulant that sent the U.S. economy into overdrive came in 1985, when the Group of Five, now Eight, industrialized nations decided to weaken an overvalued U.S. dollar. The devaluation of the dollar had a major impact on economic growth. A 7 percent reduction in the dollar's value, economists say, is like a full percentage point reduction in interest rates. A cheaper dollar can dramatically boost exports of U.S. goods, making those products considerably less expensive in markets abroad.

So as you can see, policy-makers used every form of economic trick known to man to rejuvenate the economy. The markets correctly anticipated and participated in the boom times that emerged. A reversal of many of those factors would spell the end of one of Wall Street's biggest bubbles in 1987, when rapidly rising interest rates, a crashing dollar, the threatened repeal of key tax breaks, and the scent of war combined to topple a stock market whose valuations reached historic proportions.

There is a key point to make here. Undervalued stock markets do not collapse under the weight of adverse circumstances. Just the opposite is true. Overvalued markets, particularly bubble markets, are most vulnerable to a change in circumstance. They are all "priced for perfection," so that any change in a positive forecast brings prices crashing back to earth. In the late summer and early autumn of 1987, that's exactly what happened.

Easy Money in Other Markets

A glaring example of overvaluation occurred as a result of the high oil prices that crippled the U.S. economy from the mid seventies until 1983. As the United States suffered with painfully high oil prices, OPEC nations were reaping untold billions in petroleum profits. Those profits (a form of international easy money for the oil-producing countries) were the main ingredient for one of the oddest stock-market events of all time, occurring in Kuwait in the early 1980s at the height of the oil market's historic run-up.

If you'll recall the environment at the time, oil-price spikes fueled the great inflation of the 1970s and early 1980s, first thanks to the Arab oil embargo in 1973 and then with the Iranian Revolution in 1979. Both oil shocks drove crude-oil prices to then-record levels, igniting an inflationary spiral in the United States and around the world. While that caused great economic distress throughout the oil-consuming world, the oil-producing nations, particularly OPEC member states, were flush with cash. As they raked in their billions, the crude-oil money, called "petrodollars," led to a generalized prosperity in various kingdoms of the Arab world, not the least of which was the future target of Saddam Hussein, Kuwait.

One direct beneficiary of the oil rush was Kuwait's unofficial stock market, known as the Souk al-Mamakh, which author John Train called "a cauldron of speculative activity" at the time.[8] While the official Kuwaiti stock exchange was composed of more mundane firms, hot money investors raced to get in on the action at the Souk, where some of the more speculative issues jumped as much "as 100% a month or more." The Souk was the Kuwaiti equivalent of the modern-day NASDAQ, the official exchange more like the NYSE.

The oil-rich nation needed to do something with its excess cash. Some Arab nations funneled their money into American banks, which in turn loaned it to Latin American nations. In Kuwait's case, the gush of cash made its way into speculative stocks at home, causing an unusual frenzy of activity in an austere Muslim state. That the mania would peak with oil prices would be no surprise. But that it was fueled, in large part, by unchecked credit seems ironic, given the true riches of the nation at that time. A speculative bubble requires an inflation of value beyond the limits of actual wealth, as when France and Britain speculated on New World gold and silver to a degree that surpassed the considerable value of the gold and silver already in Old World coffers. In the case of Kuwait in the 1980s, the actual financial resources of the nation were enormous and posed a real challenge to speculative overextension.[9]

Train points out that the capitalization of Kuwaiti stocks exploded from $5 billion in 1980 to as much as $100 billion a year later.[10] The entire escapade was based on the easiest form of credit known to man, kited checks. One of the Arab world's richest nations financed a speculative stock-market episode with rubber checks!

Train points out that postdated checks were used by investors like cash to buy the most active and hottest stocks in the Kuwaiti market. Speculators would use the checks to buy rapidly rising stocks whose profits would cover the unpaid balances in the checking accounts. Since the stocks always went up, there was little risk of writing a bad check, or so it seemed.

Train recounts the story of a very aggressive young speculator, one Jassim al-Mutawa, who wrote $14 billion in postdated checks. The speculator, in his twenties at the time, had a brother who was eventually $3.4-billion overdrawn in his attempt to parlay kited checks into big stock-market gains.[11] Kuwait's Finance Ministry demanded that all "doubtful checks be turned in for clearance. Added up, they eventually came to over $90 billion, substantially more than Kuwait's total foreign reserves.[12]

The figures for such a small market are truly staggering, as was the subsequent crash. Kuwait shares plunged by the requisite 90 percent and never regained their former luster. The Kuwaiti Souk mania is an extreme example of how easy money, in this case very easy money, can influence, and even more important, precipitate a major bubble in financial assets.

A Yen for Action

Extraordinarily easy money also fueled the manufacturing and export juggernaut in Japan in the 1980s. The complex interaction of banking, manufacturing, and related businesses allowed Japan to manufacture a cost of capital that was, after adjusting for inflation and taxes, less than zero. Extraordinarily low after-tax capital costs can create all manner of asset bubbles. In this case, the free, not easy, money created a world-class bubble in both stock and real estate prices that only ended when the Bank of Japan began to tighten credit conditions in late 1989 and early 1990.

The Arab world parked its excess cash in Souk companies. At the end of the decade, the Japanese also had excess cash in need of an exciting investment outlet. In a choice that can no doubt be analyzed at length by students of Japanese culture, wealthy Japanese investors began to acquire museum-quality European Impressionistic paintings. Those acquisitions created a bubble in Impressionist artworks similar to the one created in Japanese stock and real estate prices, both of which peaked, coincidentally, in 1989. Michael Moses and his colleague Jianping Mei, two associate professors at the Stern School of Business, argue that the excess liquidity created by the Japanese markets helped to engender a truly remarkable bubble in art. While the average investor may not recall the excitement, the action in art, particularly in Impressionist masters, was hot and heavy in the spring of 1989. Japanese investors were among the most aggressive bidders for Impressionist works, along with newly minted billionaires in the United States and Australia. Eye-popping prices were fetched for Monet, Manet, Cézanne, and van Gogh. Van Gogh was the asset class most prized by serious collectors. *Sunflowers* and *Irises* took in tens of millions of dollars, and *The Portrait of Dr. Gachet* set a record at $82.5 million.

The Mei/Moses Art Index compiled by the two academics very clearly shows the bubble that both inflated and burst in Impressionist artworks at that time.

Mei/Moses Semi Annual All Art Index

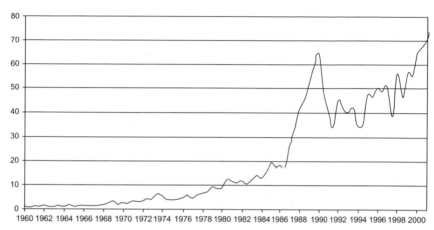

Courtesy of Michael Moses, NYU

Sotheby's

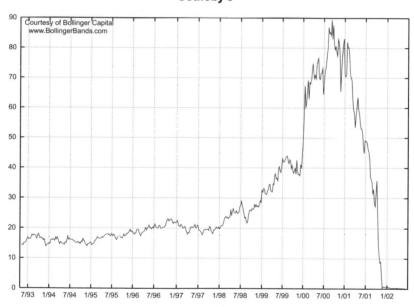

Courtesy of Bollinger Capital
www.BollingerBands.com

Not only was the art mania fueled by easy money from abroad, but the auction houses themselves helped to finance as much as 50 percent of the purchase prices of many of the most expensive works, another sign of easy money and rising prices. While the U.S. stock market was still struggling in the wake of the 1987 stock-market crash, shares of Sotheby's reflected the enthusiasm of the times.

Like the prices of Impressionist works, Sotheby shares did not regain their peak for about a decade. Of course by then, the auction house was about to become embroiled in a price-fixing scandal with its centuries-old rival, Christie's, that would send the stock plunging.

Easy Money Disguised as Costly Credit

Concurrent with all this madness was the great leveraged-buyout boom that sent selected equity values soaring in the United States. The LBO mania was driven not only by Michael Milken and his now-defunct Drexel Burnham Lambert, but by all of Wall Street, which was desperate for action after the general stock-market bubble broke in 1987. In the case of the LBO craze, it was fueled not so much by cheap capital as by available capital.

Leveraged buyouts, while not a new financial phenomenon, grew in popularity in the 1980s as corporate managers and financial engineers sought to unlock the full asset values of their companies, particularly when those values were not reflected in the company's current stock price. *Breakup value* was a term used to describe how much a company was worth when the sum of its assets were not fairly valued by investors. In an effort to unlock those values, managers sought to buy the firm for themselves, sell off various pieces, and eventually take the remaining company public again, reaping substantial rewards for their efforts.

The buyouts were generally financed by junk bonds, euphemistically referred to as "high-yield debt." The trick was to sell off enough assets to pay down the debt quickly, leaving a profitable but smaller firm that would eventually be properly valued by investors in the new public offering. The junk bonds were made readily available by Drexel's Milken and other big players in the game, who made billions in fees and from taking equity interests in the target companies.

A Potent Fiscal Stimulant: the Tax Break

It didn't matter to the borrowers that the rates of interest were often four to five percentage points above U.S. Treasury securities of comparable maturity. The high interest-rate payments were deductible as a business expense. So after adjusting for taxes, the cost of borrowing money through the junk-bond market was not nearly as high as the nominal interest rates on the bonds would have suggested. Ultimately, all that mattered was getting a deal done so that all involved could get rich from the action. And there was, no doubt, plenty of action.

Drexel's Michael Milken championed the process. He invented the so-called highly confident letter that allowed corporate managers, corporate raiders, and other financiers to declare that they had sufficient financing to buy a target company. All they had to do was produce the Milken-backed letters of credit, if you will, and they were instantaneously credible buyers. Multibillion-dollar buyouts became the rage, and many individuals, from Milken himself to his corporate raider friends to yuppie investment bankers, dined sumptuously at Wall Street's newest troughs. But the high-yield credit was not used exclusively for LBOs. Corporate takeovers of all kinds made use of the easy money. Merger and acquisition activity hit a record in 1989, topping $600 billion in the United States alone. Investors blithely ignored the fact that the costly but available credit made it difficult for a firm to survive tough times once the buyout was completed. And never mind that the activity bred all manner of abuses, from insider trading to outright extortion of company management, a process known as "greenmail." The LBO craze, we were told, would not only unlock hidden asset values but make corporate managers more accountable to stock- and bondholders as they were forced to make a company lean and mean or face the well-financed wrath of some interested party who would buy the company out from under them and do the leaning and meaning themselves.

In reality, the craze did less to rationalize inefficient industries than it brutalized them with massive debts and little room to maneuver. In 1991, an unexpected recession made the debt burdens unbearable. A record number of companies went bankrupt in 1991, many as a direct result of the largesse of Milken and others who had eagerly loaned them money for a highly uneconomic enterprise. The Milken money machine was famous for its ability to provide the financing for everything from start-up ventures to historically large-scale hostile takeovers. Drexel's list of clients reads like a Who's Who of business. Corporate raiders like Carl Icahn, Boone Pickens, and Saul Steinberg were among the most notable Milken acolytes, and businessmen like Ted Turner, Ronald Perelman, and Bert Roberts were also among Milken's A-list players.

The Milken crowd would gather every year at the Beverly Hilton Hotel for its whopping high-yield conference, dubbed the "Predators' Ball" by journalist Connie Bruck. The conferences were legendary, not only for their nonstop deal-making and money-raising but also for their parties and festivities, which raised more than a few eyebrows for their alleged salaciousness. Money, alcohol, and women flowed liberally at these events, it was said at the time. Milken's salary and bonuses near the end of his tenure topped $500 million in a single year, an astonishing amount of money even by later standards. So heady were the days of the junk-bond mania that by 1985, some 20 percent of all corporate-bond offerings were high-yielding junk securities.[13]

The high and low points of the action occurred in the very same year: 1989. The peak moment of the LBO era was the $25-billion buyout battle for control of RJR Nabisco. The deal, chronicled artfully by Bryan Burrough and John Helyar of the *Wall Street Journal* in the classic business tome *Barbarians at the Gate,* was a stunning feat of financial engineering. The buyout firm of Kohlberg, Kravis and Roberts, with the help of Milken and Drexel, outbid RJR management to take the cookie and cigarette company private in a deal that was, at that time, the largest in corporate history. The buyout was financed almost entirely by high-yielding junk bonds. The bidding war for this venerable firm was front-page news for months as the rival bidders went back and forth offering increasingly higher prices for a respected company that was troubled even before the buyout was completed. Its flagship new product in development, the Premier cigarette, was a colossal failure since it, as *Barbarians at the Gate* pointed out, "tasted like shit and smelled like a fart."[14] Cookie sales were somewhat stale as well. Two years after the LBO, the excess debt burden forced the already weak firm into a prepackaged bankruptcy and a radical restructuring of its operations. So much for unlocking the hidden asset values of RJR! Ironically, this failure meant little to Wall Street, since the deal itself was so large that nearly every major firm on the Street got a piece of the action. Later, many firms would profit from the restructuring business generated by not only RJR but other over-leveraged businesses as well. Investment bankers and brokers profited coming and going. Employees of these ravaged firms were not so lucky.

I Pledge Allegis

The low point for the LBO mania actually caused a minicrash in the stock market, almost two years to the day after the 1987 collapse. This busted buyout event centered around a company called Allegis Corporation, which was the parent of United Airlines, a car-rental firm, and a host of hotels as well. Under the leadership of Steven Wolf, who would later resurface at US Air, Allegis was a one-stop-shopping travel firm whose value at the time was said to be well in excess of its market price. The craze for airline buyouts was fostered by a couple of Milken associates, Carl Icahn, who had previously bought out TWA, and Al Checchi, who made a successful run at Northwest Airlines in 1989. When airlines suddenly became "undervalued assets" rather than unusually difficult companies to run, a feeding frenzy began on Wall Street.

That moment of hysteria began in earnest in April of 1989, when Oppenheimer airline analyst Bob McAdoo wrote a back-of-the-napkin buyout analysis of Allegis Corporation. McAdoo, whose report I was first to reveal on FNN, suggested that Allegis could support itself even if it was bought at a whopping $300 a share, more than double the price shares were selling for on Wall Street. The stock shot straight up. Immediately, the sharks started circling the company. Coniston Partners, a risk arbitrage firm that frequently raided vulnerable companies, quickly took a position in Allegis shares. Allegis management made a bid to buy out the travel giant. The run-up was breathtaking as Allegis peaked at $294 a share. For the first time, however, financing was hard to come by. At about 2:55 eastern time on Friday, October 13, Allegis management announced it could not cobble together the billions necessary to buy the company. Trading in Allegis shares was halted on the New York Stock Exchange. Stock prices promptly plunged, and for two reasons.

First, the collapse of the deal meant that speculators who had bet on the successful completion of the buyout suddenly owned stock that would be worth considerably less than $300 a share when the stock resumed trading. They were forced to sell whatever stock they could to cover their expected losses in Allegis. Second, and more important, the collapse of the Allegis deal loudly contradicted the belief that any company might be the next LBO target and have its stock price inflated irrationally. It poured cold water on the LBO craze.

A gut-wrenching sell-off ensued. The Dow Jones Industrial Average collapsed about 7 percent in just over an hour. The minicrash late on a Friday afternoon left Wall Streeters with an intense worry about another Black Monday two days hence. The minicrash occurred on Friday, October 13, a most bewitching day, not quite two years after the much bigger crash of 1987. The Dow Jones Transportation Average, which included Allegis and other hot airline stocks, suffered far worse than the Dow Industrials. From its peak of 1532 in late 1989, the average plunged about 50 percent over the course of the next few years, meeting all the requirements of a burst bubble. The takeover premium in transportation stocks collapsed. Oil prices spiked less than a year later as Saddam Hussein invaded Kuwait and the Gulf War ensued. And a recession hit the airline industry particularly hard, the combination of rising fuel prices and slowing business a potent and negative combination for travel. Had Allegis been saddled with billions of dollars in additional debt, it would likely have suffered through bankruptcy. Northwest Airlines, a highly leveraged buyout victim, went through Chapter 11 as a consequence of its heavy debt load.

The effects of the LBO bubble bursting were serious. It became increasingly difficult even for creditworthy borrowers to obtain the necessary financing to get them through the tough times that lay just ahead. In less than a year, a recession would begin that, while mild by historic standards, was deep enough to topple the firms that had most aggressively saddled themselves with high-yield debt. The collapse of the buyout boom also helped usher in a period of subpar performance in the stock market, which languished for over a year before the great bull market of the 1990s slowly began to build in 1991.

But again, easy money provided the gas that inflated another bubble. Overleverage, rising interest rates, and a changing business climate would help to pop the bubble, but on that we'll have more later.

Internal Crisis

In some cases, easy money represents a policy error or unexpected by-product of a crisis that threatens the financial stability of an entire nation. The great bull markets in stocks in the 1980s and 1990s certainly had their origins in the easy money policy responses the Fed used to combat major crises. In the early 1980s, the Fed was fighting for the solvency of American banks by cutting interest rates in the wake of a destabilizing Latin American debt default. In the 1990s, it battled to save this nation's major banks from the shadow of soured commercial real estate loans and overextended credit to heavily leveraged corporate borrowers. In both instances, the Fed aggressively lowered interest rates in an effort to bail out the financial community. Each time a profound crisis occurred, a bull market in financial assets followed the Fed's dramatic attempts to turn the tide.

One of the unexpected by-products of the Fed's rate-cutting effort in the early 1990s was to create an obscure bubble in the U.S. Treasury–bond market. In the wake of the banking problems that engulfed the nation's financial district in late 1990 and early 1991, the Federal Reserve slashed short-term interest rates in half in a little more than a year's time, from a high of 6 percent to a low of 3 percent. The so-called Federal Funds Rate, the one most closely controlled by the Fed, stayed at 3 percent for 18 months. Short-term interest rates in the United States at that time, however, adjusted for inflation, were actually closer to zero than to 3 percent. Let me explain.

Professional investors look at interest rates in two ways. There are nominal interest rates and real interest rates. Nominal rates refer to the "headline" number that you see in the bond-market page of your business section. In 1993, the Fed Funds Rate was stated as 3 percent. That's the nominal rate. But the real rate of interest reflected in that short-term yield is calculated by subtracting the prevailing rate of inflation at the time. Since 1993, inflation was running at about 3 percent annually, real short-term rates were, essentially, zero—less than that, actually, because businesspeople who borrow money to finance their businesses can deduct interest costs. So, in 1993, the real, after-tax cost of funds was less than zero.

Since short-term rates were less than zero and long-term rates were considerably higher, around 6 percent, it paid for speculators to borrow money at the short-term rates and buy bonds that offered a 6 percent yield. Smart money investors of all stripes did that with reckless abandon from 1993 until late 1994. That investment maneuver is called a "carry trade" in the bond business. It is wildly profitable when interest rates are moving in your favor, as they did in 1993. So profitable was the trade that investors rushed to buy bonds like mad, making 1993 and 1994 two of the best years for bonds since the 1970s.

But with that investment mania for bonds came several distortions in the marketplace. True, the impact on the U.S. economy was quite favorable. Banks could recapitalize their damaged balance sheets by engaging in those so-called carry trades. The 6 percent they earned on their money, plus the capital gains from their bondholdings, allowed them to recover financially while still writing off all those bad debts they had accumulated in the late 1980s and early 1990s. In addition, low rates helped fuel economic growth, making houses and cars easily affordable.

But thanks to the quirkiness of the bond market, low rates made all kinds of interest-rate derivatives extraordinarily volatile. Sophisticated investors play all kinds of games with interest-rate investments, carving bonds up into their interest-rate and principal components so that they trade as separate vehicles. These investments are called "strips," since the interest payment is stripped from the principal portion of a bond. When interest rates fall, "interest-only strips" plunge in value while "principal only-strips" gain. And just the opposite occurs when rates rise. As the distortions from the bond-market bubble grew in 1994, and threatened to again destabilize the financial markets, the Fed began to raise interest rates to cool the asset inflation that had been caused by the bond-market mania. But rising rates also affected the bond market, creating some crushing losses for speculators who had aggressively moved into principal-only securities and other derivatives. Some of those speculators included some plain vanilla money-market mutual-fund managers who failed to tell their risk-averse fund holders of their gamble. That derivative debacle left entire hedge funds, one major brokerage house, and Orange County, California, bankrupt or entirely bust.

External Shock

Even Mexico, whose currency, the peso, was tied to the dollar, suffered from the rate hikes engineered by the Federal Reserve. Countries that peg their currencies to the U.S. dollar are hostage to the Federal Reserve's monetary policies. To keep its own currency's value in line with that of the dollar, Mexico was forced to raise interest rates when the Fed raised rates and lower them when the Fed lowered them. In this way, the peso's value would remain constant. That's because the interest-rate differential between the two countries would also remain constant. Often, investors shift funds back and forth between countries when interest-rate gaps get too wide. This shifting has an impact on currency exchange rates, depressing the currency that is being abandoned for the higher-yielding one.

The rate hikes undertaken by the Fed in 1994 not only slowed down the U.S. economy and market but also pressured Mexico's economy and market. High interest rates not only depressed economic activity but also so weakened Mexico that it was forced to devalue its currency. The currency devaluation wrecked its economy. The peso crisis threatened to spread from Mexico to all of Latin America and even spill over north of the border. A weakened and highly indebted trading partner like Mexico threatened to cripple the U.S. banking system with uncollectible Latin American debts and also to cut into the highly profitable cross-border trading activity that had been stimulated by the North American Free Trade Agreement, or NAFTA.

So bad was the pain from its rate increases that the Fed was forced to play the easy money game in 1995, touching off the bubble in stocks that would last for another five years before that bubble burst in 2000. So, as it always does in a pinch, the Fed began slashing interest rates in 1995, leading to a renewed bull market in stocks and bonds that would be further accelerated by the subsequent easy money bailouts of Asia in 1997 and Russia and Long-Term Capital in 1998.

Along the way, two major international crises forced the Fed either not to raise rates as planned or to cut interest rates quickly and dramatically to offset the effects of the latest crisis. The Asian crisis in 1997 and the Russia/Long-Term Capital crisis in the following year made even more easy money available, helping to inflate the U.S. bubble even further. The topper to the easy money phenomenon came in the months leading up to the year 2000. The Fed grew the nation's money supply at a 20 percent annual rate in the final three months of the year, flooding the economy with funds. The excess liquidity found its way into the already rapidly rising NASDAQ, pushing that index up 25 percent in the first two and a half months of the year before the entire enterprise came to a crashing end.

Subsidized Bubbles

It is quite obvious how easy money can help to inflate a bubble and even push it to the bursting point if money growth, overinvestment, foreign funds, or low interest rates are left largely unchecked. But fiscal policy and government subsidies can also play a role. And like easy money, there are a variety of fiscal initiatives that can aid growth and cause overinvestment in a particular industry. Throughout history, various government initiatives, including providing full financing, allowed gold expeditions to create huge waves of speculative excess. From the South Sea and Mississippi schemes to the errant fiscal policies of the Nixon and Ford administrations, fiscal policy can play a role in asset bubbles.

More directly, however, special treatment for particular industries usually precipitates or exacerbates bubble formation. That was certainly true in the early days of canal building, plank roads, turnpikes, and, of course, railroads. Government land grants provided an enormous financial break to railroad operators, saving them huge amounts of capital that would otherwise have been associated with the development costs of their business.

The amount of land and capital the government offered to six transcontinental railroad companies was enormous. During the peak years of activity leading up to the completion of the first transcontinental link, the U.S. government doled out 131 million acres of land to six firms and $65 million in loans. States granted another 555 million acres in the same period.[15] Economic historian Robert Sobel points out that "40% of the cost of all [railroad] construction was borne by one government or another," adding that investors were so confident that the government was paying most of the construction tab they "flocked to buy railroad securities."[16]

Basically, while patrons had to pay for their trips on the railways, investors received a free ride, at least for a while. As stated earlier in the book, easy money also played a role in the build-out of the railroads, as, according to economist Robert Sobel, foreign investors were unusually keen on American railroad stocks and bonds despite their bad experience in the British railroad bubble of the 1840s. Of the $1.46 billion in foreign holdings of U.S. securities in 1869, $243 million were railroad issues.[17]

That double punch would serve other budding industries well in subsequent years. The Internet benefited quite nicely from tax incentives and easy money. Recall that the Clinton administration and Congress enacted a moratorium on Internet sales taxes as the industry was beginning to grow rapidly, allowing e-tailers to compete tax-free with their brick-and-mortar counterparts. While responding to the legitimate concern that sales taxes would hamper the growth of electronic commerce, the moratorium also inadvertently gave electronic merchants an advantage over traditional stores. In many cases, state sales-tax laws made similar goods more expensive in stores than on the Web.

This country has a long history of providing incentives to help new industries develop and mature. And many people believe that's all to the good. I'm not about to argue that point. It is, however, important to recognize that fact when analyzing the business prospects for an entire industry and when attempting to determine the trajectory of the publicly traded stocks associated with it. High-tech and biotech concerns, which have experienced bubbles of their own, have also benefited from tax breaks like the research-and-development tax credit, while oil companies, during their bubble period, also enjoyed special government-backed advantages. (It will, of course, be interesting to see whether or not the current political strife in the Middle East leads to specific tax incentives for new oil and gas production here in the United States. If coupled with a continuing easy money policy from the Fed, a hard-asset bubble could form again, just as it did in the late 1970s and early 1980s.)

Insana Insight: The three ingredients most necessary for asset bubbles to form, then, involve technological innovation, easy money, and government largesse of one form or another. When these three appear in tandem, it is fairly safe to assume, at the very least, that a raging bull market in a particular sector is coming. I should note that it takes some amount of effort to recognize these developments in the making. One must examine key economic indicators, read the newspaper, and ask questions of experts to determine whether or not there are emerging signs of a coming bubble or mania. When, however, the ingredients are evident, it is time to start looking for the investments that may be the biggest beneficiaries of a breakthrough, easy money, and government assistance. Once you find them, it is time to place a bet.

The imminent sectoral bull market may extend to an entire asset class, like stocks or bonds, in a secular bull market that lasts for many years. Certainly that was evident in the 1920s, 1960s, 1980s, and 1990s, as far as U.S. stocks were concerned. It will likely happen again in our lifetimes. The trick will not only be to recognize the environment in which that can happen but also to recognize the signs that it's time to plot an exit strategy. Which takes us to our next chapter.

7

———————

ENDWATCHING

End watching and trend watching are both part of the investment process. In the bubble phase of a bull market, end watching is even more important than identifying and acting on the beginnings of the trend. The end comes far more quickly than the beginning. And profits get taken away far more quickly than they are accumulated. The most recent example is telling. The last great bull market in stocks lasted 10 years. For those who played in the hottest sector of the market, technology and Internet stocks, it took only one year to knock the hot stocks from their peaks. In the space of only a year, the NASDAQ Composite fell 70 percent. In two years, despite some powerful intermittent rallies, the NASDAQ was still down 70 percent. In the Internet sector specifically, the bulk of the stocks that flew the highest fell 90 percent or went out of business within a year. There is a book on technical analysis called *Down Is Faster*. It details how quickly bear markets wipe out the gains built up in the previous bull market. Investors so enamored of technology stocks in the late 1990s have learned the lesson that "down is faster" the hard way, unfortunately.

The cataclysmic endings to bubbles, or manias, do not come without sufficient warnings. Indeed, big bubbles are always marked by an obvious deterioration in the positive factors that helped inflate them in the first place. In short, the same factors we examined in Trend-Watching turn negative as the end approaches.

- Money turns from easy to tight

- Fiscal policies that encouraged investment are repealed

- Innovations, inventions, or discoveries fail to deliver on their promise in time to satisfy investors

- Underlying economic conditions deteriorate

- Public participation reaches a peak

Tight Money

To my mind, the endgame in a bull market or bubble is fairly easy to spot. That is not because I fancy myself some kind of market-timing genius; far from it. But it really doesn't take much more than a cursory study of market history to find that higher interest rates or tight money bursts bubbles and brings an end to bull markets in financial assets. It's quite simple and yet investors often doubt it. Most often, rather than dealing with that fact, many investors prefer to blame their losses on the Federal Reserve, which is the bank in charge of interest-rate policy in the United States. That form of denial, however, is a counterproductive proposition for an individual investor charged with preserving his or her capital in both good and bad times.

Some of the smartest investors I know, at some of the biggest money-management firms in the world, have studied bull markets very closely. They have found that only two things cause bear markets in stocks: the onset of war and rising interest rates. War is a tough card to play, since its outbreak can be unpredictable. World War I created untold turmoil in financial markets. Its outbreak in 1914 caused the New York Stock Exchange to shut down for nearly six months. The successful prosecution of wars by the United States, as we saw later in 1917, 1941, and in the Gulf War, actually helped to reignite bull markets in equities, which is part of the displacement phenomenon discussed by Kindleberger.

With respect to bubbles, there are those who suggest that they collapse under their own weight, as in the George Jessel anecdote I quoted in Chapter 1. Once the buying power among investors is exhausted, the bubble bursts and collapses in a rather violent manner. Others suggest that the failure of a highly touted technological innovation, or merely its failure to deliver quickly on its promise, can be the catalyst. That has often been true. However, the failure of a new infrastructure development to meet heightened expectations appears to occur after higher interests rates have affected the financial markets and slowed the rate of growth in the economy.

Of course, that notion will be challenged by academics and others who believe that monetary policy is not a determinant in the formation or bursting of bubbles. However, the record is fairly clear on the matter: rising interest rates, or some form of tighter money or credit, always precede a decline in stock prices or the bursting of a bubble. I can find no examples that would suggest otherwise. It was true in America's first panic in 1792, true throughout the development of the industrial age, true in 1929, true in overseas panics—from those in Latin America at the end of the 19th century to the one in Japan at the end of the 20th—and true again with the bursting of the Internet bubble in the year 2000.

Fiscal Frights

Fiscal policy and other governmental policy changes can help precipitate a crash or exacerbate a downturn already set in motion. Or a threatened repeal of a cherished tax break can do much to temporarily derail a mania or be one of the precipitating elements of a crash. Such was the case in the leveraged buyout boom in 1987, when House Ways and Means Committee chairman Dan Rostenkowski introduced a bill to repeal junk-bond deductibility. The stocks of many buyout and presumed buyout targets plunged on the news, helping to ignite the crisis that led to the market crash in October of that year.

Rarely, however, are such policy initiatives, by themselves, able to bust bubbles or alter the course of a secular bull market. True, the Hawley-Smoot Tariff Bill arguably worsened the decline in the stock market and economy in 1930, but the bill was passed a significant amount of time after an aggressive tightening of monetary policy by the Fed, beginning in 1928. In 1962, President John F. Kennedy threatened to punish American steel companies for a planned price in-

crease, and that dramatic example of unwanted governmental inter-
ference in business prompted an important setback on Wall Street.
But it did not bring to an end a secular bull market in stocks that
would last almost until the end of the decade. As I said above, the
near repeal of junk-bond interest-rate deductions in mid-1987 helped
to cause the stock market to crash in October, but again, that factor
was an aggravating one, following a rapid rise in market interest rates
and coincident with an August rate hike from the Fed under its new
chairman, Alan Greenspan. Fiscal, trade, and general economic policies can have a powerful impact on stock prices, to be sure. But by
themselves, they are often not important enough to begin and end
major bull market moves or to create bubbles. Again, the cost and
availability of money and credit are far more important factors in financial market behavior.

> **Insana Insight:** Permit me to make one observation on mar-
> kets and interest rates as they relate to bubbles, crashes, and
> bear markets. It absolutely doesn't matter if higher interest
> rates are the cause of the crash, a symptom of one, or a result
> of an overheated economy and stock market. Too many in-
> vestors get fatally hung up on this argument. I have heard
> many raging intellectual debates and flimsy rationalizations
> explaining why raising rates won't hurt the equity markets or
> burst a bubble. Investors can argue that point at their own
> peril. Rising rates or tight money or a lack of available credit,
> a rapidly falling money supply—describe it however you
> like—they are all important signals that it is time to lighten
> one's exposure to financial assets!

Lag Times

There is a lag time between the moment when official or market interest rates begin to rise and the moment when the market succumbs to
the pressure. In 1987, it took six months of rising bond-market interest rates and an official interest-rate hike to topple the stock market.

It took over a year of a tight monetary policy in the late twenties. But a steady campaign of rising rates will do damage to financial assets, and often even hard assets. It's only a matter of time. Those who exit the stock market at the first sign of tighter money preserve their capital. Those who wait for the market to break are often surprised by the swiftness and severity of the decline. We know all too well how easy it was to get trapped in the stock market in the year 2000, when the crash finally came. One cannot get through the exit when everyone is rushing for the door at the same time!

Three Steps and Stumble

I'll provide the empirical evidence of the impact of rising rates on markets in a moment, but first a brief digression to explain a helpful rule of thumb for timing one's exit from financial assets. The stock-market technician Edson Gould, a guru in the middle of the 20th century, devised a formula known as the "three-steps-and-a-stumble" rule. The rule pertains to the relationship between interest rates and stock prices. Gould found that when the Federal Reserve raised its key interest rate (whichever rate it happened to be targeting in a particular period) three times in a row, the stock market suffered a serious and relatively lengthy setback. Conversely, he found that three rate cuts pushed stock prices meaningfully higher in the following 12 months. There have been a few notable exceptions to this. But the exceptions have most often been associated with the failure of lower rates to kick-start the markets, not the other way around. Only twice in history has an easier policy failed to help the stock market begin a long-term recovery: in 1929, immediately after the stock-market crash, and then in 2001, when the Fed started cutting rates in response to the slowdown in the economy and burst stock-market bubble.

The rate hikes are important signals for implementing an exit strategy. Bubbles will form again in the future. They won't always be in stocks, but if they are in financial assets or real assets, rising rates will likely be the most important factor that brings an end to their upward movement. It'll be true if it's real estate, gold, or oil. It has been true for all the bubbles that have materialized in the history of markets. There should be no doubt or no hesitation for individuals to act when rates start to rise.

An "EnDuering" Lesson

Examples dating back to 1792 proliferate. Historian David Cowen, using balance-sheet data from the first Bank of the United States, showed how lending restrictions in February of 1792 led to a large-scale panic in the securities market in March.

"Not only does the Bank's balance sheet provide support that the institution was reducing credit sharply in February but so do contemporary stock prices. Clearly prices would be lower, for the borrowers would be pressed for money, and therefore sell their securities to repay the Bank."[1] Stock prices in New York, Philadelphia, and Boston plunged in March. The full-scale panic that erupted amid tight credit conditions led, as noted earlier, to serious reform of this nation's embryonic securities markets.

Just as the market pendulum swings between greed and fear, the money pendulum tends to swing between cheap and dear, causing wild fluctuations in the prices of stocks and bonds. Indeed, once a bubble has been inflated, it has historically been difficult to deflate it except through extraordinarily tight money. Economist John Kenneth Galbraith captured that reality eloquently in his classic book on the 1929 crash: "A bubble can be easily punctured. But to incise it with a needle so that it subsides gradually is a task of no small delicacy."[2] In fact, the effect of "subsiding gradually" has been almost impossible to achieve. Nothing in the literature suggests that an asset bubble has ever been delicately punctured. All moments of speculative excess collapse in a highly similar manner, with catastrophic losses. The Federal Reserve, the Bank of Japan, other central bankers, indeed any lender of last resort has found this to be true. True, the elder J. P. Morgan managed to save the markets in the wake of the Panic of 1907 with massive loans to the financial community. He was, however, unable to perform a similar act of financial engineering when the market crashed 22 years later. Neither Morgan nor the Fed managed any miracles in that fateful year.

In 1968, when the market was exceptionally frothy, when "concept stocks" and "go-go" mutual funds were hot tickets, then–Federal Reserve chairman William McChesney Martin noted that it was the Fed's job to "take away the punch bowl" just as the party got started. Most often, however, the punch bowl is taken away long after the partygoers have lost their sobriety. The hangovers, inevitably then, are long and painful, leading the partiers to swear off the devil's brew forever. (Anecdotally, I should point out that the point at which the partiers promise never to do it again is usually a great time to buy the deflated asset class in question!)

THE WESTERN BLIZZARD

Market history is replete with examples of tight money panics. Again, tight money or credit comes in many forms, from rate hikes to bank failures. The latter reduced the available supply of money in periods prior to the Fed's creation in 1913. The so-called Western Blizzard of 1857 is one such example.

The late market historian Robert Sobel gives a fascinating account of the large-scale panic that followed the collapse of the gold rush in 1857. The entire period from the discovery of gold at Sutter's Mill in 1848 to the "Blizzard" reads remarkably like current times. But instead of a technological innovation being the trigger for a massive bull market and rampant speculation, it was the discovery of the yellow metal in an obscure location in northern California. We all know the story well. But the financial details of the period illustrate just how such a displacement can touch off an economic boom and corresponding bull market. Sobel describes the economic period between 1850 and 1856 as "one of unbroken prosperity." [3] Gold production surged in the period from 43,000 troy ounces in 1847 to a peak of 2.9 million ounces in 1854. [4] As the interest in railroads grew, construction boomed, from 8000 miles of track in 1846 to 30,000 miles in 1860. [5] That meant that demand for iron accelerated, and the new means of distribution enhanced agricultural prosperity as well. All in all, the economy advanced markedly. As a consequence of the economic and rapid geographic expansion of the United States during the period, the number of newly chartered state banks also grew rapidly. Foreign funds may have been instrumental in financing the railroad boom, but funds from domestic banks helped to finance not just commerce but speculation in the financial markets as well. The number of state banks more than doubled between 1844 and 1856, from 696 to 1562, while the volume of loans exploded from $264.9 million to $691.9 million in the corresponding period.[6] Sobel argues that for most of the period, paper money did not trade at par with gold, meaning that paper money creation was not as inflationary or dangerous as in the prior period of speculative excess in the 1830s. However, by the peak years of the bubble in 1856 and 1857, "there was more money about than ever before."[7] Such money creation, which nearly doubled per capita money in circulation from $6.79 in 1845 to $12.93 in 1857,[8] gave rise to a new round of excitement in financial markets, the lesson of a previous panic in 1837 having been completely forgotten.

Sobel quotes from the work of James Gordon Bennett, a muckraking journalist of the time who wrote for the *New York Herald*. Bennett was a poor-mouth and a smart-mouth who often aided and abetted the bears in raids on the stock market. His prose was striking in its anti–Wall Street sentiments. Despite his obvious biases, Bennett accurately forecast the bitter ending to the bubble of gold rush prosperity:

> What can be the end of all this but another general collapse like that of 1837, only upon a much grander scale? The same premonitory symptoms that prevailed in 1835–6 prevail in 1857 in a tenfold degree. Government spoliations, public defaulters, paper baubles of all descriptions, a general scramble for western lands and town and city sites, millions of dollars made or borrowed, expended in fine houses and gaudy furniture; hundreds of thousands in silly rivalries of fashionable parvenus, in silks, laces, diamonds and every variety of costly frippery are only a few among the many crying evils of the day. The worst of all these evils is the moral pestilence of luxurious exemption from honest labor, which is infecting all

classes of society. The country merchant is becoming a stock-jobber, and the honest country farmer has gone off among the gamblers in the western land.[9]

Bennett issued several more warnings on the financial state of the nation and was proved right by the summer of 1857, when liquidity began to dry up and stock prices began to swoon. (I should note that Sobel, in whose book the Bennett quotes appears, was among the first to recognize the seasonal drought in money that was a by-product of an agricultural economy, which the American economy still was at that time. As a consequence, the harvest period was one of notable volatility both in market terms and in terms of liquidity or money available in the nation's banks. As the harvest neared, farmers routinely pulled their money out of big-city banks to finance the labor needed to harvest crops. That put a drain on available cash in the nation's money centers. Stock prices typically fell from August to October, owing to the lack of available funds. But stock prices bottomed in October when farmers, flush with cash from the sale of their crops, redeposited the proceeds in the New York banks. Many market experts believe that this is the principal reason why the stock market has had a historic tendency to crash and bottom out in the month of October.)

But in 1857, in addition to that seasonal tendency of the market to swoon, credit began to dry up for other reasons. The Ohio Insurance and Trust Company, a key financial firm helping to finance speculative Western investments, suspended payments from its New York office. That initiated the collapse of "the web of credit" created during the boom.[10] Subsequently, poorly capitalized railroads like the Michigan Central collapsed. New York banks began to fail. Runs on financial institutions "became commonplace." More railroads went bankrupt. The failure of a large gold shipment from California to reach New York put the last nail in the market's coffin.[11] The *Central America* sank in a storm off Cape Hatteras, costing 400 lives and depositing $1.6 million in gold in a vault of water.[12] Panic ensued and stock prices plunged. Not only did the bubble burst in this country, but its explosion popped a corresponding bubble involving the Crédit Mobilier in Paris. It, too, was deflated by the ancillary effects of the Western Blizzard.[13] A worldwide panic, driven by a collapse in credit and rising interest rates, was once again a feature of the economic landscape. So profound was the panic on the public psyche that church attendance skyrocketed and even business publications like the *Journal of Commerce* published prayers asking citizens to stay away from Wall Street and use that time to engage in more metaphysical endeavors.[14] No doubt this had a salutatory effect on the "moral pestilence" Bennett had decried.

> **Insana Insight:** The bust after the boom inevitably chastens a population that, in the heady days of the bubble, thinks of little more than material gain. In the wake of their shattered dreams of riches, people seek out spiritual enlightenment. While it does not seem that this phenomenon has taken place today, the events of September 11, 2001, and the associated attack on America's financial district did lead some to question their materialism and begin to ponder other aspects of life, like family, country, and community.

Money and Morality

Moral rectitude and monetary discipline often seem to go and in hand, and many believe that social mores become far more relaxed during prosperous times than they are during times of recession or war. It is thinking like this that led some observers to note that women's hemlines tend to rise along with the stock market. Legendary hedge-fund speculator Victor Neiderhoffer observed in his book, *The Education of a Speculator,* that sexual freedom and bull markets are a function of each other. Money, it seems, is not the only thing that is easy during times of peace and prosperity. Tight money, on the other hand, tends to usher in not only bear markets but periods of self-reflection and self-restraint.

What the "Smart Money" Knows

One of the most glaring signs of the arrival of the endgame is the entrance of all public investors into the market. Full-scale participation is the hallmark of the bubble, but it happens also to be a very important sign that full potential has been reached. Individual investors, regardless of the market in which they are investing, should be aware of this. With that in mind, I would like to take a moment to show how individual investors were induced, even *seduced,* into the market.

Public Participation

One of the key ingredients in a bubble, almost by definition, is some form of mass participation. True, there have been market bubbles driven by small crowds, but the true bubbles, those of epic proportions, have always involved entire populations who were consumed by the desire to become wealthy without working. I am reminded of an old ad placed in the *Enquirer* tabloid by an entrepreneur named Joe Carbo, who offered a self-help guide entitled *The Lazy Man's Way to Riches.* No doubt Mr. Carbo earned some handsome profits selling the advice. To this day, I have no idea if anyone ever got rich the "Lazy Man's Way."

In 1928, John J. Raskob penned a tidy little piece in the *Ladies' Home Journal* entitled "Everyone Ought to Be Rich." Market historians cite this article frequently as a sign of the excesses of the time. The article described how even common folk could get wealthy by buying good common stocks. Of course, the reality is not quite so tidy. In the 1920s, it was easy to make a buck briefly, but more often than not shrewd speculators took advantage of individual investors' lack of knowledge, experience, and investing acumen. The old bucket shops of the 1920s that we looked at earlier, ancestor of the day-trading facilities of the 1990s, advertised retail services that allowed individual investors to walk in off the street and get a little action. Instead, unscrupulous types loaned their customers the money to buy stocks, then quickly cleaned out their accounts.

But the notion that the public can play Wall Street like the pros pervades market manias. From Groucho Marx commenting on the

1929 crash in his version of *Animal Crackers* to Woody Allen mocking the deathly dull 1960s cocktail-party conversations about mutual funds, when investing becomes a popular national pastime, you know you are in a bubble.

One of the clearest signs of a terminal point in the Internet bubble occurred at a funeral. Late in the craze, the *San Jose Mercury News* ran a story about a young man trading stocks over his cell phone at his grandmother's funeral. He generously involved the rest of his bereaved family in the action! Such an obvious shift in the national character, in which both traditional values and traditional valuations get ignored, is often quite indicative of the bubble's terminal phase. That in this instance two terminal events took place simultaneously only adds to the irony.

An Affair to Remember

The degree to which investor interest in the stock market grew was never as strong as it was in the 1990s. Starting with the mania for mutual funds to the rise of the individual investor as savvy day-trader, public participation in the stock market hit an all-time peak in the year 2000. The process, of course, was aided and abetted not only by those who wished to prey on the public but also by those who truly believed that Wall Street was becoming a more democratic institution. I must admit that I am among those who believe the individual investor now has access to more and better information than ever before. That is a truly important development. But I also believe that professional investors will always have some sort of information advantage. To me, that means that while individuals can become smart and successful investors, they will never be able to "outtrade" professionals, contrary to the beliefs of the late 1990s.

But how did the public come to believe that making money was easy on Wall Street? Bubbles, as stated, rely on the psychology of the crowd to turn bullish toward whatever asset is in vogue at the moment. Without full public participation, bubbles cannot inflate to their fullest.

A lot of factors caused the public to play. The Motley Fools, who challenged Wall Street's conventional wisdom, and the Beardstown

Ladies, who made investing seem simple, were among the most staking examples of the popular belief that with a little work, one could get fabulous returns in the stock market, just like the pros. *Beating the Street* by mutual-fund maven Peter Lynch whet the public's appetite in 1994. Then *Dow 36,000* (1998) by pundit Jim Glassman and *Dow 40,000* (1998) by money manager David Elias encouraged individual investors with the false hope that stocks were poised for a decades-long rally that knew no bounds.

Dow 100,000!

Let me deal with the latter works first. While I greatly admire and respect the ideas of both Glassman and Elias, they based their work on a concept known as "linear extrapolation." In other words, their predictions of Dow 36,000 or 40,000 assume that because the market has gone up on average 10 percent a year, it will continue to do so. Even at a compounded 8 percent annual return, a Dow that was sitting at 10,000 in 1999 would double in nine years and then double again in another nine. (The so-called rule of 72, a mathematical formula, shows how compounding works. Simply divide the number 72 by the expected rate of return and you'll find out how long it takes to double your money. At 8 percent, money doubles every nine years.) Using such methods, Glassman and Elias showed how easy it would be for the Dow to hit those lofty price targets.

Of course, the problem with linear extrapolation is that it fails to take into account a break in the prevailing trend and gives investors the false idea that one can bank on compounding to bail them out of investing mistakes. Let's examine a couple of cases in point. In the 1920s, when John J. Raskob was preaching that everyone ought to be rich, the Dow vaulted to a high of 381 (September 1929). Using Glassman and Elias's approach, the Dow should have hit a high of 1524 by 1947. The crash and Great Depression, however, unexpectedly intervened. The Dow plunged to 41 by the summer of 1932. It did not reach 381 again until 1954. It did not even approach 1500 until the mid-1980s, nearly 40 years after it "should have" had it compounded at an 8 percent annual rate.

Similarly, in 1966, the Dow touched 1000 for the first time in the midst of a roaring bull market. Again, using simple compounding rules, it should have vaulted to 4000 by 1984. The road to 4000 between 1966 and 1984 was interrupted by the Vietnam War, the Arab oil embargo, raging inflation and unemployment, the Iranian hostage crisis, and the deepest recession since the 1930s. The Dow first touched 4000 10 years after it "should have," in early 1994.

I don't doubt that the Dow will one day reach 36,000 or 40,000. And while it may happen on the predicted timetable, it should be obvious that history, not even financial history, doesn't move in a straight line. Indeed, that is the whole point of this book, to disabuse people, specifically investors, of the notion that markets are a one-way street. In 1966, the Dow hit 1000. It hit 1000 again in 1968, then failed to surpass that level twice in the 1970s and again in the early 1980s. Essentially, the Dow moved sideways from 1966 to 1984—*18 years*—the same time it should have taken to double twice!

> **Insana Insight:** As optimistic as the bulls appear to be, I should note, the bears are equally pessimistic at market bottoms. That is something all investors should remember as they become increasingly disaffected with a particular asset class. As many have written before, headlines in 1982 declaring "the death of equities" paradoxically signaled that the universally unloved stock market had nowhere to go but up. Everyone who wanted to sell stocks had already sold them, creating the perfect environment for a meaningful bottom in the market.

Fools and Females

But getting back to the various lures that pulled Main Street toward Wall Street in the 1990s. The Motley Fools were one of the greatest new acts of our investing age. Two savvy brothers, Tom and David Gardner, wrote several books and launched an extremely popular web site that criticized Wall Street's less-than-insightful analysis and replaced it with their own brand of "foolish" thinking. The self-styled

Fools challenged Wall Street's conventional wisdom, claiming that individuals who did their own research could far outperform professional investors who relied on the big-time analysts on the Street. And for a time, the "Fool Portfolio" outperformed many professionally run portfolios by a wide margin.

The Fools were an instant hit on Main Street. Their books were bestsellers. Their web site, originally established on AOL, grew rapidly and expanded beyond the proprietary on-line service. Tom and David Gardner were frequent guests on TV, radio, and at financial seminars. Their Motley Fool chat rooms were home to thousands of novice and experienced investors who gathered electronically to share ideas and, in some cases, tout stocks that appeared ripe for big moves. Indeed, the Fools were among the first to discover Iomega, a once-small disk-drive maker whose stock price was one of the early indicators of the coming technology boom.

Iomega was a sleepy little technology company until the mid-1990s, when investors suddenly discovered the maker of "Zip Drives" that allowed users to expand their computer memories greatly and inexpensively. The Zips became must-have computer peripherals. As sales soared, so did Iomega shares, hitting a peak of nearly $140 a share in early 1996. Iomega devotees, known to many as the "Iomegans," constantly talked up the prospects for the company's stock, despite its lofty valuations and soaring price. Indeed, Iomega was a fine company, and indeed, it was growing amazingly fast. The problem, in the minds of professional observers, was that the stock's growth far outpaced the company's growth in sales and profits, a disquieting divergence.

Iomega was also the cornerstone stock in the Fool Portfolio. The Motley Fools were, for quite a time, Iomegans in funny hats. (The Fools wore 16th-century fool hats with bells attached as a reminder that Shakespeare's fools were actually the characters with true wisdom, while the princely folks around them were often the most obtuse.) But the joke would ultimately be on the Fools and the Iomegans. Iomega shares began to fall as growth prospects for the company's products appeared to slow. True believers that they were, both the Fools and the Iomegans denied the possibility of a change in the company's fortunes. Iomega, like many tech firms, stumbled. Investors, even wise ones, had overstayed their welcome in Iomega shares.

Iomega

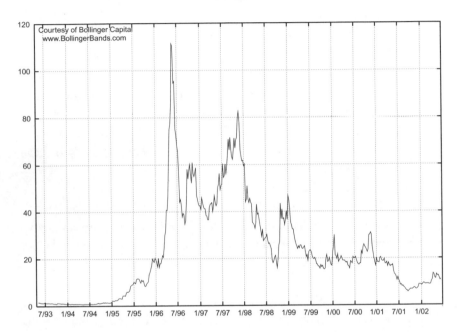

The Fool Portfolio, which once vastly outperformed other pools of money, fell sharply. A series of miscues led to further declines. While Tom and David's business continued to grow, signs of difficulty began to show. Suddenly it appeared that investing "foolishly" was actually . . . foolish. Investing was not a simple proposition even for wise investors. It seemed they had as much difficulty as the pros in understanding how to navigate a fluid marketplace where product cycles can shift with the prevailing winds.

By the time the Internet bubble crashed and technology companies of all stripes tumbled dramatically, the Motley Fools business model was also in trouble. The decline of the self-reliant day-trader led to plummeting interest in stock-market chat rooms and Internet financial communities. In 2000 and 2001, The Motley Fools began to retrench and reorganize, shedding scores of workers and drastically paring back its operations. Investors, including the Fools, learned never to confuse brains with a bull market. In a bull market, particularly a great bull market or bubble like the one witnessed in the 1990s, it's easy to make the wise look foolish and the fools look wise, but in most cases only temporarily.

Legendary investor Warren Buffett looked foolish to some people for a few years, since he failed to capitalize on the Internet trend. Mr. Buffett, who publicly claimed not to understand the Internet business, chose instead to buy shares in companies whose business models he understood thoroughly. Some observers thought the greatest value investor of our generation was out of touch with the new reality of both the business world and the marketplace. But Buffett's seemingly obsolete wisdom ruled the day. Shares of his holding company, Berkshire Hathaway, soared as technology stocks plunged. While countless Internet millionaires and billionaires have come and gone since then, Buffett remains the second-wealthiest man in the world. Seeming foolish for adhering to principle can look unwise in the heat of the moment. But being foolish during that moment can be disastrous.

No group ever made seeming wise look quite as easy as the Beardstown Ladies. A group of grandmas from the Midwest raced to the top of the nonfiction (at least it started that way) bestseller list in the mid-1990s, with an investment guide that bore their name. The Ladies, it seemed, had parlayed a small, regular series of investments into a winning portfolio that, like the Fools,' far outpaced the gains scored by stock market professionals. With their investment club meeting on a regular basis and picking good, solid stocks, the Beardstown Ladies' portfolio beat the S&P 500 a number of years running. Outperforming that benchmark, I might add, was no mean feat in the mid-1990s. To recall: the stock market's main barometer was in the process of delivering unusually strong gains of at least 15 percent a year, far above the normal 10 percent returns delivered in modern times.

The Ladies were the darlings of both Wall Street and Main Street. They proved that the average investor could match the pros with a little homework and a regular, disciplined approach to investing. Alas, again, it was not to last. As it turned out, the Beardstown Ladies had been counting their regular contributions to the fund as gains. So in addition to the capital appreciation they might have seen in the fund, their monthly investment was goosing their returns, an accounting error that professional money managers are not allowed to make. (Although we have since seen how accounting tricks have helped a lot of firms look more savvy than they actually were—another hard-learned lesson of the 1990s, I'm sad to say.) When it was discovered that the Ladies were inadvertently miscalculating their results, a re-examination of their portfolio showed that rather than outperforming the S&P during the period in question, they underperformed it by a fairly wide margin.

Still, individuals remained convinced that they could play with the big boys, and the stage was set for the biggest suckers' rally in the history of Wall Street. The individual investor was hooked. The stumbles along the way, whether they came from the Motley Fools or the Beardstown Ladies, only emboldened investors to strike out on their own, determined to win on Wall Street. It was a challenge for the individual to attempt to beat the professionals at their own game.

There were, by the way, countless signs of a top and countless opportunities for individual investors to exit the market before the serious damage was done. In addition to numerous anecdotal signs of trouble, from homeless people inquiring about Internet stocks to the more important fundamental signs like rising interest rates, classic signs emerged that should have been heeded by individual and professional investor alike. The signs always emerge. What is remarkable is that few pay attention. In the spring of 1928, Charles Merrill published the following letter warning investors to exit the stock market because of a buildup of serious imbalances, not unlike the imbalances that would cripple the stock market in the future. Of course, few listened and many were hurt.

NOW IS A GOOD TIME TO GET OUT OF DEBT

We think you should know that, with a few exceptions, all the larger companies financed by us have no funded debt. This situation is not the result of luck but of carefully considered plans on the part of the management and ourselves to place these companies in an impregnable position.

The advice we have given important corporations can be followed to advantage by all classes of investors. We do not urge that you sell securities indiscriminately but we do advise in no uncertain terms that you take advantage of present high prices and put your financial house in order. We recommend that you sell enough securities to lighten your obligations or, better still, to pay them off entirely.
        CHARLES E. MERRILL

Courtesy of Merrill Lynch and Robert Farrell

Similarly in April of 2000, another market guru, Abby Joseph Cohen, who correctly called the stock market's bottom and imminent long-term bull market in 1990, issued a serious warning to investors . . . right at the top of the cycle. Cohen's warning was veiled to an extent. She suggested that investors reduce their exposure to technology stocks just as they hit their peak. It is important for individual investors to understand Wall Street's coded language when it comes to calling a top. As one of Wall Street's most influential voices, Ms. Cohen was no doubt under plenty of pressure, both from her firm and even from the government not to cry fire in this crowded movie house called the stock market. Given her stature and influence, issuing a blanket sell order at the time could very well have caused a panic. Indeed, during times of serious market trouble in 1998, it was believed that Cohen and her firm, Goldman, Sachs, were asked by then–Treasury Secretary Robert Rubin, to make supportive comments in order to turn the market back from the brink of collapse. Of course, there is no proof of that conversation. But extensive experience in covering such market events has led me to believe that such conversations occur at critical junctures.

Insana Insight: Cohen's sell recommendation needs to be viewed in that light. As an influential and market-moving guru, she could never say "sell everything" without precipitating a full-scale panic. But she could hint at it, which she did at 7 A.M. on March 28, 2000. That was the morning after the S&P 500 hit its all-time high of 1523, a level it has not revisited in over two years. More important, Abby Joseph Cohen told investors to "underweight" the technology portion of their portfolios by 40 percent, essentially telling them to sell their tech stocks. She also stopped forecasting a price target for the NASDAQ, the highest-flying market average of the time. That was about as big a hint as someone in her position would be allowed to give!

Few heeded her warning, and so they suffered the consequences. Those who did listen kept all their profits and escaped the enormous losses of the subsequent bear market. Investors always need to be mindful of the messages sent by influential people, regardless of their own beliefs that the good times will go on forever.

Insana Insight: What they didn't know was that in a bubble the deck is always stacked against the public. Individuals never stopped to address key issues that made the market so enticing. One question they might have asked about Internet stocks was, "If these are such great investments, why are brokerage houses selling the stocks to me, John Q. Public, instead of buying them for their own accounts?" Or, "Why are corporate insiders generously selling their shares to outsiders like me?" Individuals, time and time again, got into these stocks just as the "smart money" was getting out. And it was not as if the information about insider selling was unavailable. Several services provide that kind of data. But few chose to pay attention to it.

One of the bubble's hardest lessons is that investing is not easy. It's not a game. It can't be done with a few minutes of preparation or by reading a book by someone who says it can be. Investing has tough rules and requires great discipline. The rules are rarely, if ever, rewritten by young turks or old hobbyists, who make more money from their book writing than they ever do from investing. (I know, you're thinking the same could be said about me. But I spend my life as a writer and journalist. I don't profess to have a "system" that makes money. I argue that investing requires a deep knowledge of the markets and a healthy respect for market history . . . two things investors sorely lacked during the last great bubble experience.)

BUBBLE OR JUST PLAIN TROUBLE?

There is increasing evidence that the massive bubble in U.S. financial assets that swelled between 1995 and 2000 was not just a new technology mania that spun wildly out of control. A good portion of the hype that drove investors to a frenzied state may very well have been fraudulent. And I'm not just discussing Enron here. Accounting practices, as we have come to learn, were in many cases dubious, if not outright inaccurate. Analysts' stock recommendations often not only failed to adequately take into account the deteriorating state of a company's fundamental business, but failed to take into account the analysts' dismal, but private, views of a company's outlook. The pundits, analysts, and mutual-fund managers were, in many cases, compromised. The entire system of selling shares was biased toward short-term rewards, while the incentives for meeting one's earnings estimates were stacked in favor of company managements not long-term shareholders.

Telecommunications companies claimed phony revenues to bolster their share prices. Software firms "recognized" revenue before it was booked. Internet companies bartered ad time, counting the swaps of ad space as new sales. Fiber-optic firms swapped capacity to puff up their revenue while using accounting tricks to artificially defray costs associated with those transactions. So while it was the best of times for some, it became the worst of times for others. Company management, initial shareholders, and large fund managers sold their shares before these "accounting irregularities" became public knowledge, and hoodwinked the public in the process. For every Cisco Systems that appeared to have long-term staying power, despite a collapse in its share price, there was a Lucent or a Global Crossing.

Companies that built their fortunes on massive acquisitions were forced to write down the value of their purchases as the bubble deflated. WorldCom, an amalgam of poorly performing telecom and Internet assets, careened toward bankruptcy in 2002 under the weight of a crushing $30-billion debt burden. It spent both stock and debt to acquire company after company, then used accounting tricks, not operating savvy, to bolster earnings. The brainchild of a former high-school football coach, Bernie Ebbers, WorldCom failed to deliver on its promise of one-stop-shopping communications services and paid the price for its founder's hubris.

Lucent, the AT&T spin-off formerly known and respected as Bell Labs, was once the darling of Wall Street investors, AT&T shareholders, and Ma Bell employees, all of whom were given free stock when the phone giant's research arm was severed from the firm in 1996. The shares vaulted ever higher, making Lucent for a time the most widely held stock in America. At its price peak of over $70 a share, Lucent was among the biggest companies on the Big Board. But after booking phony revenues of over $600 million in 1999, when, presumably, the telecom business was at its strongest, Lucent shares descended rapidly until the price fell into the low single digits two years later.

And then, of course, there was Enron, most certainly the Watergate of the business world. "Enronitis," as it was described by my friend Art Cashin, was the business world's most communicable financial disease in the year 2002. It led to the collapse of Arthur Andersen, an accounting firm whose previous exploits included accounting missteps at Waste Management, Sunbeam, an Arizona Baptist church, and, possibly, Global Crossing.

Enronitis

Enron itself was a bubble within a bubble within a bubble...a formerly slumbering electric and natural-gas utility company that claimed it had transformed itself into a telecommunications power-house that also traded everything from electricity to copper to fiber-optic bandwidth. Enron had everything going for it at the height of the bubble ... a recently deregulated California power market into which it could both sell and trade electricity. It made markets in fiber optics, the hottest commodity of the late 1990s. It claimed to have earned huge sums of money from those cutting-edge operations. Some 90 percent of Enron's profits, we were told, were derived from trading power and other commodities rather than supplying the goods. In the end, of course, Enron wasn't so much a cutting-edge corporation as it was a corporation that cut corners.

Like any technology, Internet, or telecommunications company, Enron and its competitors in the energy business—Dynegy, Williams Companies, and Calpine—were betting that a developing new infrastructure in the nation's power market would allow these sleepy old companies to grow like tech firms and transform the once staid and highly regulated business of buying and selling power into a dynamic business that operated on solely free-market principles.

Wall Street, of course, eagerly embraced the concept. It presumed free-market forces would bring about a brisk competition among power-generating and -trading firms to provide electricity anywhere in the country at the lowest possible prices. No longer would businesses or consumers be obliged to buy power from local monopolies. Instead they would have their choice of power providers that would quickly serve their needs over an intricate but massive national power grid that efficiently and equitably distributed the juice anywhere it was needed. So we were told. It was another "concept" that was never questioned. The stock price told us all we needed to know. Investors embraced the notion, so who could argue with success?

Not so coincidentally, by the way, California power prices spiked terribly in late 2000 and early 2001. The California power crisis generated headlines all across the country as the market with the most competition and greatest degree of efficiency suddenly found itself in the dark. The price of a megawatt of power was electrifying to consumers from San Diego to San Francisco, streaking from a normal $30 to $50 per megawatt hour to as much as $3,500 per hour. Christmas 2000 brought an unwelcome lump of coal in California's neon stocking. (Coal stocks and fuel-cell stocks, by the way, also ran up sharply as investors looked for alternative energy sources that might provide the region with power at more reasonable prices.)

Federal regulators investigated the matter and found a poorly designed deregulatory regime was the cause of the power crisis, not manipulation or fraud by the powers-that-be in the electricity markets. Eventually, the crisis eased and Californians resumed a life that did not include rationed electricity or unaffordable power bills. Enron and other firms, meanwhile, began to unravel amid a series of unrelated matters that would bring the California power crisis back into the headlines two years later.

Enron

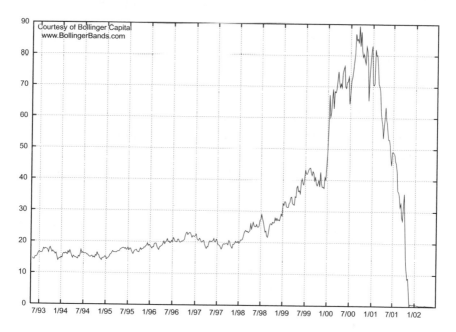

Courtesy of Bollinger Capital
www.BollingerBands.com

Enron, as we now know, was not a savvy maker of markets in power, fiber optics, and other commodities but a wildly manipulative company engaged in massive fraud on both an operational and financial level. Using complex accounting techniques, offshore partnerships, hidden losses, and inflated profits, Enron essentially puffed itself up as an enterprise, "gaming" the markets and defrauding investors of billions of dollars. Its highly touted electricity- and commodity-trading operations were a charade to impress Wall Street analysts: Enron filled its trading room with secretaries and entry-level employees who manned the computers. Unquestioning analysts recommended Enron shares based on the frenetic activity they witnessed at the new command center at Enron headquarters. Indeed, most analysts who covered the company continued to recommend the stock as it careened toward bankruptcy in the autumn of 2001. Some still recommended aggressive purchase of the shares as the price skidded to $5. None, however, seemed to notice that over the course of the previous 10 months, company officers had been unloading their own shares to the tune of a billion dollars collectively.

The story, of course, is now well known and will be the subject of books, business-school case studies, lectures, and college courses that cover everything from accounting abuses to corporate governance issues to unflattering personal profiles of those involved.

Also, as it turns out, internal Enron documents showed that the company used manipulation to help boost the price of California power, costing residents of the Golden State an additional $11 billion in electricity costs during the peak of the power crisis. Operations known as "Death Star," Fat Man," and "Get Shorty" were the code names for manipulative practices that drove energy prices damagingly higher. Some 38 rolling blackouts were called during the crisis, helping to drastically slow one of the nation's most vibrant state economies just as the recession was picking up momentum. Other firms were apparently complicit. Belatedly, the Federal Energy Regulatory Commission sought answers in 2002 after having found few abuses in its initial investigation.

Cooked Books

In the case of Andersen Accounting, the firm was shocked—shocked!—to find out that Enron executives had hidden material information from them as they prepared the company's financial statements. The firm, which had signed off on Waste Management's cooked books in the early 1990s and Sunbeam's fraudulent statements in the middle of the decade, was ultimately indicted on charges of obstruction of justice related to its alleged role in the Enron affair. Anderson partners serving Enron systematically shredded a large cache of financial documents after the Securities and Exchange Commission subpoenaed them. After an aborted effort to settle with the Justice Department, Andersen went to trial to defend its action as the work of rogue employees. One of the rogues, David Duncan, the senior partner in Houston assigned to Enron, delivered damning testimony that ultimately helped to drive the firm almost entirely out of business.

Coincidentally, as I was writing the chapter on the use of fraud to inflate bubbles, the *Wall Street Journal* delivered this damning piece on the character and nature of the entire bull market that took place from the mid-to-late 1990s:

SEC BROADENS ITS INVESTIGATION INTO
REVENUE-BOOSTING TRICKS
Securities and Exchange Commission officials, concerned about an explosion of transactions that falsely created the impression of booming business across a range of industries, are conducting a sweeping investigation into a host of practices that pump up revenue.

The inquiry is extending far beyond the disclosures by Dynegy Inc., Reliant Resources Inc. and CMS Energy Corp. that they engaged in illusory "swap" trades that boosted their apparent business. Questions about whether companies' revenues are legitimate are spreading from industry to industry, raising further questions about whether misleading practices contributed to the hyper-growth of the stock market during the late 1990s.

In other words, puffing revenues and profits was likely a regular phenomenon among the hottest companies and the hottest stocks in the market. In the bull market of the 1990s, there was no shortage of questionable activity, hype, and outright deception or fraud.

Waste Management, the big garbage-hauling firm, was forced to restate its revenues and profits from the early 1990s, thanks to fraudulent accounting practices that allowed it to exaggerate both revenues and profits. Its accountant was none other than Andersen. Sunbeam, audited by Andersen as well, and run by "Chainsaw" Al Dunlap, was another early example of how cooked books made a struggling firm's results look better than they really were. Dunlap, a veteran of many takeover battles and a protégé of deal-maker Sir James Goldsmith, used every trick in the book to boost revenues and earnings. The now-reclusive Dunlap, once a fixture on the business television circuit, hasn't been heard from since Sunbeam blew up in 1998. Dunlap filled warehouses with unsold goods, like barbecue grills, claiming that they had been sold to retailers, in an effort to boost sales and meet Wall Street's earnings expectations. The game worked for a while and drove Sunbeam shares from the low double digits toward $55 a share in 1998. Dunlap's game of making acquisitions, cutting costs, overreserving for special charges, then adding those reserves back into future earnings was a standard trick on the Street. For all his self-described turnaround expertise, "Chainsaw" Al's expertise lay more in cooking the books then in operating a company. Usually he was gone within 18 months of taking over a company, selling the puffed-up firm to an unsuspecting third party while walking away with a handsome paycheck. In the case of struggling appliance maker Sunbeam, no one wanted to buy the restructured company, forcing Dunlap to stay longer than he expected. When he ran out of gimmicks, the firm ran out of profits. The tricks were uncovered. The stock plunged. The company went bankrupt and Dunlap went underground. The stock today trades in the pennies per share.

Roll-ups

Another warning flag that was waving as the bubble was inflating centered on Cendant. The odd collection of real estate, hotel, car-rental, and consumer services companies was the brainchild of Henry Silverman, another New Age entrepreneur whose specialty was rolling up small, presumably compatible companies into one large enterprise that would likely benefit from the streamlined back-office operations provided by Silverman's holding company. The one-stop-shopping synergies that were assumed for these far-flung businesses were also one of the unique drivers behind Silverman's "vision." Along with Wayne Huizenga, Jonathan Ledecky, Bernie Ebbers, and others, Silverman was a master of the "roll-up" acquisition. "Roll-ups" allowed a deal-maker to buy up like properties in a particular business, streamline the overhead of the combined companies through centralized administrative, sales, and marketing functions, and reap huge cost savings as a result. More often than not, the cost savings and presumed synergies were illusory. Instead most roll-up experts used accounting tricks to inflate earnings. They usually cashed out of the business by selling it to another enterprise or to the public, enhancing their own fortunes long before the combined entities failed to deliver their promised growth rates.

Cendant, Silverman's biggest acquisition, turned out to be the most costly not only in dollar terms but also in terms of Silverman's reputation. When he purchased CUC International, a consumer services shopping club, he promised benefits to Cendant shareholders that would dwarf those of his previous acquisitions. CUC's mailing and shopping-club lists would provide invaluable cross-marketing opportunities for his real estate, hotel, and car-rental companies. Cost savings and operating efficiencies would boost earnings per share, a critical measure of success on Wall Street. And that success would pave the way for even greater and more profitable acquisitions down the road. As it turned out, CUC had inflated its own revenues by some $300 million in the space of only a year and Cendant failed to uncover the fraud until after the purchase. The problem sank Cendant, tarnished Silverman's reputation as a savvy deal-maker, and cost investors billions of dollars. Silverman's bank account, however, was not so unfortunate. Not only did he reap substantial compensatory rewards while building Cendant, in the form of both cash compensation and huge stock-options grants, but when Cendant's shares tanked, he simply lowered the strike prices of his and other managers' stock options. He ensured that despite his company's troubles, Henry Silverman would still make out okay. No one, of course, lowered the purchase price for Cendant's shareholders, many of whom paid upwards of $50 a share in the hope of profiting from Silverman's deal-making genius. Silverman's loss of credibility was instant and has yet to be restored.

Like Henry Silverman, Bernie Ebbers and Dennis Kozlowski were also known to be the smartest deal-makers in the business world. Ebbers, a former high-school football coach turned evangelical tele-communications guru, and Kozlowski, a conglomerator in the 1960s sense of the word, also engaged in roll-up acquisitions designed to build sprawling business empires that rivaled those of the rob-ber barons of days gone by. These days, both, of course, are hav-ing their share of troubles. In the spring of 2002, Ebbers's telecom empire was unraveling faster than a waxed string with two cups attached. The amalgamation of phone firms acquired by Ebbers was reeling under a $30-billion mountain of debt, a stock price that had plunged from $60 a share to just over $1, questionable account-ing practices, and a $388-million loan given to Ebbers by the com-pany to cover purchases of WorldCom shares on margin! WorldCom, like Cendant or Jonathan Ledecky's U.S. Office Products or Koz-lowski's Tyco International, never delivered on its promised opera-tional synergies. In WorldCom's case, the company's earnings grew as long as it could make acquisitions. With a soaring stock price and unfettered access to debt financing, WorldCom bought big brand-name companies, the largest of which was MCI, in the hope of creat-ing a one-stop telecom shopping service that would rival AT&T or the other big phone firms. The deal-making stopped in 2000 when the Justice Department blocked WorldCom's planned acquisition of Sprint, in what would have been the biggest deal in business his-tory. Without the deal, WorldCom was forced to run its voice, data, and Internet traffic businesses efficiently and profitably, something Bernie Ebbers could not do. Privately, his rivals and would-be associates expressed their concerns about Ebbers's ability to actually run a phone company as opposed to simply building up the firm's assets. His operational abilities were laid bare in 2002, when the firm teetered on the brink of bankruptcy. Debt ratings agencies slashed WorldCom's debt to junk status in the spring of that year. WorldCom was forced to tap multibillion-dollar credit lines from its banks because it could no longer borrow money in the commercial market. Restructuring of the firm's assets became inevitable as the vulture circled the carcass. Ebbers resigned as chairman and CEO in May, heavily indebted and unable to fulfill his vision. History may likely brand him not as a visionary but as an opportunist who used the bubble to enrich himself and early shareholders in WorldCom. Building a successful enterprise was a task left for another kind of executive.

Retribution

Bubbles are inflated with air, and in the case of this particular market episode it seems that corporate reports used a fair amount of hot air as well. As the revelations grew, lawsuits proliferated, congressional investigations commenced, and regulatory actions were taken. Of course, regulators snapped into action as a consequence of the Enron affair. New accounting rules were devised. Disclosure rules were modified. Congress made efforts to limit offshore incorporations and other such popular tax dodges. Conflict-of-interest rules were also changed for Wall Street analysts who, in addition to providing investment advice and analysis, had been increasingly earning their keep by helping the investment banking colleagues drum up new business. Part of that process included never issuing an offensive sell recommendation on an existing or potential client's stock. While such conflicts had been building on Wall Street for nearly three decades, the breakdown of barriers between research, marketing, and investment banking all but collapsed in the Internet bubble, leading to one of the most embarassing revelations in Wall Street history.

In the spring of 2002, New York State attorney general Eliot

Spitzer, a man whose political aspirations were said to rival those of former U.S. prosecutor Rudolph Giuliani, leveled a rather serious charge at the nation's largest brokerage house, Merrill Lynch. Spitzer contended that some of Merrill's highest-profile analysts had spent the better part of their recent careers recommending stocks they didn't believe in. The stocks were recommended, he maintained, either to induce the firms to do lucrative investment banking business with Merrill or to keep them from taking that business elsewhere.

The attorney general's proof was found in the form of e-mails from the likes of Henry Blodgett, Merrill's wunderkind Internet analyst. Blodgett, a former CNN business-news intern (not that there's anything wrong with that), made a name for himself with a bold call on Amazon.com. While at another firm, he claimed that Amazon's shares would rise to $400 in 1998 from a price roughly half that level at the time. Merrill's own Internet analyst, Jonathan Cohen, was convinced that Amazon's shares would fall. Cohen was fired, Blodgett was hired, and the rest is Wall Street history. When Amazon.com, before it crashed 90 percent in price, hit Blodgett's price target, he became an instant Wall Street celebrity and one of the highest-paid Internet analysts. Each of his pronouncements pushed stocks inexorably higher as the Internet craze grew crazier and crazier.

To be fair, at a critical point in the cycle, Blodgett tempered his optimism about Internet stocks in general, but it was his private musings that ultimately led to Wall Street's most embarassing moment. In private e-mails to clients, he admitted that pressure from management and his investment banking colleagues forced him to recommend stocks that he described as "POSs." Those "pieces of shit" he was recommending were bringing fees to the investment banking division but proved to be costly investments for Merrill clients. Some of the companies, Blodgett and his colleagues argued, were not going to survive. And yet they continued to recommend the stocks. Blodgett threatened in one e-mail to call the stocks as he saw them, despite the pressure from above, but the threat was cold comfort to the investors who lost upward of a billion dollars on the Internet stocks Merrill touted.

Comparison of Merrill Lynch's Private Comments and Published Ratings

COMPANY	DATE	CONTEMPORANEOUS ANALYST COMMENTS	PUBLISHED RATING
Aether System (AETH)	03/15/01	"might have announcement next week . . . which could pop stock . . . but fundamentals horrible" (ML82578)	3-1
Excite @home (ATHM)	12/27/99 12/29/99	"we are neutral on the stock" Six month outlook is "flat," without any "real catalysts" for improvement seen (ML 37899; ML37956)	2-1
Excite @home (ATHM)	06/03/00	"such a piece of crap" (ML51453)	2-1
GoTo.Com (GOTO)	1/11/01	Nothing interesting about company "except banking fees" (ML03806)	3-1
InfoSpace (INSP)	7/13/00	"this stock is a powder keg, given how aggressive we were on it earlier this year and given the 'bad smell' comments that so many institutions are bringing up" (ML06413)	1-1
InfoSpace (INSP)	10/20/00	"piece of junk" (ML06578)	1-1
Internet Capital Group Inc. (ICGE)	10/05/00	"Going to 5" (closed at $12.38) (ML63901)	2-1
Internet Capital Group Inc. (ICGE)	10/06/00	"No hopeful news to relate. . . . We see nothing that will turn this around near-term. The company needs to restructure its operations and raise additional cash, and until it does that, there is nothing positive to say." (ML64077)	2-1
Lifeminders (LFMN)	12/04/00	"POS" (piece of shit) (ML60903)	2-1
24/7 Media (TFSM)	10/10/00	"piece of shit" (ML64372)	2-2

From: Inquiry by Eliot Spitzer, New York Attorney General, June 2001

P.S.

In the case of Lifeminders, Henry Blodgett called it a "POS" on December 4, 2000. On December 21, in a report to investors, he recommended accumulating "LFMN" shares, calling them an "attractive investment." [1] He, of course, was not the only one to lie to the public in the interests of his employer. Worried about how some risky Internet investments could or would hurt the small investor, Merrill Lynch analysts in e-mail conversations among themselves threatened to be more frank in their assessments of a company's outlook. But when the Merrill analysts actually came to the conclusion that a company's prospects were poor, they "merely quietly stopped covering the stock, without any announcement or meaningful explanation to the retail public." [2] Few Wall Street analysts were buying the crap they were selling, but they were selling an enormous amount of it! By the year 2000, analyst buy recommendations outnumbered sell recommendations by a margin of 100 to 1!

In short, malfeasance and, in some cases, outright fraud was not simply a corporate affair. Accounting firms, Wall Street analysts, and investment bankers were, at the very least, complicit in these acts. Whether they engaged in systematic fraud remains to be determined by the courts, if it is ever determined at all.

As Wall Street seeks to restore investor confidence in the spring of 2002, one has to wonder if that will be possible for this generation of investor. Investors might repeat the old saw—"once burned, twice shy"—to their brokers as the deflating of this bubble continues for years to come.

Many of the most unbelievable stories of deception occurred not at the end of the bubble but in the middle of it. And as always, the companies involved, like Comparator Systems, Global Crossing, Enron, and, of course, MicroStrategy Inc., were poised to change the world through technology while their founders offered nearly messianic visions of the future.

Hey Saylor

MicroStrategy was part of the Internet frenzy, but its basic business was to provide productivity-enhancing application software useful to nearly any company in any industry. Its founder and CEO, Michael Saylor, was a brash, aggressive young visionary who promised to re-form the entire business world with his must-have software tools. Saylor was a technology messiah. Many said similar things about Bill Gates, Larry Ellison, David Wetherell, and others in the technology business, but Saylor, it was said, actually believed it himself. As his stock soared in 1999, Saylor's ambitions soared with it.

MicroStrategy

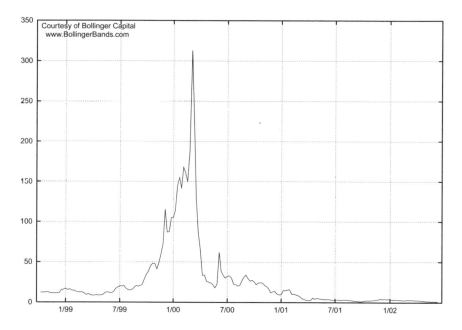

With the stock at nearly $350 a share, Saylor promised to endow a new Internet university with a $100-million grant. His ambition was to create a college that could be attended by anyone, anywhere, at any time. It would be distance learning at its finest, a grand public service delivered by a grand young man who quickly "gave back" to the community that had made him so rich. Saylor was written up in prestigious newspapers like the *Washington Post*. He appeared on

NBC's *Today Show* to announce the endowment. This 34-year-old man impressed the nation with a generosity rare at such an early age. But Saylor was only one of the young, high-tech billionaires bursting onto the national scene. In 1999, Yahoo! founder Jerry Yang was 33, Amazon's Jeff Bezos was 35, and Broadcast.com's Mark Cuban had reached the ripe old age of 39. (The old man of the group, Cuban had already made a fortune in 1990 when he sold his first company to CompuServe.) Entrepreneurs like these were able to do what no other group of successful businessmen had ever done before: give their money away as they were making it! So huge was their net worth on paper that it seemed implausible, if not downright greedy, to keep it all. Some of them gave it all away, others gave some of it away and used the rest to fulfill personal fantasies, buying sports franchises or gargantuan homes with the latest high-tech gadgetry. Saylor's ambition was to build an educational legacy that would live on far beyond his earthly existence. That ambition, that vision, would endure for all of about one week's time.

One week after Saylor announced his $100-million grant, the company announced some trouble with its financial statements. The surprise announcement caused its stock to drop 62 percent in one day, subtracting $11 billion from its market valuation and relieving Saylor of $6 billion of his personal fortune.

As it turned out, MicroStrategy's chief strategy was to inflate its revenues significantly in the late 1990s. Saylor's company disclosed what is euphemistically called on Wall Street a "revenue recognition problem." In simple terms, the company booked revenues that didn't yet exist, though they may have been promised. Computer software makers commonly sign lucrative long-term sales and service contracts with large customers. In normal times, such an arrangement helps to give a firm a solid future, provided the client renews the contract as various product and service milestones are hit. The selling firm typically recognizes only a portion of the revenue that is derived from such deals, waiting to book the rest as the contract matures. In MicroStrategy's case, however, the company puffed up its results by recognizing the full value of the contract immediately, making the software company's revenue growth look spectacular. Hence the explosion in the value of MicroStrategy's shares.

Once it was disclosed that the growth was mere puffery, Micro-Strategy shares deflated as quickly as they had expanded. In mid-2002, the stock had fallen from a high of nearly $350 a share to a buck-fifty.

Same Game

But as ever, this type of behavior was not at all unique to the great bubble of the 1990s. Major manipulations took place during the 1920s bull market. Puffed-up earnings, feats of accounting sleights of hand, and other unethical practices helped drive the 1960s bull market and the computer craze that occurred between 1978 and 1983. It is difficult to find, in fact, any bubble experience that is not rife with abuses and fraud. Incompetence may also play a part. A Morgan Stanley study published by *USA Today* on May 20, 2002, showed how U.S. companies had wasted $130 billion over the previous two years on unnecessary technology investments. Worldwide, another study estimated, as much as 20 percent of the $2.7 trillion spent annually on technology is for naught.[3]

Overinvestment was, of course, one of the key features of the technology bubble. Large and small companies alike purchased all sorts of new gear, hoping to radically improve their productivity and drive down costs. It is true that productivity rates soared in the 1990s and in the early 2000s, well ahead of the pace of the previous two decades. But those productivity gains came at a cost. The overinvestment stimulated by the technology boom will haunt many companies for quite some time.

As for outright fraud, there's no escaping the fact that the greedy moments in market history simply bring out the worst in people. As it is, it's difficult to defend against fraud even in the most austere and moral of times. But when the bubble is fully inflated, every player in the game is looking for a new and easy way to riches. In the most recent case, financial engineering, accounting gimmicks, and a collection of tax dodges aided and abetted the perpetrators.

"Insullated"

In the 1920s, as we've said, very similar games were played. Professional investors frequently banded together to generate action in selected stocks. They would aggressively bid up the price of a company's shares, making the price trend look better than it would otherwise have been. This little maneuver was, and still is, known as "painting the tape." The pros would then entice the public to get in on the action. As the public chased the rising stock with reckless abandon, the pros would abandon the stock, leaving it to fall sharply. They made a tidy sum while the public got bagged. That practice may have been duplicated in day-trading rooms and in Internet chat rooms throughout the technology boom of our time.

Conversely, groups of savvy short sellers frequently banded together in the 1920s as well, launching much-feared "bear raids," in which they would drive a stock dramatically lower. They would first sell the stock short, then spread negative, and often false, rumors about the target company. It is a practice that goes on today.

But for pure irony, one cannot find a better tale than the story of Samuel L. Insull and his Middle West Utilities Company, which flourished in the 1930s. In a highly entertaining and instructive article, the *Wall Street Journal*'s Rebecca Smith discovered Insull amid the crisis engulfing Enron in late 2001 and early 2002. In what the *Journal*'s headline writers described as "déjà vu," Smith found the uncanny similarities between Enron's Ken Lay and the aforementioned Insull.

Middle West was made up of a host of interconnected companies with interlocking boards—an arrangement mirrored, in some ways, by the web of off-balance-sheet partnerships that concealed Enron's heavy debt burden. So complicated was Middle West's structure that it took seven years for a team from the newly formed Federal Trade Commission to fully unravel its financial structure.

Other similarities between Middle West and Enron go straight to the top. Like Kenneth Lay, who resigned last month as Enron's chairman and chief executive, Middle West's Mr. Insull was a big campaign contributor, with powerful friends in Washington. Both men were successful in keeping the government out of their business dealings. Mr. Insull, for one, "was careful to regulate the regulator," Sen. Norris declared in June 1934.[4]

It would be difficult to find a closer parallel than the one between these two utilities. Mr. Insull, who left the United States for France after a series of congressional investigations into his dealings in the mid-1930s, died on a Paris rail platform of a massive heart attack. His wallet had been lifted. He was left with 85 cents in his pocket. Ken Lay's fate, of course, remains to be seen. Whether this scandal will impoverish him or let him live out his life retaining whatever riches he accumulated cannot yet be known. It has been a rare occurrence, however, for the mighty not to fall as quickly and as spectacularly as they rose.

As the postbubble events unfolded, there were more and more revelations about alleged misdeeds during the height of the action. Enron and Global Crossing were investigated for inflating each other's fiber-optic revenues, coincidentally just as the quarters in question came to a close. Using complicated "swap" arrangements, the two companies allegedly gave each other business for which no cash changed hands and no revenue or income was produced. They just showed up that way on each company's books. This, apparently, became standard practice in the communications business as the demand for results grew with inflated stock values.

What Went Wong?

One of the most egregious examples of deception or fraud was alleged to have happened at Computer Associates, once billed as the world's second-largest computer software company, trailing only Microsoft. C.A. made and sold software for large enterprises that used mainframe computers to handle a variety of complex business tasks. The firm, led by founder Charles Wang (pronounced Wong), and his number two, Sanjay Kumar, was one of the fastest-growing tech firms of the mid-to-late 1990s. Wang and Kumar were celebrated industry leaders who built an empire that enriched them and other top Computer Associates' managers beyond anyone's wildest dreams. Indeed, in 1997, the company's three top executives voted themselves a pay package that would ultimately be worth more than a billion dollars. While this caused quite a stir at the time, little was done to stop it, since the company's stock was one of Wall Street's highest flyers in the late nineties.

Computer Associates

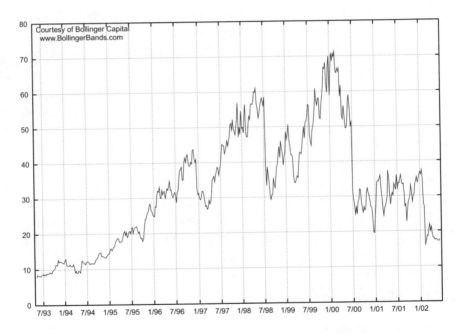

In May of 1998, the managers received a special stock award of $1 billion dollars, to be split three ways, because the price of Computer Associates shares had remained above $55 a share for the required period of time. The compensation package called for the stock to remain above that level before the execs would get their special grant. In May of 2002, federal regulators began to probe the company's accounting practices to determine whether or not the firm's managers purposely overstated revenue growth both before and after the trigger date in an effort to ensure receipt of the award. According to regulatory filings and published reports, C.A. restated its revenues for that period in May 2002, retroactively slicing $1.75 billion off its revenue line for the preceding three years, three years that included the period in question. The pay package, which was among the biggest in the computer industry, may have been nothing more than the result of still more puffery.

Tyco Troubles

One final example of a shocking transgression was uncovered in early June of 2002. The most surprising part of this story was the way it overlapped a noteworthy CEO's personal life and his professional life. Dennis Kozlowski, the former CEO of Tyco International, a mini-conglomerate that had once been billed as "the next General Electric," was indicted on June 4, 2002, for failing to pay state sales tax on a number of artworks valued at over $13 million. The controversial CEO, whose company had been frequently dogged by criticisms of its acquisition and accounting practices, though at the time of this writing had never been indicted or found guilty of abuse, was charged with tax avoidance, falsifying invoices, and other related crimes and misdemeanors. The alleged dodge deprived New York State of over $1 million in sales taxes. Manhattan district attorney Robert Morgenthau's indictment alleged that Kozlowski moved paintings back and forth from his $18-million Manhattan apartment to a company office in Exeter, New Hampshire, to make it appear that the artwork was intended to stay at company headquarters. It was immediately shipped back to Kozlowski's home, the indictment claimed. In the case of four paintings for which Mr. Kozlowski paid a modest $8.8 million, empty boxes were allegedly shipped to company HQ while the paintings were delivered to his home. Among the ironies of the allegations of Kozlowski's tax fraud is, first, that he was among the highest-paid CEOs in the nation: his compensation over the course of his career totaled several hundred million dollars when stock options and stock grants were included. Second, Kozlowski's firm, Tyco, was incorporated in Bermuda in an effort to shield it from heavier U.S. taxes, a simple dodge that Congress began examining in the aftermath of the bubble in the stock market. While the company had yet to be hammered for its obvious efforts to dodge corporate taxes, Kozlowski wasn't so lucky. The firm itself may run afoul of the law as well, since Morgenthau alleged that Kozlowski may have shifted some of the money from the corporate account to his personal account without ever repaying it. Those activities led the Manhattan district attorney to investigate possible money-laundering activities as well. Kozlowski, forced to post a $3-million bond, had pleaded not guilty to the charges at the time of this writing. He, by the way, worked out a $100-million severance package for himself as he resigned. One day later, he was indicted.

Tyco, maybe not coincidentally, was a favorite target of short sellers on Wall Street who frequently decried the company's accounting practices, the quality of its earnings, and the hefty use of acquisitions to boost both revenue and earnings growth. Some, like David Tice, of the Prudent Bear Fund, argued that Tyco's growth was all smoke and mirrors. Amid allegations such as these, the Securities and Exchange Commission reviewed Tyco's books but found no wrongdoing. The Manhattan district attorney, it appears, dug just a little deeper. The SEC reportedly reopened its investigation of Tyco's acquisition and accounting practices in June of 2002. By then, the stock had declined from its high of nearly $80 a share to a low of about $10.

Decade of Greed

In retrospect, it is becoming increasingly obvious that the bubble in stocks, in technology stocks in particular, had as much to do with very fancy accounting as with fancy new technologies. Former Federal Reserve chairman Paul Volcker, who tried to rescue Arthur Andersen from its Enron-related troubles, told me that it's a gross overstatement to assume that the bubble of the 1990s was simply a scam engineered on a grand scheme. But he did admit that the potent combination of huge stock-option grants to corporate managers and greatly relaxed accounting standards helped to distort the action in the market and misalign the goals of management and stockholders. Volcker argued, in fact, that shareholders were forced to align their interests with those of management, not the other way around. Managers benefited greatly from increased volatility in the share price, while shareholders would have benefited from a steady but true appreciation both in the stock price and in underlying corporate performance. Managers were given incentives to meet quarterly earnings targets at any cost, a behavior that, in the long run, proved disastrous for many firms as management cut corners to make the numbers look good. As we have seen from the longer-term price charts, companies that aggressively cut corners during the boom went bust when the bubble burst. More conservative companies survived the bubble largely intact.

The Securities and Exchange Commission, which, ironically, became increasingly active after the bubble burst, sued not Arthur Andersen but Ernst & Young in May of 2002 for alleged improper dealings with PeopleSoft, a large software company. The SEC alleged that E&Y had violated its independence guidelines as PeopleSoft's auditor. E&Y had been in business with the company to sell accounting software, and it should not have engaged in such a relationship with a client. Their joint venture brought in hundreds of millions of dollars in sales, a sum of money that could compromise E&Y's independence as the company's auditor. The blurring of lines between auditor and client becomes a regular occurrence when financial incentives for misbehavior grow unchecked. Why the SEC did not act during the bubble will, as ever, remain a mystery, though former SEC chairman Arthur Levitt often states that his concerns about fuzzy accounting and corporate misbehavior were thwarted by a Congress that frequently threatened to cut his funding if he complained too loudly. At a time when business wielded nearly unprecedented influence over government affairs, it is not surprising that regulators, legislators, and other officials were loath to bite the hands that fed them so very well.

The important lesson for the individual investor to understand with respect to the previous examples of fraud, abuse, and deceit is that you yourself remain your best defense against getting taken advantage of in the marketplace. Bubbles are, by their very nature, investment traps for the novice investor. They are enticing. They are exciting. Those at the top of the pyramid will be lionized for their vision, courage, and extraordinary business acumen. In that environment, it is easy for investors to trust blindly, since government officials, their peers, and even the media will heap praise upon the innovators, the risk-takers, and the captains of industry. As Kevin Phillips writes in his new book, *Wealth and Democracy,* the United States has a particular fondness for technology and infrastructure bubbles. He also notes that not since the Gilded Age have the rich and powerful wielded so much influence over government and over everyday life.[5] Against that backdrop, individual investors should be more, rather than less, wary of those in control. Bubbles, while useful in the building of transformational industries, are destructive when it comes to the financial well-being of the individual investor. As we are finding out with the daily drumbeat of headlines, the game was stacked in favor of the players at the top of the pyramid. Those at the bottom, who briefly profited from the market's rise, were trampled over when the game came to an end. The rich clearly got richer, while everyone else lost their cash.

No doubt headlines and cases such as these alienated investors in the postbubble environment. In May of 2002, some 80 CEOs stepped down from their firms; 13 of them were asked to go. It was a stunning denouement to a period that had, for a time, made heroes of the CEO. In the end, the biggest names in business had been toppled from their perches. So-called visionaries like Ken Lay, Bernie Ebbers, Dennis Kozlowski, Dynegy's Chuck Watson, and others stepped down for the good of their companies. They certainly had done plenty of good for themselves, all of it, ultimately, at the expense of shareholders and employees. Even old-guard companies from other gilded days like Kmart and Xerox were swept up in allegations of fraud and abuse. Arthur Andersen was indicted for obstruction of justice for its role in the Enron case. The watchdog closed its eyes and opened its mouth for treats. As punishment for its bad behavior, a Houston jury found Andersen guilty of obstruction of justice in June of 2002. Remarkably, neither Enron itself nor any of its executives, for that matter, had been indicted for any crime at the time of this writing. But as has always been true in speculative periods, an element of recklessness was inherent. Standards were relaxed as making money became more important than making products or providing services. Enrichment of the CEO by any and all means outweighed the legitimate enrichment of stakeholders through real profit growth and legitimate brand building.

No bursting bubble would be complete without the massive financial fraud that normally represents the terminal phase of the bear market that completes the pattern of boom and bust. On June 25, 2002, my colleague David Faber broke the story of the biggest accounting fraud in U.S. history. WorldCom, as mentioned previously, admitted to overstating its profits by nearly $4 billion over the previous five quarters. In other words, the company artificially inflated its profits by $800 million every quarter for over a year. The SEC immediately sued the phone giant for fraud. Criminal investigations ensued. The reputation of Bernie Ebbers, telecommunications deal-maker extraordinaire, lay in tatters. WorldCom shares plunged toward zero, falling to just pennies while the company's bonds, representing nearly $30 billion in debt, also collapsed in value. The firm announced the immediate layoff of tens of thousands of its employees. Bankruptcy of this once-high-flying NASDAQ pillar was inevitable. The collapse of WorldCom appeared to be the final nail in the mania's coffin. Legislative and regulatory reform was enacted as the accounts of fraud, abuse, insider trading, tax evasion, and other crimes were uncovered day after day. The pain produced from the bursting of the bubble was, sadly, commensurate with the gains experienced in headier times. At the time of this writing, most observers thought the worst of the headlines had been written. But that was only a guess.

Insana Insight: It has ever been thus. In a bubble, insiders reap the rewards while outsiders are left holding the bag. The cool and calculating make off with the big money, while the excitable players, if they're lucky, scramble for the loose change that falls from their pockets. The small investor, who during periods of excitement is often ruled by his heart rather than his head, needs to leave emotion out of the investing equation. Most assuredly the professionals are cool and calculating in their approach to amassing wealth. The individual needs to tear a page from their book. No one protects the retail investor—not corporate officers, not brokers, not analysts, not the media, not even government agencies and elected officials whose job it is to do so. An investor must use his own best judgment, all the information available (bearing in mind that publicly available information is never equivalent to insider information), and be very conservative.

9

FUTURE SHOCK

Despite the myriad lessons to be learned from the most recent bubble, history shows that there will no doubt be another one, of some kind, in the relatively near future. Of course, it won't occur in the same place as the last mania. But it will maintain the same characteristics. They key question going forward, however, is: Will we be able to identify the onset of the bubble and play it more wisely than the last, if we choose to play at all? Are the ingredients right for the emergence of another mania? Will it happen here at home, or will it happen in some exotic locale? If the latter, will we immediately forget the applicable lessons of the homegrown variety and assume, simply because the location is different, that recently learned lessons don't apply?

These are critical questions for the discerning investor. Using the criteria established by Kindleberger but modified in this work, we can examine whether or not the ingredients exist for a new asset bubble and then consider the various environments in which the next bubble may form.

1. Is there some sort of transformational technology in the works that may capture investors' attention in the near future?

2. Is there some sort of watershed event that has sparked an important change in monetary policy? In other words, was the Federal

Reserve forced to raise or lower interest rates because of an un-
foreseen event?

3. Is there some sort of watershed event that sparked a change in fiscal policy? In other words, was the federal government forced to
spend more money to offset the effects of a national catastrophe?

4. Is there an opportunity for individual investors to speculate in the
hot new asset class, which would give rise to the classic moment
of hypertrading that catapults a bull market into a bubble?

5. Will investors believe that this asset class will provide above-
average returns without interruption for the foreseeable future?

These are difficult questions to answer with a great degree of certainty, and yet, since we know from our study of history that another
bubble is on the horizon, they are questions to which we must find
answers. I have consulted with some of the most highly respected investors and market experts in the country to determine from where
the next mania might come. As you will see, the ingredients for a new
investment mania may very well be present in the current economic
environment. If some of the smartest investors I know are right, then
the next mania will come from an area of the economy that few have
found attractive in the last two decades.

TrendSpotting

Many of the smartest investors I know have analyzed the previous
questions and arrived at a conclusion that a number of developments
taking place on the financial landscape will lead to an important
shift in investor preferences, away from financial assets and toward
so-called hard assets, like real estate, gold, oil, and industrial commodities. Most investors, economists, and analysts pooh-pooh a notion of a hard-asset revival. Those investments do well only in times
of inflation, they say. And inflation, in this country anyway, is all
but dead—witness the favorable statistics on consumer and wholesale prices that have been presented throughout the course of recent
memory.

But those who entirely dismiss the possibility of such a development have not followed the thought process outlined in this book, which demands a thorough analysis of the economic environment and an insightful look into the future, as opposed to staring at the world through the rearview mirror. By using the criteria already discussed, one can determine whether there is, at least, the possibility of a shift in the prevailing winds.

Let's analyze the current economic environment to determine if the criteria for a hard-asset bubble even exist. If the criteria are not satisfied, it is a virtual certainty that such a bubble cannot form. But if the early ingredients do exist, then smart investors would be wise at least to consider the possibility. If a hard-asset bubble is beginning to form, its recurrence would truly change the way in which investors allocate their assets. Many investors currently hope that the stock market will come roaring back in a way that mirrors the behavior of the 1990s. Such optimism, while encouraged by the Wall Street community, may be misplaced. If there is a bubble forming in stocks, it almost certainly will not be in the issues that led the mania of the 1990s!

To determine whether a hard-asset bubble is even a remote possibility, we should analyze, step-by-step, the conditions under which bubbles form.

1. **Is there a technological innovation that will help inflate a hard-asset bubble?**

    Hard-asset bubbles are the only bubbles that do not require such a development. Indeed, as we have seen in the 1970s, hard assets rise in price when financial markets and technological innovations stagnate. As productivity declines and inflation accelerates, investors shift their preferences toward real estate, gold, oil, or other commodities to hedge against an inflationary environment, which some smart investors tell me is coming.

2. **Was there an important event that caused a shift in monetary policy? Did the Fed lower interest rates dramatically as a result of 9/11?**

The first question to answer is whether or not there has been some external event or some displacement that might have caused a seismic shift in government policy toward the deployment of money. Indeed, the large-scale response to the September 11 terrorist attacks surely qualifies as a catalyst for a new and different economic environment. The potential for economic catastrophe was extraordinarily high in the tense moments after the attack. The devastation to the financial community's infrastructure was unprecedented in the United States. The physical damage to the electronic payment system was enormous, while the shock to the national psyche was severe. In the week immediately after the attacks, the entire financial community was shut down. An entire population sat at home, transfixed by the events unfolding on television, too numb to go about the normal business of the day. In short, the markets closed for an entire week as economic activity ground to nearly a complete halt The danger of economic collapse was high, prompting federal officials to take heroic efforts to restore not only the physical and mechanical elements of the economy but consumer and investor confidence as well.

The Federal Reserve, under the direction of its much-respected chairman, Alan Greenspan, provided much-needed liquidity to the banking system, whose payment systems had been severely disrupted. The Bank of New York, the oldest financial institution in America, is responsible for clearing as much as a third of the trades executed in the U.S. bond market on a daily basis. The damage to its facilities put strains on the government-bond market, which is where interest rates are set in the United States. Without a fully functioning money market, the U.S. economy would not be capable of operating well, if at all. But the backstopping undertaken by the Fed kept the money markets operating smoothly, the first step in restoring the markets' ability to perform. The Fed poured billions and billions of dollars into the banking system immediately after September 11. By doing so, it ensured that anyone who wanted to take money out of the bank during those stressful times could do so. There was no cash crunch because of the damage to the physical assets of some of this nation's largest banks. As a consequence, consumers and investors did not panic and create "runs on the banks" by pulling all of their cash out at once.

Additionally, the Fed slashed interest rates to their lowest levels in 40 years in an effort to soften the blow the stock market was expected to take when it reopened on September 17. True, the Dow plunged over 700 points that day, the largest single-day point decline in market history. But the 7 percent plunge paled in comparison to other market crashes that had occurred in the past. The Fed's continued effort to lower rates gave investors some hope that the stimulative effect of falling rates would help the economy recover from a recession that was virtually assured by the September 11 attacks.

The Federal Funds Rate, the short-term interest rate directly controlled by the Fed, was dropped to a low of 1 3/4 percent, the lowest level since 1961. The decline in official rates helped to drive down mortgage interest rates and allowed homeowners to refinance their mortgages and home buyers to keep buying homes at a near record pace in late 2001 and early 2002, despite the dislocation caused by the attacks. Low interest rates encourage businesses and consumers to borrow money. That, in turn, leads to more business investment and consumer spending. Since consumer spending accounts for two-thirds of all economic activity in this country, anything the Fed does to encourage spending keeps the economy on an even keel. That's what happened after September 11. Consumers kept buying. They bought cars, homes, and refinanced their mortgages, all because interest rates fell so low.

Additionally, the U.S. Treasury took steps to help lower long-term interest rates. The Treasury stopped selling 30-year government bonds, creating a shortage of the benchmark U.S. Treasury bond. As bond-market investors scrambled to buy up the increasingly scarce "long bonds," their prices rose, and correspondingly, their yields fell, reinforcing the Fed's effort to keep rates low. The two-pronged attack on rates cushioned the economy as it weakened further and helped set the stage for an important rebound that began in early 2002.

The Fed reinforced the monetary stimulus in the form of lower interest rates by substantially increasing the nation's money supply. The growth in the nation's money stock accelerated at a 20 percent annual rate immediately after September 11, flooding the markets and economy with excess liquidity, a feat of financial engineering the Fed uses during times of extreme stress or crisis. It had infused the economy with funds in a similar manner in the months before the year 2000, in an effort to keep an expected Y2K problem from disrupting the banking system. Some economists suggested that the excess money creation found its way into the stock market in early 2000, after the Y2K problem failed to appear but before the Fed was able to drain the money out of the system. The liquidity boom, they argued, was responsible for the last big push that drove the NASDAQ 25 percent higher in the first two and a half months of the year 2000. This time, however, the Fed has been reluctant to fully drain the post–September 11 infusion from the economy, fearing that the economic recovery needs more time to establish itself.

3. **Did September 11 cause an unusually large fiscal-policy response? Or, did the federal government embark on a massive spending campaign to address concerns about 9/11?**

The answer is an unequivocal yes. The terrorist attacks that destroyed the World Trade Center towers and put a massive hole in the Pentagon had a profound and possibly long-term impact on both fiscal and monetary policies. As stated, the Federal Reserve slashed interest rates and greatly expanded the money supply. Also, federal outlays, while not jumping to an all-time record as a percentage of GDP, have accelerated at a rate that is unexpectedly high compared with the recent past. The double-digit percent increase in spending, which includes defense, homeland security, and reconstruction efforts, is among the biggest in modern memory. And prior to September 11, of course, President Bush and Congress pushed through a $1.4-trillion tax cut, which is being phased in simultaneously with other easy money measures. This is not small potatoes. Recall how quickly the 1990s economy grew without the help of tax cuts and fiscal stimulus. Monetary policy was the principle engine driving the economy in the last decade. Today it is but one tool being used to rescue the economy from the post-traumatic stress of September 11.

In addition, other inflation-inducing policies were passed in 2002. A massive $190-billion farm bill, signed by President Bush, was salted with tens of billions of dollars of subsidies for farmers. The price supports greatly counteract the natural tendency of agricultural prices to fall rather than rise, not to mention violating the spirit of every free-trade bill signed by the United States since 1986, when members of the General Agreement on Tariffs and Trade (GATT), now the World Trade Organization, began to limit or eliminate global subsidies on farm products. The bill included $83 billion in new federal spending over 10 years. That's on top of the $35 billion in new defense expenditures in fiscal 2002, $29 billion in homeland security, $20 billion on New York reconstruction, plus an additional expenditure that was approved by Congress for a host of pork-barrel projects. In the space of a single year, federal expenditures increased by at least $100 billion!

Some Keynesian or neo-Keynesian economists would argue that the "pump priming" effects of that stimulus package are likely to be large. (Keynesian economists follow the work of British economist John Maynard Keynes, whose seminal work explored the causes of the Great Depression. Keynes argued that governments could stimulate their moribund economies through massive federal spending programs and that the excess government spending, which usually produced budget deficits, acted as a tonic for both recession and depression. Such spending, he believed, provided make-work programs and expensive infrastructure projects that created jobs. Franklin Delano Roosevelt employed those techniques in his New Deal program. Other presidents and government leaders would "prime the pump," as Keynes would say, for decades to come.) Add to the explosion in federal spending the imposition of tariffs on imported steel, enacted by President Bush in mid-2002, and it's possible that the September 11 attacks induced a combustible, inflation-creating set of policies. It doesn't help that Europe, Russia, Japan, and China introduced retaliatory tariffs in response to Bush's own levies. It would appear that the early stirrings of a damaging trade war are evident as well. Protectionist measures and subsequent trade wars also add to the upward drift in prices by closing a country's borders to cheaper, imported goods. Such measures, obviously, put upward pressure on inflation. Therefore, it is altogether possible that the extraordinary easing of fiscal and monetary policies has created an environment that will help to produce some sort of distortion in the financial markets that pushes some asset values to an unexpected extreme.

Curiously, all this aggressive action has done little to excite stock-market investors. Wall Street has failed miserably, at the time of this writing, to establish a new bull market in stocks, despite the aggressive policy responses to the events of September 11. There has been only one other time in history when the U.S. stock market failed to respond to such a dramatic lowering of interest rates. That sad event occurred in the early 1930s, in the wake of the great crash and during the Great Depression. That does not mean that the massive amounts of money being poured into the economy won't reinflate a bubble somewhere. Maybe it just won't happen in stocks. As we've been saying, some think hard assets rather than financial assets will be the beneficiary of the government's largesse.

3A. Is there supporting evidence to buttress the case for hard assets?

Gross Prophet

To further underscore the case for a shift in investor preferences toward hard assets and away from financial assets, let's turn to one of the brightest economic minds I know. Consider the thoughts of bond-market guru Bill Gross. His comments to his clients in May of 2002 are a must-read for anyone hoping to catch the next big-picture play. Gross's $57-billion PIMCO Total Return Fund is the biggest individual bond fund in the country, with over $350 billion in assets. Its value and performance are shaped entirely by the outlook for the economy and inflation. The Total Return Fund has produced annual gains of over 10 percent for almost three decades with only three down years in that period. Thanks to his outstanding performance record and unusually keen economic insights, Gross is among the most respected global investors in the world, well regarded for his keen sense of timing and insightful analysis of coming economic trends. Citing a *Star Wars*–like battle between the forces of deflation and the forces of reflation, Gross suggested in May of 2002 that a cyclical upturn in inflation could damage returns on financial assets for the next three to five years. Though he does not foresee a return to 1970s-style inflationary troubles, he warned his investors to avoid domestic long-term bonds, whose returns would be significantly reduced by rising inflationary pressures.

Inflation is a friend to hard assets and a foe to financial assets. Anyone who remembers the 1970s and early 1980s knows the feeling. Inflation, which is manifested in the form of rising prices for goods and services, eats away at the purchasing power of financial assets. As inflation rises, stocks and bonds go down while the value of things like real estate, gold, and other commodities goes up. There are some very early signs that inflation may begin to stir in 2003. It is not surprising, then, that investors are having trouble explaining why stocks are going down and commodities are going up at a time when few worry about an inflation spiral. Only the early indicators are flashing warning signs. But those warning signs are coming in a period when there is plenty of money, or liquidity, to fuel an inflationary fire.

Steep Curve

One of the best single indicators of economic growth and inflation is a bond-market indicator known as the "yield curve." The yield curve measures the relationship of short-term to long-term interest rates. During normal economic times, when growth is steady and inflation mild to nonexistent, the yield curve is positively sloped, and short rates remain below long rates, but not dramatically so. When bond-market investors are worried about inflation, the yield curve is positively sloped as well, but the slope is quite steep, as these investors demand much higher yields for long-dated securities whose purchasing power could be vastly eroded by a damaging pickup in inflation. In May of 2002, as I was writing this book, a good portion of the yield curve, particularly from 3-month T-bills to 10-year notes, was very steep indeed, sending a signal of rapid economic growth but potential inflationary troubles as well. (As I pointed out in *Message,* the yield curve was inverted for nearly nine months in the year 2000, a sure sign of an economic slowdown or recession. It was, as the New York Federal Reserve suggested in an important study, the single best indicator of recovery or recession available to forecasters. It did not fail to make an accurate recession forecast in early 2000!) I should point out, however, that the lead time for the yield curve's predictive powers is 9 to 12 months, suggesting that an inflation warning issued in mid-2002 would not likely be realized until some time in early 2003.

Steep Yield Curve

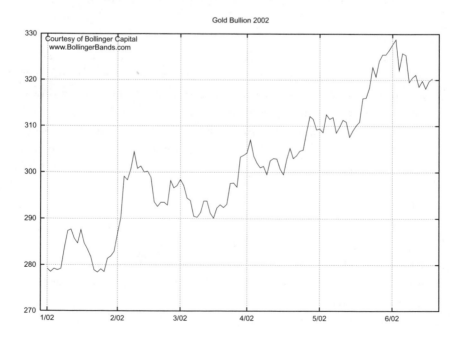

Gold Bullion 2002

Courtesy of Bollinger Capital
www.BollingerBands.com

Old Gold

Gold, the barbarous relic, was also sending some sort of signal in 2002. But gold can be a tricky commodity to watch. Because it is thinly traded and easily manipulated, the price of gold can rise for numerous reasons. In 2002, it could have rallied as citizens of economically blighted Argentina hoarded the metal as their currency collapsed in the worst economic and political crisis of modern times. Japanese investors, tired of moribund markets in their homeland, also diversified into gold. Global investors, shell-shocked from the September 11 attacks, an escalation of violence in the Middle East, and the threat of a nuclear exchange between India and Pakistan, may have purchased gold as a safe haven, just in case something in the world went tragically and dangerously wrong. But that said, gold and gold stocks made an impressive showing in early-to-mid 2002. The price of gold bullion hit a succession of multiyear highs in mid-2002, while gold stocks were among the best, if not the best, performing equity sectors of the year.

Gold Bullion 2002

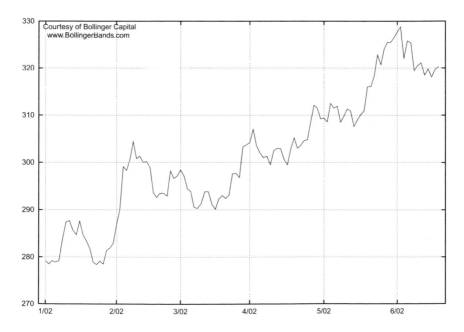

Courtesy of Bollinger Capital
www.BollingerBands.com

Gold Stock Index 2002

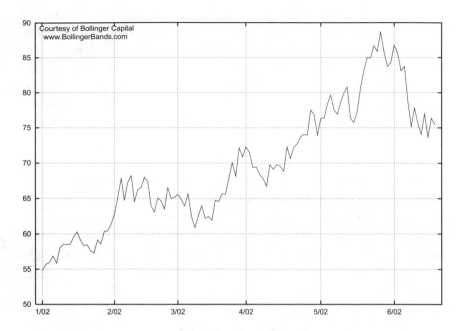

Courtesy of Bollinger Capital
www.BollingerBands.com

The breakout in gold and gold stocks has occurred several times in the last many years only to prove to be a dud. There are many arguments against gold being neither a safe haven nor an inflation hedge; if a true geopolitical or inflationary crisis does take hold in the future, it will rise again.

Gold, by the way, had been going down for as long as stocks had been going up.

If a major secular shift in investing does, in fact, take place, this relationship will revert back to a more normal spread, an environment that may include a hard-asset bubble that drives gold back toward its all-time highs of $800 an ounce, oil toward $40 a barrel or better, and real estate values higher in a meaningful way.

S&P 500 2002 (falling line),
Gold Bullion 2002 (rising line)

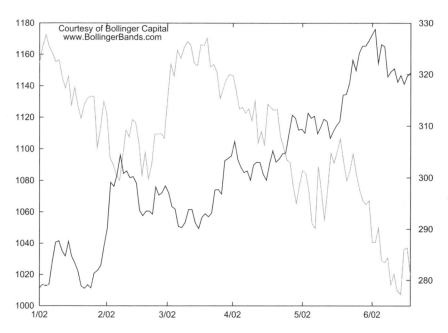

Dollar Dilemma

A weakening U.S. dollar also has inflationary implications and also suggests that hard assets may be the next asset class to have their speculative moment in the sun. Gross and others say that a yawning current account deficit in the United States, a general lack of enthusiasm for U.S. financial assets among overseas investors, and the threat of political or military instability within our borders could precipitate an important dollar devaluation. Former Federal Reserve chairman Paul Volcker told me in May of 2002 that some economists—and he didn't necessarily disagree with them—could make the case that the dollar was as overvalued in early 2002 as it had been in the fall of 1985. In September of that year, Mr. Volcker, who was Fed chairman, along with then–Treasury Secretary James Baker, met with central bankers and finance ministers from the so-called G-5 nations and decided to devalue the dollar dramatically. (The devaluation lasted about 10 years.) On an adjusted purchasing-power parity basis, which is a measure economists use to gauge the strength of a currency, the dollar was meaningfully overvalued in 2002. The risk of a dollar decline is yet another reason to look at the possibility of a secular change in the investment environment toward hard assets and away from the bubble's last winners, i.e., stocks and bonds. A declining dollar has an important impact on domestic inflation because it makes imported goods more expensive here at home. More important, every 7 percent decline in the dollar's value is said to be the rough equivalent of a full percentage point reduction in interest rates, essentially representing another form of easy money.

Indeed, the loss of a currency's purchasing power often drives domestic investors into hard assets like gold, oil, real estate, or other commodities whose values tend to rise as the currency is depreciated. Financial assets, meanwhile, tend to suffer in that environment. That trend was beginning to become increasingly evident in mid-2002 as this Reuters newswire story suggests:

DOLLAR DECLINE SETS OFF INVESTMENT SEARCH
The dollar's tumble against major currencies, threatening an end to more than six years of remarkable dominance and strength, is leading to a sharp reassessment of likely returns from global investments.

Although the U.S. currency has twice fallen sharply since late 2000 only to recover, the latest decline is being seen in many quarters as a more sustained trend.

If it proves so, the implications for global stock and bonds will be large, changing the price of investments and whatever rewards they might eventually reap.[1]

A big drop in the dollar, like a run-up in government spending and extraordinarily low interest rates, is an inflationary factor that could produce a decided shift in the quality of the economic environment facing America today. While all of this sounds reasonable on paper, are there any market-based signs that could suggest such an inflationary bubble is in the making? If we use some of the techniques I described in *The Message of the Markets,* the simple answer is, again, yes.

Soft vs. Hard

Whether or not hard assets as opposed to financial assets will reach new extremes in price depends on whether the benign, disinflationary, and innovative environment of the previous 20 years contains, or if, instead, a paradigm shift occurs that resuscitates inflation. Bond guru Bill Gross, for the first time in many years, appears to think the latter environment is more likely than the former. Using *Star Wars* characters to describe the battle between the forces of deflation and reflation (read *inflation*), Gross says the reflation camp is manned by Jedi knights who "bear the swords of inflation. September 11, domestic terrorism, a potential Iraq invasion (which would drive oil and gasoline prices higher), and the upward reversal in defense expenditures as a percentage of GDP." These, he says, are perhaps the "easiest" inflationary forces to agree on. "War, or preparation for war, is inflationary—always has been, always will be."[2] Gross and others have noted that in addition to those factors, the expansionary monetary policies of the world's central banks, many of which are keeping interest rates, in real terms, near zero, also constitute a potential inflationary factor.

So, What's the Next Bubble?

If, indeed, the forces of inflation defeat the forces of deflation, or recession, which assets will likely benefit from the events that have created such expansive monetary and fiscal policies? Again, hard assets like real estate and commodities are set to benefit. Real estate has already shown a peculiar strength in an economic environment that is normally hostile to property price appreciation.

Corroborating Evidence

For the first time in modern history, housing sales and prices not only failed to weaken at any point during the recession but actually managed to advance. Such a phenomenon has never taken place in modern American economic history. Real estate mogul Sam Zell told me that in his decades as a real estate expert, he has never seen this kind of resilience during such a difficult economic period. It is true, I should note, that residential real estate is most often a lagging, rather than leading, indicator. In some cases, real estate sales and values may not decline until one or two years after the peak of an economic cycle. In this instance, however, real estate went on to have two record-setting or near-record-setting years after the economy peaked in the fourth quarter of 1999. As a *USA Today* article suggested in mid-2002, the pace of home-price appreciation throughout the recession not only exceeded the prevailing inflation rate but also expanded at a rate of 6 percent, which outperformed most other asset classes in the United States. However, the recent action in home sales and housing pricing is not yet indicative of a bubble. There hasn't been the type of speculative trading of houses as there was in stocks, nor is the action yet reminiscent of the regional housing bubbles that occurred in California, New York, and Boston in the late 1980s.

Ed Yardeni, chief market strategist for Deutsche Bank Capital and a widely respected economist, makes the case that housing and housing stocks may continue to do well for quite some time despite the widely accepted view that housing activity and the appreciation in housing stocks were beginning to falter in mid-2002. Yardeni argues that with mortgage rates remaining below 7 percent, cheap by historic standards, and a record backlog of homes on order, waiting to be built, the outlook for housing remains quite strong.

Yardeni, by the way, was the first after the stock-market bubble burst to suggest that a housing bubble might very well be the next investment phenomenon. His view was supported by many newspaper and wire-service articles that appeared throughout the year. Some identified how hot properties in New York City, despite the lifestyle concerns created by 9/11, were still selling briskly and at above-market prices. Around the country, meanwhile, the median price for a single-family home rose to a record $147,500, up sharply from its previous high.

Surprisingly, in Silicon Valley, where the dot-com bust was felt more acutely than anywhere else in the nation, real estate prices and sales have continued to rise rapidly. Smallish Silicon Valley homes have sold recently for well over a million dollars, sold above their asking prices, and sold within only a few days of being listed. That type of behavior is entirely anomalous given the economic circumstances that have arisen in the post–technology bubble environment.

No doubt, the run-up in real estate could very simply be the result of an extended lag time between the peak in stock prices, the economic cycle, and the expected bust in land prices. Or something entirely different and unexpected could be in the making. But it remains possible, given all the efforts undertaken by policy-makers to kick-start the economy, that the excess cash is now going into real estate. The government, it seems, may be providing the necessary liquidity for a new bubble in the housing sector. Certainly, there is mounting evidence that this is the case. Investors have become so disenchanted that they are redirecting their available funds into their homes instead of into stocks. Rather than gamble on Wall Street, which has been tarnished in their eyes, individuals want to bet on a sure thing. The *New York Times* and other newspapers have suggested that investor psychology has changed dramatically as a consequence not only of the bursting of the bubble but of 9/11 and other unsettling events around the world, prompting people to reevaluate their priorities. Home and hearth have always supported the individual investor, and hence there may be a decided shift in investor preferences. Again, this moment could signal the beginnings of a secular change in investor preferences, where hard assets—"stuff," as economic historian Jim Grant calls them—outperform financial assets for the first time in decades. While many observers are breathlessly waiting for that new bull market in stocks to begin, a major new bull market in real estate and other hard assets may already be starting to form.

Real Benefits

In addition to the favorable macroeconomic and macropolicy influences on real estate, one must remember that it is the only investment that is heavily subsidized by the federal government. While the bull market in stocks was raging, few individuals noticed the tax advantages of buying and holding real estate. True, home ownership reached record highs along with the stock market. But individuals were merely purchasing places to live at that juncture, not speculating in real estate. As investors shift their preferences, they will likely be reminded by real estate brokers and others who stand to benefit from the coming boom that real estate is the only investment that gives the investor a large tax break. As many know, the interest-rate deductions on a mortgage are so generous that by the time a mortgage has been fully paid, the U.S. government has picked up 40 percent of the tab.

Insana Insight: One can make a very powerful case that the ingredients for a bull market in hard assets, particularly real estate, are present. Whether they coalesce to produce a bubble remains an open question. But a quick glance at the criteria should help to clarify the situation.

Active Ingredients

To believe that the ingredients exist for a bubble in hard assets, including real estate, land, and commodities, requires a distinct shift in thinking about financial markets. Between 1982 and 2000, stock prices had returned more than 15 percent annually. They returned more than 17 percent in the 1990s and more than 20 percent between 1995 and early 2000. Those outsized returns helped to make investors believe that the only asset class in which to invest was stocks. But in the current environment, one can successfully argue that the innovative, disinflationary environment that prevailed in that time period may be disappearing and will instead be replaced by a more inflationary or reflationary set of conditions, at least for a time.

Real Estate Bubble Checklist

External Shock?	Yes
Monetary Stimulus?	Yes
Fiscal Stimulus?	Yes
Economic Conditions?	Favorable
Speculative Public Participation?	Not Quite Yet

Speculative Fever?

4. **Are there signs of speculative activity in hard assets?**

Now that we have identified and examined the emergence of the ingredients that could ignite a bubble in real estate and commodities, the question remains: Are the characteristics of a bubble yet in place? We have to answer no, there is not sufficient speculative activity. True, in most parts of the country, residential real estate is as hot as it has been in decades. Counteracting that fact, however, is a strong decline in the demand for, and price of, commercial real estate. Luxury home activity cooled in mid-2002 as well. Housing rentals in New York's upper-crust vacation community, the Hamptons, were off by as much as 50 percent in the summer of '02, while rental prices were down by 25 to 45 percent. Still, sales of second homes and vacation properties remained generally brisk throughout the year, indicating a willingness of real estate investors to own rather than rent additional properties.

Fevered trading, or flipping, of homes remained notably absent in mid-2002. That was, by the way, a dominant feature of the Los Angeles– and New York–based real estate mania that peaked in 1989. Individuals speculated in real estate by buying starter homes and reselling them at a large profit, sometimes in as little as a few months. The proceeds were reinvested in more expensive dwellings, with the expectation of repeating the practice. While that action is absent, it is also far too early to be expected. The speculative action—or "overtrading," as it is called—becomes a feature in the final leg of the bubble, not in its early stages.

The same can be said for commodities like gold and oil. Bullish trends have not become so firmly ingrained in the investor's psyche that he or she is willing to make aggressive speculative bets that what is going up now will continue to go up forever. Such a positive-reinforcement loop requires both time and price appreciation. As UBS PaineWebber's Art Cashin told me during the last bubble, the fear of looking stupid has to outweigh the fear of losing money before the masses begin a full-scale foray into a particular asset class. As yet, most investors are afraid of missing the next bull market in stocks, not a coming bull market in real estate or commodities.

Fed Factor

As a consequence of considerations like these, many investors believe a residential real estate bubble may be on the immediate horizon. Federal Reserve chairman Alan Greenspan, however, has his doubts. He told a congressional committee in the spring of 2002 that a national housing bubble was both unlikely and extraordinarily difficult to bring about on a national scale. It is interesting to note, though, that the housing market has been acting in a rather unpredictable, even peculiar, way during the recent recession.

My views and the views of billionaire investor Sam Zell and some others already mentioned are a bit different. While I agree that the action in housing to date has not shown the characteristics of a bubble, I would stress that no bubble simply starts out as a bubble. It takes time for the ingredients to mix and coalesce. The point of this entire exercise to identify the ingredients and characteristics of a bubble before the bubble is obvious. The other point is to recognize the signs that the bubble is about to burst. Mr. Greenspan correctly asserted that it is difficult for an entire nation to experience a real estate bubble. Most real estate bubbles in this country, unlike, say, Japan, have been regional in nature. The Fed chief also noted that it's often prohibitively expensive to trade houses like stocks; the associated costs are high, property tends to be illiquid, and houses, unlike stocks, are lived in, giving them a necessary utility value that keeps people from rushing in and out of them. However, having witnessed firsthand the bubble in Southern California in the 1970s and 1980s, I know it is possible for people to trade houses like stocks or commodities, if the ingredients are right. There are already anecdotes of individuals trading in and out of hot properties in places like Miami and other enticing locales. They are flipping condos to capture fast and easy profits rather than buying residences to settle in.

5. **Will investors believe the asset class provides above-average returns for the foreseeable future?**
    Again, it is too early to tell. But the point of identifying an emerging bubble is to capitalize on it *before* everyone recognizes it. By the time an entire population believes in the new paradigm, whatever it is, it is too late to get in.

Additional Thoughts, Thinking the Unthinkable

Sadly, it now seems plausible to believe that the geopolitical environment will favor hard assets in coming years, if past parallels are any guide to future realities. The 1970s were filled with political and military dislocations that helped to spark an inflationary bubble, which crested in 1980 with gold at $800 an ounce, silver at $50 an ounce, oil at $35 a barrel, and both inflation and unemployment in double digits. The 1970s followed a great bull market, even bubble, that was fueled by rising productivity, low interest rates, technological and financial innovations, and very heavy public participation. After that bubble burst, there were two oil shocks, increasingly hostile actions in the Middle East, the enlargement of the Vietnam War, and economic policy mistakes that made hard assets far more attractive than financial assets. Some fear that a replay of those more challenging times may be in the offing.

In recent months, rising military tensions from New Delhi to New York, from Palestine to Punjab, and from Buenos Aires to Bethlehem, have turned the world on its head. Indeed, the entire notion of lasting peace and prosperity now seems like a pipe dream based on the enticing but elusive goal of spreading capitalism and democracy to every corner of the planet. Frances Fukayama's bold prediction of "the end of history," in the early 1990s, based on the fallacious assumption that armed conflict was about to cease, now appears at best premature and at worst hopelessly naive. The euphoria that followed the death of communism and the fall of the Berlin Wall ushered in an extended period of peace and prosperity, to be sure. But it also unleashed a resurgence of hostilities in the developing world, hostilities that the struggling superpowers' rivalries had managed temporarily to overshadow.

As we've stated, rising tensions in the Middle East could lead to a widening conflict between Israeli and Arab interests. The situation is reminiscent of the 1970s, when such tensions led to an Arab oil embargo, frequent clashes between Israel and neighboring states, and a revolution in Iran. Today, the threat of another Arab oil embargo is bandied about by everyone from Saddam Hussein to Saudi Crown Prince Abdullah. The rise and explosion of Islamic fundamentalism, whose expression on September 11 may set the stage for an East-West showdown, may not augur well for a return to the disinflationary nineties, but instead to something reminiscent of the inflation-dominated seventies and early eighties, when commodities like oil, natural gas, and gold became increasingly scarce and far more precious.

A "dirty-bomb" attack against New York would obviously have disastrous implications for the country, in social, political, and economic terms. Imagine the response to the financial community not only being destroyed but becoming uninhabitable for some unknown number of years. As unthinkable as this is, even a near miss could greatly alter the landscape in such a fashion that investors and consumers would scramble to hoard all manner of tangible assets—from history's only sure form of money, gold, to safe residential properties, to food.

Insana Insight: It sometimes seems cold or callous to consider the economic implications of such tragic events. But investors need to examine them to determine how they might shape the investing landscape in the years to come. Many have lost considerable sums of money as a consequence of a burst bubble in stocks. There is no need to have more wealth destroyed in what could be a far more challenging environment, especially for those of us are nearing retirement age and simply cannot afford another devastating loss of capital. This is no time to bury one's head in the sand. It will be far easier to maintain a higher standard of living in our so-called golden years if we actively seek out emerging opportunities.

Markets and Other Manias

We've examined the possibility that a new bull market/bubble is forming in places that haven't seen a bubble for about 20 years. But there are still some who wonder where the emerging hot spots in the stock market are, given the poor performances of the major averages. If, indeed, another secular bull market in stocks is on the horizon, one has to examine where it might occur. We have made the case that there is plenty of liquidity, or money, sloshing around the world right now to provide fuel for any number of different asset classes. Despite the massive bear market in the most popular stocks of the last bubble, countervailing forces have offset the negative-wealth effect. I have detailed those already, so there is no need to belabor the point. The question, however, that is important for investors is whether or not the favorites of the last experience will be the favorites of the next experience. It appears that the answer to that question is no. While I will hold out the possibility that certain technology stocks may have become sufficiently undervalued to warrant inspection, the impetus for another technology bubble does not seem evident.

Insana Insight: The questions we ask about stocks are the same as those we asked about other asset classes. But since the environment has changed so dramatically, one has to consider additional questions when trying to identify large new opportunities in the stock market.

1. **Are there new inventions that appear to be creating new investment opportunities in the near future?**

   There is no "killer ap," or important new technological application, on the horizon that will cause the type of excitement that inflated the Internet bubble. Venture capitalist Roger McNamee says another tech bubble is a good 10 years off for that simple reason. Some venture capitalists believe that nanotechnology will provide the next secular long-term investment opportunity. Nanotechnology involves using microchips the size of atoms or molecules to achieve the same results as larger chips have done in recent times. The implications are clear and, of course, staggering. Not only will new technological innovations shrink in size, but their power and speed will be greatly increased. Nanotechnology is going to be the stuff of pop science and pop culture in the near term, which will greatly enhance its appeal among individual investors. Some venture capitalists believe that a new wave of stock offerings among nanotech companies will rejuvenate the entire tech sector and launch another major frenzy for technology investments. Roger McNamee disagrees. He doubts that nanotechnology will deliver a near-term speculative event of any magnitude, though he concedes that interest in this technology may lead to some excitement in the investing world. McNamee thinks that nanotechnology is still too embryonic to bring to the market, and so any excitement surrounding it remains many years off. He is, instead, among those who think a hard-asset bubble will produce the next major excitement in the investing world.

2. **Was there an event that caused monetary policy to become easy?**

   The answer again is yes . . . 9/11. The question remains open as to whether investors will direct the money they have as a result to stocks or to other assets.

3. **Was there an event that caused an easing in fiscal policy?**

   The answer again is 9/11. Obviously the big pickup in defense spending has already pushed up the shares of defense and defense-related firms along with companies that provide security services.

Whether that forms a minibubble in the near future is an open question. Some say it is a good bet.

The Big Picture: Can There Be Another Stock-Market Bubble?

If a stock-market bubble is on the horizon—and I am among those who believe that bubbles of different varieties can exist simultaneously—it is possible that it will take place in a region of the market that has remained unexploited for a number of years. In this regard, past history can again be useful. Small-cap stocks have not outperformed large-cap stocks for at least a decade, but in early-to-mid 2002, there were signs that they would take over where their big-cap brothers left off. By May of 2002, small stocks were among the only sectors of the market to show positive returns. In truth, small stocks had been generally outperforming big stocks, since the autumn of 1998, but that went largely unnoticed or was obscured because of the bubble in a handful of big-cap names. Only after nearly three years of steady declines in the stock market's most popular averages did investors and commentators begin to notice the action in small and midsized stocks.

Sweat the Small Stuff

It is interesting to note that at the end of another big bubble, in 1975, small stocks took over from big stocks and provided an extraordinary performance. Between 1975 and 1983, in the wake of the collapse of the so-called Nifty Fifty, small stocks went on a tear, rising over 1000 percent and producing average annualized returns of over 33 percent! Consider the following chart depicting the periods in which small stocks outperformed large stocks. In many cases, the environments bear some similarities with the current environment. There are periods in which the differences are greater than others, but when the shift favoring small stocks emerges, the level of outperformance can be astonishing. In the 1975 to 1983 time frame, I should note, small stocks put in their most impressive performance despite the bubble in hard assets that was occurring simultaneously. Some analysts may accuse me of data mining here, selectively choosing like environments while ignoring important differences. My intention is not to state definitively that these bubbles are on the horizon, but only that their occurring is entirely possible and plausible. The intent is to awaken investors from their bear market slumber to an understanding that investing is a dynamic, not passive, undertaking. Those who fail to learn from the past, and who also remain preoccupied with past successes, will fail to identify and profit from emerging opportunities.

. . . As This Can Be One Of The Best Periods Of Outperformance Ever!

PERIOD	DURATION IN YEARS	CUMULATIVE RETURN	ANNUALIZED RETURN	ANNUAL EXCESS RETURN
1932–37	4.8	946.0	62.5	16.0
1940–45	6.0	534.1	36.0	13.9
1963–68	6.0	267.7	24.2	10.8
1975–83	8.5	072.6	33.6	14.5
1991–94	3.3	142.8	30.8	11.3
1999–02	3.0	30.3	9.2	16.5
Average	5.7	592.6	37.4	13.3

Source: CRSP, The University Of Chicago, Frank Russell Company, Prudential Securities

The Biggs Picture

Some market experts, particularly those adept at identifying bubbles, think there are some other candidates for the next market mania. Barton Biggs, chief global strategist at Morgan Stanley, has a few thoughts on this. Biggs has a long and successful track record spotting market excesses before they go to extremes and warning investors about the eerie, historical parallels that crop up time and time again. In the 1980s, his analysis of Japan's speculative bubble, which he was able to understand as it was inflating, won him great praise. Biggs often identifies bubbles or manias long before they become apparent to anyone else. His thoughts on these matters are sought out by some of the best-known money managers in the world.

These days Biggs is betting that the next likely bubbles will occur in smaller sectors of the U.S. stock market and in overseas markets as well. He believes that biotechnology stocks will have yet another day in the sun, thanks to the peculiar characteristics of investing in science "projects." It's true that biotech has experienced two bubbles since the late 1980s. The first "biotechnomania," as it was dubbed at the time, gave birth to companies like Amgen, Genentech, and Chiron. Bioengineered drugs like TPA, Epogen, and Nupogen were developed and helped both heart-attack and cancer patients. As with all bubbles and busts, scores of biotech companies that went public in the late 1980s and early 1990s went out of business, as we noted earlier in the book. For every blockbuster drug or company, of which there was only a handful, there were equally spectacular blowups, with billions of dollars lost in the process.

Similarly, genomics companies were all the rage at the height of the most recent tech boom. Celera Genomics led the way in the identification and mapping of the human genome. It is widely believed, though not yet proven, that the full mapping of the genome will allow pharmaceutical firms to discover and/or create targeted compounds that will cure everything from obesity to cancer to AIDS. It is from this launching point that Biggs thinks another wave will come.

One of the peculiarities about biotech that Biggs notes is that the science is nearly impossible for everyone, from the most sophisticated investor to the layperson, to understand. As was the case in the first wave of biotech investing, and in Internet investing as well, the more incomprehensible sounding the project, the more allure it has for investors. The reason is simple. You can't argue with the experts projections if you don't have the requisite knowledge to intelligently challenge their assumptions. So, when a company's founders and stock-market promoters begin to make fantastic predictions and offer hope to the hopeless, the project can take on a life all its own.

Those of you who experienced the bubbles in biotech, the Internet, and genomics know that this is true. The early days of biotechnomania included promises of miracle cures. The Internet, like every other major infrastructure project before it, offered a technology that would make business more efficient, life easier, and community relations more harmonious. (Remember the tract on plank board roads? Similar promises were made then as well.) The genomics promoters talked of a meaningful extension in the human life span. At the height of the mania, even laypeople were discussing the possibility of beating once-incurable diseases and living well past 100 years. Biggs assumes the next wave will be even more intense.

And this is not simply because the hype will be greater but because a real breakthrough may very well be on the way. Whether it's a serious drug to treat obesity, one of the leading health problems in America today, or some other blockbuster new drug, the first hint that a marketable product is at hand will touch off a new biobubble. Biggs has done thorough analysis of the biotech arena. He believes that a breakthrough in obesity treatments may be near. An event such as this, in which bioscience apparently triumphs over a major health problem, could touch off a new tidal wave of enthusiasm for biotech shares.

4. & 5. Are there signs that investors expect big returns for engaging in speculative activity?

If there is a bubble coming in small-cap stocks or biotech or nanotech stocks, there are no current signs of speculative activity. In all these cases, while a future bubble is possible, none of the statistical or anecdotal indicators that show a speculative frenzy is imminent are evident.

COUNTRY-FUN REDUX:
IS AN EMERGING MARKET BUBBLE ON THE HORIZON?

Biggs also believes that overseas markets, especially Russia and China, are ripe for bubbles. The Russian market is an interesting case. Russia, whose stock market soared in the mid-1990s, has gone through convulsive changes in the last half decade. Recall in 1998, the country's unexpected debt default and currency devaluation that sent world markets reeling only a year after the Asian currency crisis had similarly disastrous consequences. The Russian stock market, among the best-performing markets in the world between 1995 and 1998, collapsed with the ruble. The benchmark RTS Index plunged 90 percent from its high and languished for several years as twice-burned foreign investors pulled their capital from the highly risky markets of Asia, Eastern Europe, and Latin America.

Russian Stocks 2002

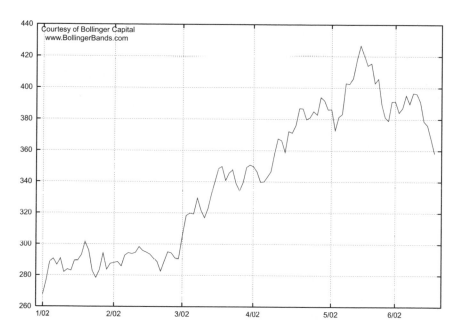

As a consequence of this economic disaster, Russia was forced to radically restructure both its political and economic policies. Prior to the presidency of Vladimir Putin, Russian industry was controlled largely by the so-called oligarchs, organized-crime figures who essentially plundered the economy, stole foreign-aid money, and did little to modernize the country's inefficient, formerly state-run enterprises. But Putin, a former KGB agent who cozied up to Western interests, has made some progress in establishing the rule of law and much-needed property-rights protections, and helped to limit, somewhat, the influence of the oligarchs, at least so I am told. Since the 9/11 attacks, Moscow has taken additional steps to open its antiquated energy industry to American oil companies and modernize. With new promises to provide badly needed non-OPEC oil supplies to the United States, relations between Moscow and Washington have never been more cordial. Indeed, if Russia can become a significant oil exporter to the West, its revenues from energy products will soar, helping to finance a much better way of life for its people. Consider that the average selling price for a barrel of crude oil, inside Russia, is $5; the market price of around $25 on world markets would lead to a windfall, making Russia very much like the OPEC countries. Some say that the RTS Index, which returned to the top performers' list in 2002, albeit from a much lower base, may be poised for a spectacular bull market run.

The same, it seems, can be said for China. China, whose market rally paused noticeably in 2002, is unlike Russia, however, in several respects. First, its market has been going up steadily for a number of years, without a significant crash, despite the travails of the markets adjacent to it. Second, its economy, while having slowed a bit from its late 1990s/early 2000s growth pace, continues to expand at a healthy high-single-digit pace. China, as Russia may do several years from now, is benefiting from its new status as a member of the World Trade Organization, a membership that brings Beijing more deeply into the 100-plus-member-nation trading system. China is also benefiting from renewed growth in the emerging markets of Asia and in Japan. A rejuvenated Pacific Rim will only strengthen the nation's growth prospects in the years ahead.

As more evidence of excitement in emerging markets materializes, U.S. investors who grow weary of below-average rates of return in U.S. financial markets may set their sights on more exotic locales. One could envision an environment where the strong performance of emerging markets leads U.S. investors into so-called exchange traded funds, or ETFs, which are an easy and inexpensive way to dabble in the offshore action. ETFs, which are not entirely dedicated to overseas opportunities, have products, however, that are based on stock-market averages from many of the world's markets. Buying an ETF is like buying a foreign stock-market average, but it's as simple to buy as an individual stock. Just like closed-end country funds were the rage in previous emerging market manias, ETFs may become the rage if overseas markets prove to be the site of the next major asset bubble.

The single most important impediment to an emerging market bubble at the time of this book's writing is the looming threat of nuclear war between India and Pakistan. By the time this book is published, the two nations may already have exchanged nuclear fire, ushering in a new departure from the conventions of modern warfare. As mentioned earlier, a nuclear exchange between India, one of the world's largest emerging markets, and Pakistan, one of the world's most troubled, would likely create almost unimaginable distortions in the markets.

For example, commodities would no doubt replace financial instruments as the investments of choice, as savvy traders bought up supplies of foodstuffs and other goods that could be gravely impacted by a thermonuclear explosion. In April of 1986, the Chernobyl disaster in the Ukraine, the "breadbasket" of the Soviet Union, destroyed important farmland, forcing the U.S.S.R. to buy wheat from Western nations. The increased demand for wheat sent prices skyrocketing. The price of rice on world markets began to rise in May/June 2002 amid fears that a nuclear incident on the subcontinent would create a similar shortage in Eurasia. Of course, there would be additional consequences to such devastation. World stock markets would likely plunge. Gold and, in particular, silver would very likely soar. Indians, more than most other nations, are big buyers of the metal, both as an investment and for adornment. Their rush into precious metals could be precipitated by a protracted conventional war with Pakistan as well as by nuclear war, since the Indian rupee would probably decline sharply in either case. Currency crises often cause affected citizens to seek the safety of precious metals, at least until the crises pass.

In the absence, however, of such an unthinkable catastrophe, a bubble in emerging markets can still be envisioned. The catalysts are obvious. Emerging market nations are again beginning to grow at rates faster than those of their developed-nation counterparts. There is a surfeit of liquidity worldwide. Investors and professional money managers are desperate to find more productive and rewarding ways to utilize their capital. Also, most emerging market nations have suffered through serious but cleansing bear markets over the last four or five years. At the very least, a substantial rebound could be in the offing, helping to facilitate the kind of investor enthusiasm required to touch off another bubble.

I should add that 9/11 could also be the catalyst for change in the United States as well. With mature nations, the United States in particular, suddenly appearing to be more vulnerable than invincible, global investors may worry that dollar-denominated assets are no longer the gold standard they appeared to be in the 1990s. Coincident with stagnation in U.S. financial markets, there could very well be a mass exodus from the dollar, which we discussed earlier, and a reallocation of assets toward those nations that are less likely to be troubled by war or terror—nations like Russia, China, Korea, or Singapore. Such a development would be consistent with an accompanying rise in commodity prices and even real estate. Again, while it is difficult and even painful to contemplate a prolonged period of stagnation or extreme two-way volatility in U.S. financial markets, one has to examine the possibility that the next bubble may inflate an asset class, or group of asset classes, that has been out of favor for some time.

Indeed, one could make the case for just such a scenario if the next bubble occurs as the result of a displacement that leads to a cyclical, if not secular, upturn in inflation. In 1982, it was unthinkable that financial assets would be the home of the next major bubble, but that is exactly where the bubble(s) formed over the next 18 years. The stock-market bubbles in the United States and Japan in the 1980s were the product of a disinflationary environment that lasted for nearly two decades. There were intermittent bubbles in harder assets, like real estate or art, but those were the financed by the profits derived from the bubbles in the equity markets, not from an inflationary spiral. The excess profits derived from stock-market gains were plowed into other assets—real estate and art—and the existence of each of those bubbles was entirely contingent upon the health of the underlying bubble in stocks. At this point in time, many find the idea that a hard-asset bubble is forming to be implausible, since most modern investors have little experience with a bubble of that type.

Younger investors have forgotten, or never heard, the tales of American citizens melting down the family silver in the early 1980s to cash in on the run-up in precious metals. Those individuals, who had also speculated in oil and gas limited partnerships, alternative energy investments, and other hard-asset schemes, found it unthinkable to buy stocks or bonds at the peak of the oil and gold bubble of the late 1970s and early 1980s.

For Argument's Sake

One could argue that I am making a contrarian point only for the sake of being contrary. I would argue that for the first time in two decades, the ingredients for a hard-asset bubble are more numerous today than they have been in decades. It is not a firm projection that I am making. That is not the role of a journalist. However, one has to recognize when the winds of change are blowing and at least consider the possibility that a new bubble is unlikely to form in the same place where it most recently burst.

The Next-to-Last Finale (There Will Be More)

To sum up, it seems entirely possible that another asset bubble will be visited upon us before we are prepared for it. Despite the reservations of some of the most well-educated and well-respected economic observers of our time, real estate and hard assets may be in the beginning stages of a new secular move higher in price. And while I agree that it is extraordinarily difficult to create a nationwide bubble in real estate, I can't help but wonder when I see that during this most recent economic slowdown real estate prices have done what they failed to do in all other recessions of the modern era . . . go up at an astonishingly fast clip.

Are the ingredients for a real estate and hard-asset bubble evident? To repeat, the answer is yes. Interest rates are low. Mortgage financing is not only cheap but readily available. Tax incentives remain strong. Tax policies are helping to prime the economic pump. Deficit spending by the federal government on all manner of programs, from defense to airport security, are providing support to a number of different industries and helping to restore the jobs that were lost during the recession. If, indeed, government-financed job growth picks up, the communities most closely associated with increased defense spending will likely lead the most expansive phase of a real estate bubble, just as they did in the 1980s.

In the absence of a major technological or financial innovation, one could also argue that gold, oil, and other commodities could also enjoy their own speculative day in the sun, since stocks have few catalysts to propel the major averages considerably higher so soon after the recent bubble burst. The big-cap names that were the drivers of the most recent stock-market mania could very well be sidelined for a number of years while other investment vehicles replace them as the principal objects of speculation. (Again, though, small and medium-size stocks could rally amid a bubble in other asset classes, as could biotech and nanotech stocks.)

This outlook could, as always, be drastically altered by several events. The world could suddenly become peaceful again, with potential conflicts resolved amicably and satisfactorily. Terrorism could cease to be a threat in the world's developed nations, thereby lessening the need for a huge increase in defense spending, particularly in the United States. The Federal Reserve could raise interest rates abruptly while contracting the nation's money supply sharply, killing off any incipient inflationary pressures before hard-asset prices spiral higher. And a technological innovation could reenergize equity investors so that they race back to the equities markets.

For that to happen, of course, the stars would have to align themselves in perfect order. The fortuitous set of economic and political circumstances that led to the stock-market bubble in the last decade would have to reemerge intact, aided and abetted by government policies. Investors, burned by the stunning collapse of equity values and incensed by corporate greed and, in some cases, corporate malfeasance, would have to shed all their worries about Wall Street and dive back in, willing not only to invest, but to speculate, in stocks as they did at the peak in the year 2000.

Such as scenario is unlikely, at best. History shows us that while bubbles occur with ever-greater frequency, they often change shape in order to entice as many players as possible into the game. The subtle shifts in style and the changes in asset class allow even sophisticated investors to believe that, somehow, this bubble will be different from all the rest. As a consequence, traders and investors will overstay their welcome.

But an investor's job is not to hope that the world will become a more beneficent and benign place, but to accept the world as it is and uncover the opportunities that emerge in a changing set of circumstances. The bubble of an era just passed is not the most likely bubble to form in the near future. But as surely as day follows night, another investment bubble will begin to form before our very eyes. We have the historical evidence to back up that claim. We know that the next bubble will lure us in, offering a new set of get-rich promises that seem as plausible as the promises that so recently disappointed us. We will choose to lose money rather than look dumb as all our friends and neighbors make a killing. We know all that.

The real trick for any investor is to approach the coming bubble with the foresight that is created by hindsight. We can choose to play in the next game, confident in the knowledge that the next bubble, no matter what the asset class, will be no different in character from the last. We will know that when an entire nation believes that a single asset class has nowhere to go but up in price, the bubble is fully inflated. And knowing this, as we see conditions change, as interest rates move higher or as a meaningful event alters the investing equation, we will exit the playing field gracefully, without worrying that we will miss the final leg up.

Those who look objectively at the world can remain rational when the next bout of irrational exuberance takes hold. Those of us who use history as a guide can gamble in the next wave of speculation more confidently or choose not to play at all. Those who understand the consequences of extreme behavior in the markets can save their hard-won profits by recognizing those extremes and excesses before becoming excessive themselves. Not all of us, of course, will be so sensible or so wise. But a few of us might be.

Lest we forget how bubbles begin and end, here is a graphic reminder of the pattern. The *Bank Credit Analyst,* a financial newsletter, published this picture in mid-2002, showing how all bubbles trace out the same exact patterns. The newsletter's composite of the Roaring Twenties stock-market bubble, the bubble in oil and gold in the 1980s, and the bubble in Japan's Nikkei later that decade underscores the point of this book. Bubbles are repetitive. Bubbles begin and end in exactly the same manner. And those who fail to understand that historical imperative are doomed to lose money. It's as simple as that.

After the Bubble: The Long Hangover

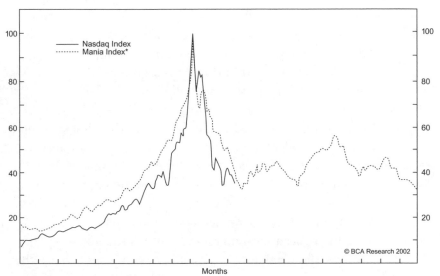

*A composite index of peaks in gold & silver (1973–1986)
Japanese Nikkei (1982–1995) and Dow Jones (1922–1935)
Note: both series are indexed to 100 at their respective peaks

All bubbles appear enticing as they develop. They excite investors and lure them into the notion that riches can be had for the asking. The parabolic arch that all bubbles exhibit leads the uninformed investor to believe that "trees grow to the sky," as they say on Wall Street. But as the picture clearly illustrates, those trees are torn down at the roots by the time the frenzy is over. If there is one picture that all investors should keep in their heads, you've just seen it.

ENDNOTES

CHAPTER 1: "IT'S NEVER DIFFERENT THIS TIME"

1. Richard J. Anobile, ed., *Hooray for Captain Spaulding,* Darien House Books, 1974, p. 83.
2. ———. *The Marx Brothers Scrapbook,* Darien House Books, 1973, p. 146.

CHAPTER 2: WHAT IS A BUBBLE?

1. Larry Neal, *The Rise of Financial Capitalism,* Cambridge University Press, 1990, p. 13.
2. Charles P. Kindleberger, *Manias, Crashes and Panics,* p. 19.
3. Ibid., p. 15.
4. Greg Ip, *Wall Street Journal,* December 30, 1998.
5. Mark Boyar Research, *Wall Street Journal,* December 30, 1998.

CHAPTER 3: PAST AS PROLOGUE

1. David Cowen, *The Origins and Economic Impact of the First Bank of the United States, 1791–1797,* Garland, 2000, p. 13.
2. Ibid., p. 36.
3. Ibid., p. 37.
4. Ibid., p. 39.
5. Ibid., p. 102.
6. Ibid., p. 102.
7. Ibid., p. 99.
8. Edward Chancellor, *Devil Take the Hindmost,* Farrar Straus & Giroux, 1999, p. 123.
9. Ibid., p. 124.
10. Daniel Klein, John Majewski, *Economy, Community and Law: The Turnpike Movement in New York, 1797–1845,* June 1991, n.p., p. 17.
11. Ibid., p. 2.
12. Daniel B. Klein, John Majewski, *Plank Road Fever in Antebellum America: New York State Origins,* 1994, p. 58.

13. Reprinted from the *Washington Post,* July, 15, 1990.
14. *Plank Road Fever,* p. 41.
15. Ibid., p. 49.
16. Ibid., p. 48.
17. Ibid.
18. Ibid., p. 51.
19. Ibid., p. 45.
20. Ibid., p. 62.
21. Ibid., p. 63.
22. *Wall Street Journal,* April 17, 2000.
23. Robert Sobel, *The Big Board,* The Free Press, 1965, p. 82.
24. Ibid., pp. 87–88.
25. Charles R. Geisst, *Wall Street,* Oxford University Press, 1997, p. 76.
26. Ibid., p. 9.
27. Ibid., p. 10.
28. Ibid., p. 18.
29. Ibid.
30. Ibid., p. 19.
31. Ibid., p. 23.
32. Ibid., p. 23.
33. Ralph C. Epstein, *The Automobile Industry,* Arno Press, 1972, p. 163.
34. Ed Kerschner, Thomas Doerflinger, "Net for Naught," PaineWebber, May 10, n.p., 1998, p. 3 research paper.
35. Ibid., p. 3, quoted from Jonathan Hughes, *The Vital Few,* 1966, Oxford University Press, Chapter 7.
36. Ibid., p. 4.
37. John Brooks, *Once in Golconda,* Allworth Press, 1969, p. 42.
38. *The Big Board,* pp. 231–232.
39. Ibid.
40. Ibid.
41. Robert Sobel, *RCA,* Stein and Day, 1986, p. 48.
42. Ibid., p. 49, quoted from *Historical Statistics of the United States.*
43. Ibid., quoted from "The Coming Shake-out in Personal Computers," *Business Week,* November 22, 1985, p. 85.
44. *Business Week,* March 2, 1992, p. 66.

CHAPTER 4: TINY BUBBLES

1. Laura Jureski, "No Exit," *Forbes,* March 23, 1987.
2. Michael Siconolfi, Michael R. Sesit, Roger Lowenstein, "Japanese Buying Fuels Spain Fund Frenzy," *Wall Street Journal,* September 27, 1989.
3. Bram Rosenthal, "Beanie Boom," *Montreal Gazette,* September 26, 1998.
4. Ibid.

5. Richard Gibson, "Bear Market?," *Wall Street Journal*, September 25, 1998.
6. All stats from Jenny Booth, "Intrigue as Beanie Poll Casts Doubt on Toy's End," *The Scotsman*, December 30, 1999.

CHAPTER 5: THE BIGGEST BUBBLE OF THEM ALL

1. Ron Chernow, *New York Times*, September 2, 1998.
2. Ibid.
3. Reprinted from the *Washington Post*, July 15, 1990.
4. John Kenneth Galbraith, *The Great Crash of 1929*, Mariner Books, 1954, p. 6.
5. David Sylvester, *San Jose Mercury News*, March 4, 2001.
6. David Kilpatrick, *Fortune*, October 11, 1990.
7. Mark Boyar & Co. Research, April 30, 1999.
8. Hal Varian, *New York Times*, February 8, 2001.
9. Kenneth Gilpin, Todd S. Purdum, *New York Times*, May 1, 1985.
10. Ibid.
11. Lawrence Magid, "On-Line Services Leaping Forward," *Los Angeles Times*, July 13, 1989.
12. Ibid.
13. Federal Reserve Bank of San Francisco Economic Letter, March 10, 2000.
14. Ibid.
15. Robert Samuelson, "Wall Street Scapegoats," *New York Post*, June 20, 2002.
16. Greg Ip, Dow Jones Interactive, *Wall Street Journal*.
17. Robert Sobel, *The Big Board*, The Free Press, 1965, p. 355.
18. Cited in *The Big Board*.
19. Ibid.
20. Art Cashin, *A View of Wall Street from the Seventh Floor*, Greenwich Publishing Group, 1999.
21. Howard Kurtz, *The Fortune Tellers*, The Free Press, 2000, p. 265.
22. Robert Samuelson, "Wall Street Scapegoats," *New York Post*, June 20, 2002.
23. *Wall Street*, 1997.
24. *The Great Crash*, p. 61.
25. Ibid., p. 65.

CHAPTER 6: TRENDWATCHING

1. *The Great Crash*, p. 29.
2. Edward Clendaniel, *Forbes ASAP*, March 25, 2002, p. 30.
3. *The Origins and Economic Impact of the First Bank of the United States*, p. 89.
4. Ibid., p. 90.
5. John Kenneth Galbraith, *A Short History of Financial Euphoria*, p. 58.
6. Ibid., p. 59.
7. *The Great Crash*, p. 22.

8. John Train, *Famous Financial Fiascoes,* Fraser Publishing Company, 1995, p. 18.
9. Ibid.
10. Ibid.
11. Ibid.
12. Ibid.
13. *Wall Street,* p. 341.
14. Bryon Burrough and John Helyar, *Barbarians at the Gate,* HarperCollins, 1991, p. 112.
15. *The Big Board,* pp. 87–88.
16. Ibid.
17. Ibid., p. 82.

CHAPTER 7: ENDWATCHING

1. *The Origins and Impact of the First Bank of the United States,* p. 98.
2. *The Great Crash,* p. 25.
3. Robert Sobel, "Panic on Wall Street," *Barrons,* p. 80.
4. Ibid.
5. Ibid., p. 80.
6. Ibid., p. 92.
7. Ibid.
8. Ibid.
9. Ibid., p. 96.
10. Ibid., p. 99.
11. Ibid., pp. 99–103.
12. Ibid., p. 103.
13. Ibid., p. 104.
14. Ibid., p. 108.

CHAPTER 8: BUBBLE OR JUST PLAIN TROUBLE

1. Daniel Kadlec, " 'Buy!' (I Need the Bonus)," *Time,* May 20, 2002.
2. Affidavit in Support of Application for an Order Pursuant to General Business Law, Section 354, New York State Attorney General, Elliott Spitzer.
3. Jim Hopkins and Michelle Kessler, "Companies Squander Billions on Tech," *USA Today,* May 20, 2002.
4. Rebecca Smith, "Enron's Rise and Fall Gives Some Scholars a Sense of Déjà Vu," *Wall Street Journal,* February 2, 2002.
5. Kevin Phillips, *Wealth and Democracy,* Broadway Books, 2002, p. xvi.

CHAPTER 9: FUTURE SHOCK

1. Reuters News, London, May 30, 2002.
2. Bill Gross, "Investment Outlook, Episode II," May/June 2002.

INDEX